DEAR BARACK

DEAR BARACK

THE EXTRAORDINARY PARTNERSHIP OF BARACK OBAMA AND ANGELA MERKEL

CLAUDIA CLARK

DISRUPTION
BOOKS

AUSTIN   NEW YORK

Published by Disruption Books
New York, NY
www.disruptionbooks.com

For ordering information or special discounts for bulk purchases,
please contact Disruption Books at info@disruptionbooks.com.

Library of Congress Control Number: 2021905553

Print ISBN: 978-1-63331-057-5
eBook ISBN: 978-1-63331-058-2

Cover and text design by Kim Lance

Photo Credits:
Cover, Adobe Stock photo by Reuters/Anton Denisov
vi, Official White House photo by Pete Souza
vii, Offiical White House photo by Pete Souza
101, Official White House photo by Pete Souza
106, Offiical White House photo by Pete Souza

First Edition

DEDICATION

To John Lewis, Stacey Abrams, Beto O'Rourke,
and the other thousands of everyday citizens
who tirelessly and bravely continue to fight for
the right of every American to cast their ballot
and ensure their voice is heard.

"Our state leaders and legislatures must
make it easier—not harder—for more Americans to
have their voices heard. Above all, we must exercise
our right as citizens to vote, for the truth is that
too often we disenfranchise ourselves."

BARACK OBAMA

"Well-behaved women seldom make history."

LAUREL THATCHER ULRICH

"Always be more than you appear
and never appear to be more than you are."

ANGELA MERKEL

President Obama and Chancellor Merkel enjoy a walk on the grounds
of Camp David during the May 2012 G8 summit.
(Official White House photo by Pete Souza)

Chancellor Merkel and President Obama continue their talk after a meeting with world leaders at a 2014 NATO summit in Wales. The continuation of the NATO alliance would become a core issue for both leaders over the course of their terms in office. (Official White House photo by Pete Souza)

CONTENTS

AUTHOR'S NOTE

I come from a family of political activists who have a keen interest in world affairs. My great-grandmother marched for women's suffrage; my grandfather was a union shop steward for a tool and die-maker factory in Michigan; and my mother, a gifted linguist who taught French on three continents, answered President John F. Kennedy's call to join the Peace Corps, where she taught English until she became gravely ill with malaria and had to return to the United States. I grew up with their stories of activism and service, so it seems only fitting that I would also share those interests.

I became a feminist at the age of five after my mother bought me a book about "mommies at work" when I had told her I wanted to be a nurse and not a doctor when I grew up because girls became nurses, while boys became doctors. Later, I formed one of my earliest memories at seven years old when a breaking news story about the Iran hostage crisis interrupted my Saturday morning cartoons. Even at that age, I followed the developments to the best of my ability—to the point that more than a year later, when the hostages were released, I faked sick from school so I could watch the news coverage. That interest in both politics and foreign affairs followed me as I grew older. As a teenager, I became engaged in political activism for the first time— I protested against restrictive legislation on women's reproductive rights, led anti-censorship campaigns at my high school, and interned for my state representative during my senior year. At age seventeen, I watched and cheered from my home in Michigan at the historic moment when the Berlin Wall came tumbling down.

I was fascinated by the German culture and people long before my move to Germany in 2017, largely because of my uncle, who had been stationed in Germany for most of my childhood, where he met, married, and had two children with a German woman. In August 1990, the summer before my senior year of high school, my mother, my stepfather, my best friend, and I made our first trip to Germany to visit them. I instantly fell in love with the country and promised myself I would live there someday. The Berlin Wall had been down for almost a year at that point, but there were many parts still intact, so I chipped off a white piece of concrete that fit inside the palm of my hand— today it remains one of my most prized possessions.

All around Berlin, I looked around and saw the sharp contrast between East and West. For all intents and purposes, the Wall was down, and Berlin was a united city. However, even as a seventeen-year-old girl, I clearly saw the stark difference between the former Soviet-controlled East Berlin—with its dreary buildings, unkempt properties, and lack of businesses—and the flourishing, free West Berlin. It was a mind-opening experience: at that moment I learned the importance of living in a free society and took to heart the lesson that democracy and freedom should not be taken for granted. Although we spent only a few days in Berlin, I knew I would eventually return, and I wondered whether the stark contrast between West and East would be as evident when I did.

In college and graduate school, I studied history and public policy and continued my political activism in my spare time. Fortunately for me, Michigan State University had been selected as one of the venues for the 1992 presidential debates, so I very briefly met Bill Clinton as a nineteen-year-old college sophomore. By 1993, I had devoted so much of my spare time to political causes that the local Democratic Party presented me with the Geraldine Rappaport Award for Young Democrat Volunteer of the Year. Two years later, the mayor of Lansing called for a city council resolution declaring a Claudia Clark Day as thanks for all the activism in which I had engaged as a student.

Following graduate school, I spent most of my early working life in political campaigns for progressive candidates and causes across the United States, eventually settling in the San Francisco Bay Area. Like many, I became an enthusiastic supporter of Barack Obama. I volunteered on his campaigns and followed his career closely. All the while, my obsession with Germany and my desire to move there remained close to my heart.

As a champion for women's rights, I followed closely the career of Angela Merkel. I admired her dual-faceted professional life: her careers as both a scientist and a politician. Personally, I am awful in math and science—I even tried to persuade my high school physics teacher that forcing anyone to take physics was torture and thereby unconstitutional. Nevertheless, because of my own shortcomings, I really admire women who excel in traditionally male-dominated fields, and the fact that Chancellor Merkel has a PhD in physics made me respect her greatly. Given Merkel's combination of scientific training and political achievements, there are few people I admire more—even though her politics often are more conservative than mine.

As I watched Obama and Merkel's final joint press conference in November 2016, I was immediately struck by how visibly upset Merkel appeared when questioned by the media about this being their last such event together in an official capacity. In both the days leading up to that final event and the days that followed it, I could not help but notice stories in the media regarding the strong bond between the two leaders. Journalists often noted Merkel's use of the affectionate phrase "dear Barack," and Business Insider ran a story titled "16 photos that demonstrate Obama and Merkel will truly miss one another," which illustrated to me that others had also witnessed the chemistry between them.

I kept these images in the back of my mind but did not dredge them up again until March 2017, during Merkel's first trip to Washington, DC, to visit President Donald Trump. I watched as Trump refused to shake Merkel's hand, and noted the stark contrast compared to her interactions with his predecessor. It was then that I realized Obama and Merkel had a truly memorable relationship—one that deserved special recognition, one that should be memorialized in some way. I recalled that books had been written about the relationship between President Franklin Delano Roosevelt and British prime minister Winston Churchill, and considered the many parallels between the two sets of leaders. In both scenarios, the leaders came from allied countries, belonged to opposing political parties, and governed in troubling times, but despite the odds, they managed to form strong bonds with one another. And I began to think maybe a book about Merkel and Obama's friendship would be a project worth pursuing.

Still on the fence, however, I began to research whether such a book had any merit, a burdensome task for someone who had only ever written a one-hundred-page master's thesis. I was also aware that I was an unknown author and yet I was attempting to undertake a massive work of nonfiction involving two of the most powerful people in the world.

While I pondered whether I were up to—or qualified for—the task, I heard in April 2017 that Obama planned to make his first overseas trip since leaving office a visit to Berlin, where he would reconnect with Merkel and speak in honor of the five-hundred-year anniversary of the Protestant Reformation. Finally, I was convinced. Obama's first official overseas trip as a private citizen was to Germany and to see Merkel. Surely that indicated their partnership was strong enough to warrant the time and energy required to embark on such an ambitious project.

The timing was nearly perfect. By the fall of 2016, for a variety of reasons, my husband and I had already realized that our "eventual" move to Germany would be sooner rather than later. In May 2017, when my husband was offered a job in Bavaria, he enthusiastically accepted. Excited about starting a new life, and knowing my German skills were somewhat lacking, I needed to find something productive to do that would not interfere with my language classes. Based on my research, I now firmly believed there would be enough interest to make writing a book a worthwhile undertaking, and at last I made the decision to start this project.

Less than a year later, from the other side of the Atlantic, and only six months after our move, I turned over a 250-page manuscript for review by the first of two editors and a translator, and I began a process about which I knew nothing—how to get a book published.

I think it is worth mentioning what this book is and what it is not. Although it is a book about two politicians, it is not a "political book" per se. The book discusses politics and policy issues, but only with respect to how those matters impacted the partnership and friendship of these two leaders. One does not have to agree with all (or any) of the policies they have supported to get something valuable out of this book.

As a historian, I have learned that famous people—whether politicians, movie stars, or athletes—are, above all, human beings. They make mistakes, or they believe or do something contrary to what we want or even expect. So, while I clearly like and respect both Obama and Merkel very much, both have made decisions and taken sides on policy issues contrary to what I would have preferred. Nevertheless, I find the leadership and life stories of these two individuals extraordinary, and the bond they formed is quite simply exceptional.

When I embarked on this project, someone told me a good piece of nonfiction should do three things: entertain, educate, and inspire. Whether or not one supports the Obama and/or Merkel administrations, I hope I have managed to achieve these three goals.

Truthfully, of the three criteria, entertainment proved to be the biggest challenge. Between the Great Recession and Putin's illegal annexation of Ukraine, the times Obama and Merkel faced were hardly a joking matter. Nevertheless, when a humorous comment or event took place in the midst of the trying times, I did my best to capture it.

The educational component proved to be a bit easier. If a reader learns a new fact, personal or professional, about either Obama or Merkel, or simply gains a better understanding of a foreign policy issue after reading this book, then that mission has been achieved.

The final piece, and, to me, the most important, is to ensure the work is a source of inspiration. Both Germany and the United States have stains on their histories that endure today. If the formation of such a formidable bond between the first Black president of the United States and the first female chancellor of Germany—people from two countries that have fought two long and bitter wars against one another—does not provide hope and inspiration for what is possible, then I am not sure what does.

Admittedly, my own life-defining moment was not as exciting as Senator Obama's keynote speech at the 2004 Democratic National Convention, or the collapse of the Berlin Wall in Merkel's situation. Yet, little did I know at the time, my fascination with that final press conference between Obama and Merkel following the 2016 US election would be my moment of inspiration.

President Obama campaigned on a message of hope, with the campaign slogan "Yes We Can." After years of blood, sweat, migraines, tears, more migraines, more tears, and more migraines, this book is my contribution to the inspiration he has provided to a generation.

INTRODUCTION

W ith all the authority, respect, and prestige the president of the United States possesses, it would seem to be the world's most desirable position—one to which anyone would aspire. Yet what people fail to realize is the incredible amount of isolation that accompanies this level of power. Between the Secret Service and a press corps that follows the president's every move, most levels of normalcy are abandoned once one becomes an official presidential candidate. It is a position few have held and few understand. President Harry Truman described the loneliness of the Oval Office when he claimed, "If you want a friend in Washington, get a dog."[1]

Perhaps in an attempt to overcome their alienation, it has become common for US presidents to form close bonds with their foreign counterparts. President Franklin Delano Roosevelt and British prime minister Winston Churchill formed such a bond during World War II, followed by President Ronald Reagan and British prime minister Margaret Thatcher in the 1980s and, most recently, President Barack Obama and German chancellor Dr. Angela Merkel.

Unlike Roosevelt and Churchill, or Reagan and Thatcher, who became close friends upon their first official meeting, it was well into Obama's first term as president before he and Merkel developed a close rapport. When Obama visited Berlin as a presidential candidate in July 2008, his aides understood the importance a backdrop played in the midst of a political speech and wanted him to share his message of hope with the German people in front of the Brandenburg Gate, a symbol of how the West overcame the Cold War. However, Chancellor Merkel, a straitlaced, no-nonsense leader, was less mesmerized by Obama than her fellow citizens and denied the request. Undeterred, Obama's campaign staff settled for the foot of the Victory Column instead, where he drew a crowd of more than 200,000 people.

Pundits argued that Merkel's refusal created tensions so strong it seemed unlikely the two would ever recover. According to the press, Merkel and her aides argued that Obama was "touchy,"[2] while Obama's aides described Merkel as "difficult."[3] This was the first time the press would misinterpret their relationship—but not the last. Over the course of their eight-year working relationship, their partnership evolved from one of extreme apprehension to one of profound respect and admiration. In fact, Obama's former deputy national security advisor for strategic communications, Ben Rhodes, in his memoir *The World as It Is: A Memoir of the Obama White House*, recalled seeing a tear in Merkel's eye as she said goodbye to Obama for the final time of his presidency.[4] And Obama's final phone call to a foreign leader was to the German chancellor the day before he officially left office.[5]

Beyond their key personality and cultural differences, there were political and ideological conflicts as well. For a start, Merkel belonged to Germany's center-right party, the Christian Democratic Union (CDU), and Obama was among the more progressive members of the United States' center-left Democratic Party, which already held more progressive views than Merkel's CDU.

When elected in 2008, Obama inherited the biggest financial crisis since the Great Depression of the 1930s. He and Merkel had opposing ideas on how to address that crisis, both domestically and in Greece and other European countries. Nevertheless, these leaders, both known for their pragmatism, understood the historical significance of the relationship between their two countries and knew that it would be in their mutual interests to work with one another successfully. Fortunately, the two learned not only to work with one another but to respect one another—and sincerely like each other.

One has only to type "Merkel and Obama" into any search engine today, and the results are autofilled with words like "romance" or "partnership." In anticipation of their final press conference together, on November 17, 2016, media headlines like **OBAMA LANDS IN BERLIN FOR FAREWELL VISIT TO CLOSEST ALLY MERKEL** (*China Daily*)[6] and

16 HEARTWARMING PHOTOS OF BARACK OBAMA AND ANGELA
MERKEL'S FRIENDSHIP (Business Insider)[7] summarized the friendship
the world had come to witness firsthand. Interestingly enough, Obama and
Merkel's relationship managed to capture the attention of the pop culture
media as well as the mainstream media: the United States' long-running satirical television show *Saturday Night Live* and Germany's satirical *Heute Show*
both highlighted the friendship of the two leaders in several skits.

For anyone who sought further evidence of this mutual affection, Obama
and Merkel—sharing the podium that last time in Berlin—did not disappoint
the press or the world. Responding to a journalist's question about Obama's
imminent departure, Merkel replied:

> *Now, taking leave from my partner and friend, well, yes, it is hard. If
> you've worked together with somebody very well, leave-taking is very
> difficult. But we are politicians. We all know that democracy lives off
> change. So, in the United States of America, the Constitution has very
> clear stipulations on this. It's a tough rule—eight years and that's it.
> Out goes the president and a new one comes in. . . . But personal—we
> have freedom of movement in the whole of Germany, so if we want to
> see each other, well, I'm game.*[8]

As Merkel spoke, the cameras shifted their attention to Obama, who
stood to her right and made a phone gesture with his hand—implying he and
Merkel would continue their relationship after he left office. As Obama made
this motion, the noise from the journalists' cameras was deafening. These
photos captured attention in newspapers not only in Germany and America
but around the world—including France's prominent *Le Monde*, accompanied by the headline DANS SES ADIEUX À L'EUROPE, OBAMA LOUE
MERKEL, 'PARTENAIRE EXTRAORDINAIRE' (OBAMA PRAISES
MERKEL AS AN 'EXTRAORDINARY PARTNER' IN HIS FARE-
WELL TO EUROPE).[9] The images vividly demonstrated the partnership
and friendship between the two that the world had grown to expect over their
eight-year working relationship.

If one single event could be classified as the "reset" in their relationship, it would be Merkel's trip to Washington, DC, on June 9, 2011, to receive the prestigious Presidential Medal of Freedom—the highest honor a president can bestow on a civilian, and one rarely granted to non-US citizens. Here they began to refer to one another as "Angela" and "Barack," and their relationship publicly transformed into a friendship and a partnership both. Eventually, Merkel began to use the informal second-person pronoun *du* (meaning *you*) rather than the more formal *Sie* when she publicly addressed the president, and she routinely referred to her friend as "*lieber* Barack" or "dear Barack." Obama returned the compliment when he referred to Merkel as one of his best friends on the international stage. The shift in protocol did not go unnoticed by the media, the public, or political advisors around the world.

That June 2011 award ceremony may have been the turning point, but their relationship was by no means linear. Just as Roosevelt and Churchill disagreed over issues such as colonization, and Reagan and Thatcher disagreed over policies with regard to Argentina, Obama and Merkel had their differences—most notably the tensions that arose when Merkel and the Germans learned the United States had wiretapped her personal cell phone. Over the years, the two would disagree on other issues, from austerity versus growth models in reviving the global economy to policies on Libya and Ukraine. What is important is that, despite these disagreements, the two leaders continually restored their friendship and partnership—which made their bond stronger than ever.

During the eight years the two worked together, Obama granted Merkel the distinction of being the first German chancellor to speak before a joint session of the US Congress and only the second German citizen to receive the highly coveted Presidential Medal of Freedom. Meanwhile, on the other side of the Atlantic, Obama was the first US president to visit the former concentration camp of Buchenwald, as well as the first to visit and cosponsor the Hannover Messe technology fair. Tellingly, Merkel eventually authorized Obama to speak in front of the Brandenburg Gate, and stood at his side when he did so.

All these events occurred in addition to the traditional meetings, summits, and conferences where leaders of the free world could expect to meet. Whether Obama laid a white rose on the tomb in Buchenwald or they exchanged a toast in Washington at Merkel's state dinner, the two stood side by side. It was apparent in everything from their body language to their words and their demeanors that the two had a mutual affinity and respect for one another.

This book explores how their relationship evolved, transforming them from world leaders skeptical of one another to good friends and close confidants. According to Rhodes in *The World as It Is*, "There was no foreign leader [Obama] admired more. Like him, she was a pragmatist, driven by facts, dedicated to international order, deliberate in her decision making."[10] The American magazine *Politico* argued that Merkel became Obama's "go to" person. Whenever a complicated issue arose, Obama demanded that his aides find Merkel for her input.[11]

Over the years, Obama and Merkel developed a friendly, informally competitive relationship with one another. Aides have revealed that the two often spent the first few minutes of meetings, video conferences, or telephone calls attempting to "one up each other" on which of them had spent more time reviewing the intelligence briefing book.[12] When one examines the obstacles these leaders faced and the differences of opinion they held, the fact that they remained such good, loyal friends and partners speaks volumes about the strength of their friendship and the amount of respect and admiration they felt toward each other and their respective nations.

What was it about the chemistry between Obama and Merkel that captured the world's attention? As Stefan Kornelius points out in his book *Angela Merkel: The Chancellor and Her World*, the private Obama was quite different from the passionate and charismatic public Obama. Behind closed doors, the president tended to be extremely introverted, with his primary focus on his wife and family. In the early years of his tenure, other world leaders such as British prime minister Gordon Brown and French president Nicolas Sarkozy had trouble connecting with Obama on a personal level—to the point where they wondered aloud among themselves if Obama's "awkward, cold and unapproachable" temperament amounted to a personal attack directed toward them.[13] Unbeknownst to Sarkozy, Obama had already begun to form opinions about his colleagues. Obama admitted in his autobiography, *A Promised Land*, that while he had appreciated Sarkozy's enthusiastic and early support for him and his campaign, Obama realized Merkel would be the person to whom he could turn. "It wasn't hard to tell which of the two European leaders would prove to be the more reliable partner," he wrote.[14] According to Kevin Liptak, a CNN White House producer who wrote the article "How Obama and Merkel Learned to Love One Another," the bond Obama formed with Merkel was something unusual for him: "a genuine international friendship that both have leveraged to their own advantage."[15]

When one considers their different political ideologies, and the fact that the two got off to such a rocky start, it seemed highly unlikely that they would forge such a strong bond. Yet as Kornelius argues, "It would be . . . correct to say that human factors can even influence relationships between heads of government, and that Merkel and Obama may be more similar than they are [willing] to admit."[16]

Both were classic political outsiders who experienced an unimaginable rise to power. They have similar approaches to solving problems: Merkel, a physicist by training, used her scientific background in her approach. She would acquire, research, and study all the possible evidence surrounding an issue before she made or acted on a decision—something that Obama's aides claimed he appreciated. Like Merkel, Obama hesitated before making decisions when he could see the possible consequences.[17] Furthermore, both leaders are cerebral realists, highly analytical, and objective.[18]

Yet while their shared personality traits and problem-solving approach certainly explain the nature of their relationship, it was only part of the equation. The core values shared between the United States and Germany—freedom, democracy, and human rights—also played a significant role in their relationship. As someone who had grown up in the former East Germany, Merkel very firmly believed that she would not hold the position of chancellor, nor would her country be a free nation, were it not for the United States. It is safe to say that Merkel's background as the first German chancellor from the former East Germany meant she already placed a higher value on the relationship with America than her predecessors did. Based on her fondness and gratitude toward the United States, she might have had more of an incentive than her European peers to work harder at establishing a relationship.

From Obama's standpoint, he repeatedly stated that he admired Merkel for overcoming the hardships of her life to become who she is. While some of that can be attributed to the history of the two countries they represented, it was much more than that. Merkel was not only the first former East German but also the first woman to lead Germany—and Obama was the first Black politician to be elected US president. As Obama first stated and as Merkel repeated:

> *The arc of our lives speaks to this spirit. It's obvious that neither of us looks exactly like the leaders who preceded us. But the fact that we can stand here today as President of the United States and as Chancellor of a united Germany is a testament to the progress, the freedom, that is possible in our world.*[19]

But why revisit the story now?

Whereas several authors have already written about Merkel and Obama as individuals, and many about the history of diplomacy between Germany and the United States, this book is primarily about the relationship between Obama and Merkel. The focus here is on their working relationship and their friendship—and the rapidly changing environment of global politics makes such a book seem timely and appropriate.

Since World War II and the formation of partnerships and alliances such as the North Atlantic Treaty Organization (NATO) and the European Union (EU), the world has not seen another widespread war. Partnerships such as those between Thatcher and Reagan and now Obama and Merkel have played a significant role in maintaining peace and harmony throughout Europe and the United States. However, the rise of radical ideology and terrorist activity has replaced traditional warfare. Since the September 11, 2001, terrorist attacks in the United States, an increase in terrorist groups and activities has created an upsurge in anti-immigrant, nationalist, and isolationist movements across these regions.

The June 2016 Brexit vote, in which the citizens of the UK voted in a controversial measure to leave the EU, and the November 2016 election of Donald Trump in America based on his isolationist principles demonstrate this shift in values. Similarly, far-right presidential candidates bid unsuccessful, but noteworthy, campaigns in France and the Netherlands in 2017. The prevalence of anti-Semitism in Poland has reached heights not seen since World War II, and most recently, Austria elected a chancellor with an openly nationalist, anti-immigration stance. What used to be deemed necessary political alliances among world leaders and countries have been replaced with nationalist and isolationist philosophies as countries attempt to keep their borders safe. While organizations such as NATO were paramount in maintaining the peace in the decades that followed World War II, relationships among political leaders such as Angela Merkel and Barack Obama played an equally important role.

More recently, the Trump administration's policies, such as the controversial 2017 decision to move the American embassy in Israel to Jerusalem, created worldwide opposition—including from Germany. In response to these policies, the German foreign minister reported, "Germany can no longer simply react to US policy but must establish its own position. . . . [E]ven after Trump leaves the White House, relations with the US will never be the same."[20] Now, in light of these drastic shifts in foreign leadership and policy, it is crucial to study and remember the importance of alliances between countries and world leaders.

Unlike previous wars, the dangers that face the world today involve more than invading one another's borders. Today's wars and attacks target the values and the way of life of America and its allies. Moreover, with the omnipresence of the internet and social media, terrorist attacks can be planned by anyone, from anywhere. It is imperative that countries maintain effective working relationships with allied countries and their leaders, as the inability to share intelligence with partners, and the risk of alienating those partners, is dangerous not only to the security of one country but to the greater world. Furthermore, as the world becomes more globalized, issues such as climate change and economic downturns impact every nation, not just one or two.

To face these realities, ensuring that world leaders and countries work together and form partnerships is more crucial than ever before.

1

"THE ARC OF OUR LIVES"

Nothing illustrated the difference between the free and communist states during the Cold War more than the completion of the Berlin Wall in August 1961. While the Wall provided an obvious physical barrier that separated friends, families, and compatriots from one another, it also visually symbolized the stark contrast between the free Western world and the communist Eastern Bloc. Angela Kasner, who had just turned seven when the communist government of the German Democratic Republic built the Wall, later recalled its construction as her first political memory.

On that notorious Sunday morning, August 13, as the Kasner family prepared for church, they received the news that the communist regime had erected what it called an "anti-fascist protection wall." Angela later recalled:

> *My father was preaching on that Sunday. The atmosphere was horrible in the church. I will never forget it. People cried. My mother cried too. . . . What had happened was almost unprecedented in human history. A whole country had been turned into a prison. In addition to fortifying the border with barbed wire and control towers, the whole of West Berlin was surrounded by a 155-kilometre-long wall four meters high.*[1]

Over the twenty-seven years that Germany remained divided by that concrete wall, both the American people and their government took various measures to demonstrate their support for the Germans' quest for democracy and unity. The United States and West Germany had grown to become strong allies in the years following World War II, and Americans vehemently opposed the authoritarian actions taken by the East German government.

In 1960, as a symbol of solidarity with their Western allies, American citizens had sent a Freedom Bell, modeled after their own Liberty Bell, to their friends in Berlin. More notably, then–US president John F. Kennedy gave one of his most poignant addresses in front of the Brandenburg Gate in 1963 with his "*Ich bin ein Berliner*" speech, in which he passionately declared before a crowd of thousands of Berliners that those "who really don't understand . . . what is the great issue between the free world and the communist world—let them come to Berlin."[2] President Ronald Reagan made a similarly emotional plea in 1988, to Soviet leader Mikhail Gorbachev, when he stood before the Wall and demanded, "Mr. Gorbachev, tear down this wall."[3] A year and a half after Reagan uttered those words, millions of East Germans experienced freedom for the first time in twenty-seven years when the Berlin Wall crumbled in November 1989.

It is fair to say that perhaps nobody benefited from its collapse more than the thirty-five-year-old Angela Merkel. The fall of the Berlin Wall paved the way for Merkel, a trained physicist from the former East Germany, to eventually become the first female chancellor and the first former East German to serve under a unified and free Germany. As Merkel rose through the political ranks, her political opinion of America centered around the Cold War and the support Americans offered to her country when it had been divided by a concrete barrier that represented an ideological chasm. She firmly believed that the United States played a crucial role in her freedom and, ultimately, her success. And thus she has long believed that transatlantic relations lie at the heart of German foreign policy.[4]

This belief would help her forge future relationships with all the American presidents she worked with during her tenure.

Angela Dorothea Kasner was born on July 17, 1954, in Hamburg, Germany. Her father, Horst Kasner, was a Lutheran minister who had agreed to the unusual relocation from the free West Germany to the communist-controlled East. Because of the urgent need for Protestant clergy in the Soviet-occupied zone, Reverend Kasner went to the East to settle, leaving his wife, Herlind, who was seven months pregnant with Angela, behind in Hamburg.[5]

Hans-Otto Wölber, one of Reverend Kasner's senior colleagues in Hamburg (he later became bishop of that city's cathedral), told his young colleague that he was needed in East Germany. As Reverend Kasner was originally from the East, he was easy to persuade—though he joked that those who traveled to the East were "normally total idiots or Communists."[6] However, his main motivation had been religious. "I would have travelled anywhere to preach the word of our Lord, even to Africa," he once said.[7] When Angela was only eight weeks old, Herlind and her infant daughter—carried in a bassinet—made the journey to join Reverend Kasner to begin their new lives.[8] It was unquestionably a controversial decision, and one he would later regret.

Once in the East, Angela's father ran a seminary and a center for the mentally disabled, and, while Angela's mother had been a trained English and Latin teacher, the communist controlled government refused to allow her to work, and she remained at home with the children. Reverend and Mrs. Kasner raised Angela and her younger brother and sister in the small agricultural East German city of Templin, approximately fifty miles north of Berlin, where the family lived a comfortable middle-class life—including the rare luxury of owning two cars.[9] Although East German residents had more freedom from governmental control than people in other communist countries, conditions were still far from ideal.

Reverend Kasner agreed with the principal teachings of the socialist doctrine, but he vehemently opposed how the communist government implemented them. Among the many restrictions placed upon its own people, the East German government forbade public discussion of politics, shot and killed citizens for attempting to escape, and spied on its residents. Nonetheless, Angela's father often held "politically charged" gatherings at his seminary, and the Kasner dinner table often hosted heated political debates.[10]

Raised during the Nazi regime, Angela's mother insisted on protecting her children from the propaganda of the communist government. When the children returned from school, Herlind held daily debriefings with Angela and her siblings, where the children informed her of everything they had learned in school, so she could correct them as necessary. Angela referred to these two-hour sessions with her mother as the time where they "despoke."[11] It was her mother's way of minimizing the "brainwashing" her children were exposed to in the government-controlled schools.

Even with more relaxed restrictions than in other communist countries, clergy and their families faced additional persecution and discrimination other citizens did not. Moreover, the communist regime did not welcome Reverend Kasner or his family. His religious affiliation combined with his West German roots created such suspicion that the Stasi, or the East German secret police, had an active file on the minister's every move.[12] The fact that Angela opted to be confirmed by the Lutheran Church rather than participate in the typical East German coming-of-age ceremony known as *Jugendweihe* undoubtedly added to these suspicions. In 1968, Reverend and Mrs. Kasner signed up fourteen-year-old Angela to participate in the Free German Youth. Although her involvement later raised questions about her allegiance among her political rivals, her parents' sole purpose had been to ensure Angela would be able to attend university; students who failed to join the communist youth organization often found it difficult to get accepted into institutions of higher education.[13] Such participation proved to be so important that, according to an article written by George Packer for the *New Yorker*, Merkel herself once admitted that her participation in the Free German Youth was "seventy per cent opportunism."[14] Merkel's parents clearly disagreed with the policies of the Soviet communist dictatorship, but they understood the necessity of at least pretending to play by the government's rules in order to help their children get ahead—astute and necessary skills for an effective leader, or a politician.

From an early age, Angela excelled in both math and Russian. As political science professor Matthew Qvortrup claimed in his book, *Angela Merkel: Europe's Most Influential Leader*, her parents encouraged Angela's studies because "learning Russian was not just an opportune way of conveying that she—and by implication her family—was toeing the party line, it also allowed her the opportunity to read critical authors, such as Leo Tolstoy."[15] One of her former math teachers recalled her as one of the "most gifted" students he had ever taught, and she did well enough in her Russian studies that she qualified for the Russian Language Olympics in school when she was only fourteen years old.[16] It seemed that Angela had inherited her mother's gift for languages—a skill that would prove to be one of the most useful in her later life as a politician.

Although it would be many years before Angela took an active interest in politics, the political teachings of her family impacted her academic path when she entered university. "I wanted to study physics because the East German regime couldn't simply suspend the rules of elementary arithmetic and the laws of physics," she explained.[17]

Given Angela's chosen field of study, she surprised her parents with her decision to attend Karl Marx University in Leipzig. At age nineteen, Angela found Templin too claustrophobic. "I wanted to be away," she said later, confessing that "above all, I wanted to get out of this small town."[18] Angela had a challenging relationship with her father, and he had begun to regret his decision to move the family to East Germany. According to Qvortrup, he worked too hard, and as a child, Angela did not see much of him. As Angela recalled later in an interview, "Work and leisure became indistinguishable and became as one. And sometimes, I think, the responsibilities were, possibly, sacrificed for the sake of his work."[19]

On August 4, 1961, shortly before the communist government built the Berlin Wall and changed seven-year-old Angela's life forever, Barack Hussein Obama II was born in Honolulu, Hawaii. His father, Barack Obama Sr., was a member of the Luo tribe from the Kenyan village of Allegro who met and married his mother, Stanley "Ann" Dunham, in 1960 while the two were students at the University of Hawaii.[20]

When Barack's parents married, miscegenation was still a felony in more than half of the United States, and in his autobiography *Dreams from My Father*, he expressed bewilderment that his grandparents even grudgingly allowed their daughter to marry someone from a different race.[21] The marriage did not last long, and his parents divorced in 1964. His father returned to Kenya, where he married again. Barack saw his father only one time after that, when he visited him in Hawaii at Christmas in 1971. His father was killed in a tragic car accident in Kenya in 1982, when Barack was only twenty-one years old.[22] The absence of his father in his daily life would prompt Barack to go on a truth-seeking mission. One could argue that the answers he found on this journey laid the foundation for the career path he would eventually take.

Although Barack's parents did not officially divorce until March 1964, the couple formally separated in 1962 when Barack's father moved to complete a master's degree in economics at Harvard.[23] Later, in 1964, Barack's mother married Lolo Soetoro, a geologist from Indonesia, and in 1967 the family moved to Jakarta, Indonesia. His stepfather worked as a tunnel and road surveyor for the army, while his mother taught English for the US embassy.[24] According to Obama, Lolo treated him as his own son but remained distant:

> *He didn't talk much but he was easy to be with. With his family and friends, he introduced me as his son, but he never pressed things beyond matter-of-fact advice or pretended that our relationship was more than it was.*[25]

Although for very different reasons, young Barack, much like Angela, had a strained relationship with the father figures in his life.

Ann appreciated Lolo's kindness to her son, but she felt alienated and lonely in her new country. Obama later acknowledged that one way his mother managed to address her own loneliness had been to focus on her son's education. The family lacked the financial resources to send him to a private international school, so his mother supplemented his Indonesian education with materials from an American correspondence school. During the family's time in Indonesia, Barack's mother realized that "his true life lay elsewhere"[26] and assumed her son's best chance for success was back in the United States. She began to give him English lessons five days a week, from 4 a.m. to 7 a.m., while he ate breakfast.[27] Like Angela's parents, who encouraged their daughter's studies of Russian to ease her life in communist East Germany, Barack's mother understood that fluency in English was essential for his success in the United States. And just as Angela's parents attempted to counter the teachings of the East German communist dictatorship, Barack's mother tried to contradict the racial stereotypes that existed in American society.

As Obama later professed, his mother believed that any type of bigotry was wrong and that everybody should be treated as a unique individual regardless of race.[28] Ann routinely bought her son books, magazines, and recordings about key civil rights leaders, including Dr. Martin Luther King Jr. and gospel singer Mahalia Jackson.[29] Because his mother and his grandparents shielded Barack so effectively on the issue of race, he later admitted that as a child, the fact that "my father looked nothing like the people around me—that he was black as pitch, my mother white as milk—barely registered in my mind."[30] Ann understood the obstacles a Black child faced in white America and wanted to do her part to protect her son from the misinformation and inaccurate racial stereotypes in the real world.

During the summer of 1971, between Barack's fourth and fifth grades of school, he returned to Honolulu to live with his maternal grandparents in order to attend the prestigious private school Punahou. A ten-minute walk from his grandparents' two-bedroom apartment, the acclaimed Punahou was one of the oldest private schools west of the Mississippi River, and the best in Hawaii.[31] For the first three years, Barack lived with his mother and his half sister Maya Soetoro, but in 1975 his mother and sister returned to Indonesia, and Barack remained in Hawaii with his grandparents to finish high school.

His mother spent most of the next two decades in Indonesia, divorced Lolo in 1980, and earned a PhD in anthropology in 1992 before she died of gynecologic cancer in Hawaii three years later. Given the encouragement and support she had given Barack in his early years, it is tragic that she did not live long enough to see her eldest child become the first Black president of the United States.

Barack graduated from high school in 1979 and moved to the Los Angeles suburb of Pasadena to attend Occidental College, a small liberal arts school. After two years he decided he wanted to be in a larger city, so he moved to New York City and transferred to Columbia University in 1981. After he completed his bachelor's degree in political science in 1983, Barack worked as a writer, financial researcher, and project coordinator for a community activism group until 1985.

In June 1985 he moved to Chicago, Illinois, to work as a community organizer for a church-based organization, The Developing Communities Project, with the mission of improving lives in eight Catholic parishes in Roseland, West Pullman, and Riverdale on Chicago's South Side. During his three-year tenure, he helped set up a job training program, a college preparatory tutoring program, and a tenants' rights organization.[32] But it was also here that Barack found himself without an identity. He felt empty and, as he characterized it, "stripped of language, stripped of work and routine—stripped even of the racial obsessions to which I'd become so accustomed. . . . I had been forced to look inside myself and had found only a great emptiness there."[33]

At the recommendation of his colleagues, he went to Kenya in the summer of 1988 in an attempt to address his feelings of emptiness and come to terms with his father's life and death. The information and stories Barack collected from his father's extended family during his trip that summer became the premise for his first memoir, *Dreams from My Father*.

When Barack returned to the United States in the fall of 1988, he entered Harvard Law School. During summers, he returned to Chicago, where he worked as an associate at the law firm of Sidley Austin. In 1989, Barack met fellow lawyer Michelle LaVaughn Robinson, his assigned mentor while he worked as a summer associate. Born in Chicago on January 17, 1964, she had graduated from Princeton University cum laude with a degree in sociology in 1985, and went on to graduate from Harvard Law School in 1988. Their relationship started with a business lunch and then a community organization meeting, where he first impressed her.

In 1990, the *Harvard Law Review* panelists selected Barack as the organization's first Black editor. Barack's selection granted him a great deal of national media attention, which ultimately resulted in him receiving a publishing contract for *Dreams from My Father*. Barack graduated from Harvard with his law degree in 1991 and returned to Chicago. He taught constitutional law at the University of Chicago Law School from 1992 until 2004, when he joined the small law firm of Davis, Miner, Barnhill & Galland, a firm of just thirteen attorneys that specialized in civil rights litigation and neighborhood economic development. Meanwhile, in his personal life, Barack married Michelle in October 1992 and went on to have two daughters, Malia Ann (born in 1998) and Natasha (known as "Sasha," born in 2001). It is worth mentioning that Michelle, with two degrees from Ivy League colleges, is one of the most educated first ladies in the history of the United States. The husband of a gifted lawyer, son of an academically accomplished mother, and grandson of a respected matriarch—Madelyn Dunham, who passed away just one day before his election—Barack was clearly far from intimidated by bright, educated women, which could also help to explain the respect and chemistry between him and Merkel.

During her first year at university in Leipzig, Angela met Ulrich Merkel, the man who eventually became her first husband and whose surname would later become one of the most famous in the political world. According to Qvortrup, Ulrich noticed Angela from afar, as she worked as a barmaid while she attended school, but they did not begin to date until after a school excursion together to Leningrad in 1972. Both recalled their time together at Leipzig as "carefree." They traveled, to the extent the government permitted them, but they also saw movies together and attended theater productions just like any other normal couple. In 1976 the pair moved into a small apartment, where they shared a living room, kitchen, and bathroom with two other couples.[34] They married in September 1977.

Both Angela and Ulrich obtained jobs at the Academy of Sciences in Berlin—Ulrich as an assistant at the Central Institute for Optics, and Angela as an assistant with the Section for Physical Chemistry. Both focused on their careers rather than their relationship, however, and they eventually drifted apart. After four years of marriage, Angela abruptly left their apartment. Ulrich described the circumstances as follows:

Suddenly one day she packed her bags and left the apartment we shared. She had weighed up all the consequences and analyzed the pros and cons. We split in a friendly manner. We were both financially independent. There weren't too many things to be divided between us.[35]

By most accounts, Merkel had a successful career as a quantum physicist. She worked for one of the most prestigious academies in Germany and was a published researcher. Yet Merkel realized spending her career as a scientist was not what she envisioned for herself. As she stated, "The prospect of another twenty-five years of carrying out scientific research on a shoestring budget was not enticing."[36] Fortunately for her, the world as she had always known it began to change, and opportunities would soon open that would help her find her true calling.

Despite rumblings in the political realm that the East German government was on the verge of collapsing, misunderstood orders by the Communist Party spokesman caused the Berlin Wall to fall sooner than anyone anticipated. As a result of a spokesman's premature announcement that East Germans could now travel freely to the West without papers, the Berlin Wall began to fall on the night of Thursday, November 9, changing the lives of millions of people.

In his 2013 BBC documentary *The Making of Merkel*, Andrew Marr recounted that while thousands of citizens flooded the gates to have their passports stamped as proof they had been present on that historic night, Angela continued with her usual Thursday ritual—a sauna followed by a beer with a co-worker.[37] Angela's apathy toward the collapse of the Wall did not last for long. She was just thirty-five years old—"young enough," as one of her friends and colleagues later pointed out, "that [she] could reestablish [herself] with a new career."[38]

The leap from physicist to politician seemed an unlikely one, but as Marr stated, "She wanted to use power—before the Wall came down, she wanted power over molecules to change the world, and after the Wall came down, she wanted to use power on a wider stage."[39] Despite the restrictions of the East German government, Angela had grown up in a politically aware family. The seeds of political interest had already been sown. Once those constraints were lifted, and Angela could freely discuss politics, she found her true calling.

Angela obtained her political start with the center-right group *Demokratischer Aufbruch*, or the Democratic Awakening. According to her account, she walked into their campaign office and asked how she could assist. The West German government had donated boxes of computers to the organization, so Angela helped unpack and set up the computers. She further added that setting up those computers permitted her to use her scientific expertise to get involved in the political process. In a 2004 interview, she described this time as "the magical experience of new beginnings. You will never live through something as beautiful as that again."[40]

Angela Merkel's political career accelerated at an unprecedented pace. She went from unpacking boxes at a campaign office to holding a cabinet position in a mere six months. Marr argued that the million-dollar question is, how did Merkel go from just another member of East German society to a leading figure in German politics in such a brief period? There is only one logical explanation: she happened to be the right person at the right place at the right time.[41]

In 1990, under the leadership of Lothar de Maizière, East Germany held its first and last multiparty election. Upon his victory, de Maizière appointed Merkel as his deputy spokesperson in the new, pre-unification caretaker government. In April of that year, much to the surprise of many, Merkel joined the larger, overwhelmingly male-dominated Christian Democratic Union. Helmut Kohl, head of the CDU, also led the growing German reunification movement. In the first federal election following reunification in 1990, the citizens of the Vorpommern-Rügen region elected Merkel to the Bundestag, or the German Parliament, and the citizens of Germany elected Kohl as the first chancellor of their united country.

When he formed his cabinet, Kohl wanted a woman and a former East German. He selected Merkel, whom he appointed as minister for women and youth. He became her mentor, and referred to Merkel as his *Mädchen* (girl) and introduced her accordingly. But in 1994, he promoted Merkel to the Ministry for the Environment and Nuclear Safety, which gave her greater international visibility and a platform from which to build her political career. During her tenure in this position, she orchestrated the second major global climate change conference in Berlin, which resulted in the first international promise to reduce greenhouse gas emissions.[42]

Merkel understood that she owed her political career to Kohl, but she also acknowledged that she had to break free from *der Dicke* (the Fatty), as the corpulent chancellor was known in government circles. "To put it diplomatically," she said, "I knew that I had to fight to be seen as an individual. Not in the eyes of Helmut Kohl, but in the eyes of other people. People already had a fixed and predetermined view of who I was; a token woman on the left. All this annoyed me."[43]

The time would eventually come for Merkel to prove not just to Kohl but to the rest of the political world that she would not settle for being a "token" woman—rather, she would prove herself a viable asset to his cabinet and administration.

When Kohl lost the 1998 election to opposing Social Democratic Party (SPD) leader Gerhard Schröder, the CDU appointed Merkel as its secretary general. Then, in 1999, it was discovered that the CDU had received donations into a secret slush fund, which Kohl used to reward his friends. Kohl refused to identify the donors, claiming he had given his word the donations would be anonymous. Most party members wanted the scandal to remain quiet, but Merkel had other ideas or, some argue, future aspirations.

Merkel turned on her mentor when she wrote a scathing editorial that appeared in the December 22, 1989, edition of the *Frankfurter Allgemeine Zeitung*. She insisted that Kohl step down as head of the party and encouraged the party to move forward without him, writing:

> *We can only build a future on a foundation of truthfulness. Helmut Kohl must accept this realization; the CDU must accept this realization. Incidentally, only by doing so will the party manage to avoid exposing itself to attack every time another news item about alleged donations surfaces.*[44]

As one can imagine, Merkel received incredible criticism for writing this piece. To many, her actions were opportunistic, even Machiavellian. To others, the article reflected a woman who had been undermined and underestimated one too many times—it demonstrated that she was more than a token woman or East German, but rather a competent politician with goals and aspirations of her own. Regardless of one's position, most agree it was the turning point of Merkel's career and positioned her to run for chancellor.

Merkel's decision to join the conservative CDU had startled many people from the beginning. In addition to the party's overwhelmingly patriarchal hierarchy, the CDU was also a socially conservative party with Catholic roots and strongholds in the western and southern parts of Germany. Merkel, on the other hand, was a centrist Protestant who originated from northern Germany. Additionally, her "living situation" created quite a controversy among other party members. Many people did not think that a forty-five-year-old divorcée, who lived with her divorced boyfriend, set the ideal example for the conservative party. When questioned about it, she merely replied that since she had already been married once, it would be prudent not to rush into anything.[45]

Nevertheless, she routinely found herself addressing questions about her private life—questions Qvortrup claims she most likely never would have had to answer if she were a man. A career woman who had grown up with a more enlightened view of the role of women, she found it hard to be continually bombarded with questions about her family and private life, especially as she felt them to be irrelevant. "No, I had not concluded that I did not want to have children," Merkel answered repeatedly in some form. "But when I went into politics I was thirty-five, and now it is out of the question."[46] Nonetheless, as a leading figure in a party that appealed to the conservative values of *Kinder, Küche, Kirche* (children, kitchen, church), Merkel realized that if she were going to become a true leader in the German political arena, she would have to address the marriage concerns.

On December 28, 1998, Angela Merkel and Professor Joachim Sauer surrendered to societal pressure and married in a ceremony so small that they even excluded their own families.[47] Perhaps Merkel's willingness to marry and adhere to societal norms was analogous to the lesson her parents had taught her with respect to dealing with the communist government: sometimes one must at least pretend to go along with people or principles—if for no other reason than to make one's life easier.

Perhaps one of Merkel's most admirable characteristics is the combination of her opportunism and pragmatism—a combination that has helped her achieve high ranks in the political world. As legal scholar Guido Calabresi describes her, "She doesn't take on fights she can't win. . . . There are a couple of examples out there, lying in their coffins, of people who got in her way."[48] Kohl was the first in a long line of politicians—both German and worldwide—who underestimated Merkel. Gerhard Schröder, the SPD leader and German chancellor from 1998 to 2005, publicly called her "pitiful."[49] But Merkel would eventually have her day.

After the 1998 defeat and the subsequent scandal, the CDU ousted both Kohl and his successor, Wolfgang Schäuble, from its leadership and elected Merkel to replace Schäuble. She became the first female leader of the German party on April 10, 2000. By the 2002 election, Merkel's ambition to become chancellor was well known, but she lacked the support of most minister-presidents (heads of state government) and other party leaders. That year, however, in addition to her role as CDU leader, she became leader of the opposition in the Bundestag. And on May 30, 2005, Merkel won the CDU/CSU nomination to challenge the incumbent, Chancellor Schröder of the SPD.

On the eve of the September 18, 2005 election, opinion polls expected Merkel to win a decisive victory. Nonetheless, the result was close enough—with the CDU/CSU winning 35.3 percent (CDU 27.8/CSU 7.5) of the second votes to the SPD's 34.2 percent—that both sides declared victory. Neither the SPD–Green coalition nor the CDU/CSU and its preferred coalition partners had enough seats to form a majority in the Bundestag.

After three weeks of negotiations, the two parties reached a deal where Merkel became chancellor and the SPD held sixteen seats in the cabinet. The majority of delegates (397 to 214) in the newly assembled Bundestag elected Merkel as Germany's next chancellor. At 11:52 a.m. on November 22, 2005, in one historic moment, Dr. Angela Dorothea Merkel became the first former

East German chancellor, the first woman chancellor, and—at age fifty-one—the youngest.[50]

Obama's political career began in 1996 when the residents of the South Side of Chicago elected him as their state senator. After his election, he sponsored legislation to increase tax credits for low-income workers, negotiated welfare reform, and promoted increased subsidies for childcare. Obama served as an Illinois state senator until 2002. He faced his first political defeat in 2000 when he ran an unsuccessful campaign to unseat four-term Democratic US Congressman Bobby Rush. Although the defeat by a margin of four-to-one humiliated Obama, he regrouped and, in August 2002, began to raise funds and create a campaign committee to launch his formal campaign for the US Senate. He officially announced his candidacy in January 2003.[51]

Obama's real rise to political fame came when he delivered the keynote speech at the Democratic National Convention in Boston in July 2004. In what became known as his "Audacity of Hope" speech, he passionately argued that "there's not a liberal America and a conservative America; there's the United States of America. There's not a Black America and white America and Latino America and Asian America; there's the United States of America."[52] Four months later, he was elected senator in a landslide victory.

Endlessly encouraged to run for president following that speech, Obama officially announced his candidacy on February 10, 2007. As a backdrop for his announcement, he chose the symbolic Old State Capitol building in Springfield, Illinois, the same building where President Abraham Lincoln had delivered his historic "House Divided" speech in 1858. In a campaign speech that projected themes of hope and change, Obama, the first Black presidential candidate to receive a nomination from one of the two major parties, emphasized rapidly ending the Iraq War, increasing energy independence, and reforming the healthcare system.[53]

Just as Merkel grew tired of having to address questions about her personal life—primarily about her decision to marry and not have children—Obama had to address issues of his race and ethnicity. As a candidate, he never skirted around the issue of his race, nor did he ever make it the forefront of his political campaign and his candidacy—until Reverend Jeremiah Wright, the minister of the church Obama and his family had attended for twenty years, went on the record with some racially charged comments in March 2008. The backlash from the media over the comments "threatened to derail Obama's insurgent campaign,"[54] according to E. J. Dionne and Joy-Ann Reid, editors of a collection of Obama's greatest speeches. Among the litany of comments Reverend Wright made, he blamed the United States' own "terrorism" for the 9/11 terror attacks and argued that Black Americans lived in a country that treated its citizens as less than human, and thus should sing "God Damn America" instead of "God Bless America."[55] Obama responded to the crisis with his speech "A More Perfect Union," delivered at the National Constitution Center in Philadelphia, on March 18, 2008.[56]

In this inspirational speech, Obama refused to apologize for the country's past sins—instead he argued that only because of the greatness and uniqueness of America could someone with his unique background even have the opportunity to run for president:

> *I am the son of a Black man from Kenya and a white woman from Kansas. . . . I've gone to some of the best schools in America and lived in one of the world's poorest nations. I am married to a Black American who carries within her the blood of slaves and slave owners. . . . I have brothers, sisters, nieces, nephews, uncles, and cousins of every race and every hue, scattered across three continents. And for as long as I live, I will never forget that in no other country on Earth is my story even possible.*[57]

He passionately proclaimed that one of the primary goals of his campaign was to help Americans create a more tolerant, more just, and more prosperous nation together, regardless of race, ethnicity, or national origin. Obama touched on the criticism he had received from some groups for being "too Black" even as he was defined by others as "not Black enough." Despite the differences in America, Obama pointed out, the one thing everyone had in common was wanting a secure future for their children and their grandchildren, and he hoped his campaign would help people focus on that rather than on their differences.

He emphasized the need for members of the Black community to embrace the challenges of their past without becoming victims of it.[58] Obama understood that the roots of racism and the struggle for equality were deeply embedded in American society and that one election would not erase everything, but it would be one step of many over the years. He charismatically argued that racial equality would occur when America realized that one group's ambitions need not cancel out another group's—that investments in the welfare of every American would advance the interests of the entire country.[59]

During both the primary process and the general election, Obama's campaign set numerous fundraising records, and on June 19, 2008, Obama became the first major-party US presidential candidate to turn down public financing in the general election since the modern system was created in 1976. Barack Obama became the first Black president on November 4, 2008, when he won both the popular vote 52.9 percent to 45.7 percent and the electoral vote 365 to 173 against the Republican challenger, Arizona senior senator John McCain. Following his astonishing victory, at noon on January 20, 2009, Barack Hussein Obama II was sworn in as the forty-fourth president of the United States.

Although not quite as fast as Merkel's rise to power, Obama's movement up the political ranks was by all accounts remarkable. Moreover, unlike Merkel, who had barely won her election in 2005, Obama won his historic 2008 election in a landslide. Given the record-breaking amount of money Obama managed to raise, combined with his unprecedented route to the White House, it was clear the American people were willing to take a chance on the young, relatively inexperienced senator, regardless of—or perhaps partly because of—his race. With his speeches and campaign promises, Obama had managed to win over the American people, but he would have a hard road ahead of him in patching up the relationship between the United States and its European allies—most particularly Germany.

While those relationships stood on shaky ground, one thing was certain: Obama and Merkel were unlike any of their predecessors. As Obama once said to his German counterpart, remarking on the progress of the twenty-first century and the extraordinary historical and personal circumstances that had prepared both leaders for public service, "Wars can end. Adversaries can become allies. Walls can come down. At long last, nations can be whole and can be free. Madam Chancellor, the arc of our lives speaks to this spirit."[60]

2

"I TAKE RESPONSIBILITY"

JANUARY-APRIL 2009

U S president George W. Bush had just won reelection for his second term when the Bundestag swore in Merkel as Germany's newest chancellor in November 2005. Due to the Bush administration's decision to invade Iraq in 2003, the relationship between the United States and Germany had become strained for the first time since the Cold War. But, although most European leaders viewed Bush as "Satan's representative on earth,"[1] Chancellor Merkel gave the president more leniency than her colleagues.

Nonetheless, Merkel had her differences of opinion with the American president about the Guantanamo Bay detention center, and she had no problem expressing them. In an interview Merkel granted to the German news magazine *Der Spiegel*, she managed to effectively strike the right balance, acknowledging the threat of terrorism while simultaneously rejecting Bush's militaristic approach. "An institution like Guantanamo cannot and must not continue in the long term," she said. "Other ways and means of dealing with the prisoners must be found."[2]

As a consequence of isolationist policies implemented by the Bush administration, by 2009 many world leaders were pleased to see him go and hopeful that President Obama would restore the alliance between the United States and the EU that Bush had all but destroyed. Merkel, however, remained the notable exception. She and Bush had a close relationship, and it seemed clear that she would miss him.[3]

Something one should always keep in mind with respect to Merkel and her attitude toward the United States is her East German roots. As someone who lived under a communist regime, she remains extremely grateful toward the United States, and as such, somewhat prejudiced, so her opinions often seem more tainted by bias than those of her European counterparts. Nevertheless, despite her fondness for Bush, Merkel understood that many of his policies alienated not only many of her colleagues but her fellow citizens as well.

Yet, after Obama had been elected, Merkel realized that she needed to walk a fine line because, despite her reservations about the new president, her citizens were incredibly fond of Obama. In fact, according to an article by Ralf Beste, Dirk Kurbjuweit, Christian Schwägerl, and Alexander Szandar in *Der Spiegel*, "85 percent of the German population would have also elected Obama. Hardly any other issue enjoys such widespread consensus in the country."[4] It is true that part of Obama's allure for the German people came from their hope that Obama would restore the closeness between the two nations that Bush had damaged. However, as it became abundantly clear during the course of his presidency, Obama had a genuine affection for the German people. They sensed that and clung on to the spirit of hope it inspired. It was evident that the Germans' admiration for Obama was contagious, and their leader fully realized this.

Following Obama's inauguration in January 2009, Merkel granted an interview to Spiegel Online where she acknowledged the significance of Obama's historic victory and claimed that his inauguration as the first Black president was "a truly great hour for America" and that it "offered a multitude of opportunities."[5] Without mentioning Obama's predecessor by name, she took a swipe at Bush and his policies when she stated that she hoped Obama understood the complex problems of the world could be solved only through collaboration and dialogue with others.

The German chancellor chose her words diplomatically. On a personal level she had a close relationship with Bush, but on a professional level she understood the challenges some of his policies had created. Therefore, she managed to discuss the downfalls of the Bush administration, but by failing to mention him directly, she did not openly offend him. Merkel simply listed the issues—in Afghanistan, in Iran, and in relations with Russia—that needed immediate and ongoing attention, saying, "I hope our cooperation will be characterized by listening to one another and taking decisions on the basis that any one country can't solve the world's problems on its own, but that we can only do it together."[6]

Although Merkel acknowledged that the violent situation in Afghanistan continued to be problematic, and offered to provide nonmilitary assistance to the region, she remained unwilling to reconsider sending more military troops after the change in US administration and said, "We took our decisions based on our capabilities, our skills—not on who is president."[7] Although there had been speculation from the media and key leaders that Obama would insist on more military involvement from the United States' European allies, that was not the case.

A February 2, 2009, article published by *Der Spiegel* discussed Merkel's indifference to the newly elected president, as well as the increasing conflict between the two leaders over Germany's refusal to accept Guantanamo detainees:

> *There is not even a trace of enthusiasm for the man on whom the world's hopes are now pinned. Merkel is not prepared to quickly accommodate the Americans on the first concrete issue for trans-Atlantic relations, namely the acceptance of detainees from Guantanamo.*[8]

Given the fact that Merkel firmly disagreed with the Bush administration on the Guantanamo prison, arguably, from the US perspective, it seemed that at the very least she could have assisted in the closure of the facility.

Obama and Merkel spoke via telephone for the first time in an official capacity the last week of January 2009, and during their twenty-five-minute conversation, they addressed the hot-button issues: the year-old economic crisis, Iran, Afghanistan. The February 2 piece in *Der Spiegel* indicated that Obama took every opportunity during their conversation to make abundantly clear that he had no intention of bombarding Merkel with demands, but rather would seek to persuade her instead.[9] Merkel later told her staff that Obama had failed to make one single request—not even for additional German troops in Afghanistan—during the course of their call. Moreover, the piece argued, there were two striking components to the conversation between Merkel and the new US president: "Obama's tone, and the silences in between his sentences." Unlike previous administrations, which tended to only make demands of allied nations, Obama had listened as well. The United States no longer wanted to be "the skunk at the garden party," explained Germany expert Jackson Janes of Johns Hopkins University, who was interviewed by *Der Spiegel*. "The White House of Barack Obama is a house with two buttons, not just a 'send' button."[10]

Listening rather than merely dictating demands to allied nations is a trait that Obama employed many times throughout the course of his presidency and, as it turned out, one that Merkel greatly appreciated and respected. Despite the cordial conversation between the two leaders, however, both were slow to cast judgment on their new colleague. Merkel feared that the overwhelming furor among the German people was really nothing more than "an overly hasty expression of admiration for the new president, who—so people believe—has got to be better than his predecessor."[11] Unprepared to make any hasty rulings or let down her guard, she instead adopted a "wait and see" attitude toward the new president. Journalist and political advisor Sidney Blumenthal wrote as much to Hillary Clinton, who was secretary of state at the time, when he described Merkel's skepticism:

> *[Diplomat John Kornblum says] she dislikes the atmospherics surrounding the Obama phenomenon, that it's contrary to her whole idea of politics and how to conduct oneself in general. She would welcome a more conversational relationship with you.*[12]

On the other side of the Atlantic, the American president and his staff were equally dubious of the German chancellor. Although her refusal to permit Obama to speak in front of the Brandenburg Gate as a presidential candidate may have set the tone for their future working relationship, the new administration's skepticism toward Merkel went deeper. On a personal level, Obama's staff viewed her refusal to visit Washington, DC, following his inauguration as "rude and impolitic," according to *Der Spiegel*. [13] From a military perspective, the Obama administration resented Germany's "checkbook diplomacy," the piece continued, and viewed the German government's approval of €50 million for a trust fund to help build and train the Afghan army (rather than deploy additional troops to south Afghanistan) as a way to "buy its way out of its responsibilities."[14]

At this point in the Obama–Merkel working relationship, however, the biggest point of contention concerned the economic crisis that would come to be known as the Great Recession. Merkel had a reputation for procrastination while she analyzed and, in her colleagues' eyes, overanalyzed a situation. Many of her peers, both within and outside Germany, found this "inactivity" tactic annoying. The economic crisis was one such scenario, and Washington officials firmly believed that Merkel's lack of political or economic expertise also caused her to procrastinate, which only exacerbated the problem. It is worth noting that in the beginning stages of their working relationship, Obama tended to side with Merkel's European allies on this issue, but in later years Obama, and the public at large, would recognize this tendency toward deliberation as a trait he and Merkel shared, and it would become one of the things he valued most about her.

The Great Recession had begun in December 2007 when an $8 trillion housing "bubble" in the United States burst. The economic impact proved to be disastrous not just for the United States but for the entire world. Before the catastrophe, the US unemployment rate had been at a modest 4.9 percent, but by October 2009 that number had climbed to a staggering 10.1 percent.[15] The average numbers were similar for the EU nations, with Spain being hit the hardest with an unemployment rate that reached 18.7 percent (37 percent for youths) in May 2009.[16] Despite the worldwide impact of the recession, the euro remained stable—with Germany playing a significant role in that outcome.

Nonetheless, ahead of the G20 summit, the German government tried for several weeks to marshal support for a "Charter for Sustainable Economic Activity," whose core principle was that nations should not become so indebted that they are unable to recover. Germany and France also fought for stricter economic regulation. More specifically, European leaders on the whole wanted European-level supervision of bank behavior, expanded hedge-fund regulation, and the freedom for banks to retain a higher amount of equity capital. Prior to the April G20 summit in London, several EU leaders met in Brussels to propose a plan to negotiate a unified strategy that would address the economic crisis. Merkel took the lead, having emphatically expressed her desire that the nations of the EU speak with one voice. The group quickly determined that further economic stimulus packages would not be implemented and that the EU wanted to take the lead and reform the world's financial markets.[17]

Given their adamant opposition to additional stimulus packages, the EU leaders grew increasingly concerned about the position of the United States— especially after they heard reports that Obama's secretary of the treasury supported the International Monetary Fund (IMF) recommendation that all nations should spend 2 percent of their gross domestic product on an economic stimulus package.[18] The regulation of hedge funds and taxation became the biggest sticking points between the Americans and the Europeans because the Americans felt stronger economic contributions, via economic stimulus packages, would provide better and more sustainable economic growth than mere regulations. According to a document leaked to Secretary of State Hillary Clinton, Merkel had a "profound belief that the Obama administration is on a disastrous economic path."[19]

In anticipation of the upcoming G20 summit, the German chancellor granted an exclusive interview with the *New York Times*, published with the eye-catching headline MERKEL IS SET TO GREET, AND THEN RESIST, OBAMA.[20] Such a headline expressed the apprehension she held toward working with the new president. During the hour-long interview, Merkel reiterated her position: She had no plans to encourage the European Central Bank to follow the Federal Reserve in pumping money into the system. Nor would she permit Germany to pay additional money toward the economic bailout. Finally, she hoped Obama would keep his word and control the American debt created by his proposed domestic stimulus plans.[21]

Although the Americans remained hesitant about the proposed reforms, the German government expected Obama to join the finance-reform movement at the 2009 G20 London Summit on April 2. Many of Merkel's initial concerns with the new president rested on fears that he talked a good talk but, she dreaded, would be unable to deliver on his promises. Her final remarks in the *New York Times* article demonstrated her reluctance to take Obama at his word. This time, she had deployed her "wait and see" attitude toward the American president. There was no question that Merkel and Obama had a significant difference of opinion on how to address the economic crisis. But Merkel was unprepared for the humility with which Obama addressed and acknowledged the crisis, and she did not foresee his willingness to work toward ensuring a similar disaster did not happen again.

When the world leaders met in London at the beginning of April, it was evident from the start that the summit comprised two factions: the United States and Great Britain versus France and Germany. Obama and British prime minister Gordon Brown had repeatedly indicated that increasing regulation and eliminating tax havens played a secondary role to economic stimulus packages, while French president Nicolas Sarkozy and Merkel insisted the opposite. Germany and France refused to pump money back into the economy without assurances in the form of stricter regulations that would ensure such a crisis would not happen again.

In a joint press conference, Sarkozy and Merkel made it clear that they spoke as one with respect to financial market regulation. According to *Der Spiegel*, Sarkozy proclaimed that "[w]hen it comes to the regulation of the financial markets, there will be no room for negotiation."[22] Merkel seconded her French counterpart and added that additional regulation should not be debated and anyone who "doesn't understand that is paving the way to the next crisis."[23] As *Der Spiegel* characterized the meeting, "Sarkozy and Merkel went on a warpath."[24]

While the media certainly captured the opening tone of the summit, reporters never lost sight of the purpose of the meeting. The press illustrated that, despite the conflicts and disagreements among various world leaders, the ultimate goal had been to find a successful package that would help stimulate national economies and prevent the world from going into a major recession. In fact, *Der Spiegel* described tensions being so high, with people arguing and making slanderous accusations against one another, that it was surprising anyone left London on speaking terms. At one point, Argentina's president Cristina Kirchner became defensive and attacked Merkel over a perceived disagreement on whether to assist African nations. *Der Spiegel* recounts her statement as follows:

> *"What Merkel is saying makes it sound like I don't want to help the African countries. . . . And by the way,"* [Kirchner] *said looking at Merkel, "I'm not angry at anyone."*[25]

The solution to the economic crisis proved to be such a challenge that even when leaders were on the same page, arguments arose as to the most effective way to address the problem. For example, both Brown and Sarkozy agreed that leaders should publish a public list of banks that refused to comply with the policies agreed upon in London, yet they disagreed on the specifics with regard to *how* to publish such a list. Sarkozy had promised his government that the list would be made public and would be part of the communiqué, while Brown stated that the list was already available with the Organisation for Economic Co-operation and Development (OECD) and therefore it was unnecessary to make it part of the communiqué. After the two exchanged heated words, Brown tried to calm his French counterpart down. "Nicolas," he said, "keep in mind what it was that we agreed on here. The era of banking secrecy is over."[26] The one obvious takeaway from these controversial exchanges was that, despite the disagreements over the ways to achieve that goal, all the G20 participants shared the same vision and a goal of doing whatever was necessary to stimulate the economy for their countries and their people.

After numerous hours, many disagreements, and even more compromises, the world leaders managed to settle on a strategy to solve the greatest economic crisis since the Great Depression of the 1930s. In the end, nations pledged to introduce greater regulation of financial markets, ban tax havens, and grant loans to poorer countries. The German contribution would come from the vaults of the central bank, the *Bundesbank*, rather than from the federal budget. The G20 leaders also approved the creation of a new international supervisory authority, the Financial Stability Board. And Sarkozy was satisfied that the G20 communiqué would refer to the list of tax havens published by the OECD.[27]

The results produced at the London summit were by no means perfect. For example, the leaders failed to offer a solution to the growing imbalance of the world economy between nations with large consumer debt, such as the United States, and nations like Japan and Germany with a large export surplus.[28] The *Der Spiegel* authors pointed out that, while the world leaders at the summit had avoided open conflict with one another to reach an imperfect but workable agreement, their heated debates had in some ways only exacerbated existing economic differences:

> *The world we saw in London was a world in transition. It was no longer the old world of nation states, but it was also not yet a new world capable of thinking in harmony.*[29]

Amid all these agreements and concessions, the most significant event came when Obama spoke up at the conclusion of the summit. While Merkel, Brown, Sarkozy, and other G20 members had been engaged in heated exchanges over the correct solution to the economic crisis, Obama remained unusually quiet. That silence ended, however, when Italian prime minister Silvio Berlusconi looked directly at the newly elected US president and told him that because the economic crisis had begun in the United States, Obama had an obligation to address it.[30] Much to the surprise of everyone in the room, especially Merkel, Obama replied, "It is true, as my Italian friend has said, that the crisis began in the US. I take responsibility, even if I wasn't even president at the time."[31]

The US president's admission may go down in the history books as one of the most significant confessions by a world leader in modern times. According to *Der Spiegel*, by taking ownership of the worst economic crisis in nearly one hundred years, Obama had admitted that while other countries shared some responsibility for the crisis, the bulk of the problem resulted from the United States and its endless need for profit.

Obama's ability to confront the problem head-on rather than skirt away from responsibility sent a signal of hope to the other G20 members that perhaps he would implement policies to prevent such an economic collapse from happening again.

Merkel immediately telephoned her finance minister to inform him of Obama's confession.[32] While it would be some time yet before she would let down her guard around the US president, his admission of guilt and willing-ness to take responsibility perhaps laid the foundation for the relationship that later developed.

After the summit ended, Obama's final words of encouragement to his colleagues, about how to address their respective media, must have left an impression:

> It is important that we do not sell short the results of this summit. The press would like us to have conflicts. Instead we have attained great achievements. And it is important that we exude confidence.[33]

As the *Der Spiegel* journalists argued, Merkel, mindful of the number of compromises reached among world leaders, focused on those accords and kept in mind the advice Obama had given when she offered the German media her depiction of the events that transpired at the London summit. She said that a "very, very good compromise" had been reached, an "almost historic compromise."[34]

Given all the arguments and the compromises the G20 members endured during the summit, it would not have been unreasonable for them to return to their home countries demanding an increase in their annual pay. In truth, the results of that summit likely saved the world markets from complete disaster.

Immediately following the G20 summit in London—the very next day, in fact—Obama and Merkel had the opportunity to meet again with other world leaders at the Strasbourg–Kehl Summit, in honor of NATO's sixtieth anniversary. The jointly hosted conference took place April 3–4, 2009, in the German city of Baden-Baden and the French city of Strasbourg. While in Baden-Baden, Obama and Merkel held their first bilateral meeting, which they followed up with a press conference.

In accordance with tradition when a foreign dignitary visits another country, Merkel greeted the American president and First Lady Michelle Obama with a full military ceremony. People crowded the streets, waving American and German flags and chanting "Obama." The two leaders shook hands with spectators and posed with their spouses for the obligatory media photos. By all accounts, the scene demonstrated exactly what one would expect for a visiting leader of an allied nation—especially for someone as popular as the American president.

Merkel's husband, Professor Joachim Sauer, also attended the ceremony. His attendance spoke to the importance of the event, as he usually remained absent from his wife's public appearances. In fact, he had not even taken time off work when Merkel was sworn in as Germany's first female chancellor.[35] Because of Sauer's frequent absence from the public spotlight, the German tabloids had dubbed him the "Phantom of the Opera."[36] As with many "firsts" in the relationship between Obama and Merkel, this was the first time Professor Sauer made a public appearance at an event the US president also attended, but it would not be the last.

Following the military reception and the informal "meet and greet" on the streets, Merkel and Obama held a thirty-minute press conference where they both made statements and addressed journalists' questions. The chancellor noticed the admiration Germans continued to show toward Obama.

When Merkel welcomed the American president in her opening comments, she acknowledged the excitement of her citizens over his visit:

> *I think you've seen that the press was actually showing a great deal of welcome to you, and you saw the people along the way who were waiting for you for many hours with their little flags waving. And we're pleased to have you.*[37]

Following her welcoming comments, Merkel summarized the topics she and Obama had discussed in their recent private meeting, most notably with regard to Afghanistan and the results of the G20 summit. When she addressed the issue of the ongoing conflict in Afghanistan, Merkel reiterated Germany's continued support and "responsibility" in solving the crisis. Merkel characterized the recent G20 meeting in London as productive because

> *the United States has shown that they are willing to cooperate, too, to show that spirit of cooperation. I think that this is a common task, indeed, for us to shape an alliance in this cooperative spirit, because this . . . transatlantic relationship is also one that helps us to overcome the current financial and economic crisis.*[38]

If one reads between the lines, Merkel's comments are a tribute to Obama's confession at the summit. The chancellor discussed the importance of the long friendship and partnership between Germany and the United States, and, clearly, she hoped the promise Obama made to restore the strained relationship between the countries would prove to be sincere. Although Merkel's praise of this relationship with the United States was open and genuine, her comments about the president were cordial but much more cautious. She had not been ready to completely let down her guard around the new American president, but the ice had begun to thaw.

During Obama's ten-minute speech, he shared the unpleasant news that he had learned earlier that day: the latest jobs report indicated that the United States had lost 663,000 in the previous month alone, which "pushed our unemployment rate to 8.5 percent, the highest in twenty-five years"; he also revealed that the United States had "lost 5.1 million jobs since [the] financial crisis and recession began."[39] Despite the gravity of the topic at hand, Obama did his best to make light of the seriousness of the situation. In response to a reporter's question regarding the economy, he replied:

> *Now, the US will remain the largest consumer market, and we are going to make sure that it's open.... It's not the Germans' fault they make good products that the United States wants to buy. And we want to make sure that we're making products that Germans want to buy.*[40]

At this, Merkel broke out of her reserved shell for a brief time to laugh.

In his remarks, Obama talked about NATO. He argued that it had been the most successful alliance in modern history but also acknowledged, "If NATO becomes everything, then it's nothing."[41] He thanked Merkel and the Germans for the support of activities in Afghanistan with regard to resources as well as troops. "You just heard Chancellor Merkel emphasize that at its core, what has made NATO so effective is the Article 5 principle that if one ally is attacked, then all allies come together to deal with the problem," he said. "That is the essence of a successful alliance."[42]

Politicians on both sides of the Atlantic had speculated that Obama would ask for more resources in Afghanistan and that there would be pushback as European allies denied the request. From both Merkel's and Obama's comments, however, there did not appear to be conflict over troops. Rather, Merkel, as an ally and a NATO member, knew Germany had a duty to support the American mission in Afghanistan, and Obama understood and appreciated that Germany provided what support it could.

Obama and Merkel differed in one notable way that was evident from the start: the way they answered journalists' questions during press conferences. Merkel would often give very short and precise answers, whereas Obama had the American politician's skill of answering everything but the question asked—in fact, he had it down to a fine art. His answers tended to be long and detail oriented, peppered with data on any number of relevant issues.

Obama, aware of this tendency, owned it during this press conference. When a German reporter asked him, "What does this mean, in concrete terms, for the Europeans and NATO?"[43] Obama simply replied, "I think that was an indication that my answers have been too long. So I'll make this one quick."[44]

Later press conferences and appearances reveal an affection between Obama and Merkel, who seem to enjoy extending compliments to each other. Yet from the very beginning Obama referred to Merkel as his "friend," a compliment Merkel would not return until much later:

> *I want to thank Chancellor Merkel for her leadership, her friendship ... I have been spending quite a bit of time lately with Chancellor Merkel and continue to be impressed with her wisdom and leadership and diligence in pursuing the interests of her people.*[45]

According to German historian Hans W. Gatzke, "Americans are more willing to use the term friendship than most Germans."[46] Journalist Lisa Schwesig shares the perspective of a German etiquette and manners expert, who argues, "Compliments are not in keeping with the German way.... Germans are brought up to be humble and not to stand out." In addition, Schwesig says, a compliment carries the danger of being misunderstood. According to her expert source, "Many people are afraid to offend someone with a compliment or become too personal."[47] So it is not surprising that Obama had been more open than Merkel to expressing a budding friendship between them.

Following their joint appearance, Merkel and Obama had one more opportunity to work together at that time, in Strasbourg on the next day of the NATO summit. Although pundits argued that tensions were still high between them, Obama intervened on behalf of Merkel to help avert a disaster that day.

Twenty-seven of the twenty-eight existing NATO members were prepared to support the nomination of Danish member Anders Fogh Rasmussen as the next secretary general to head the transatlantic military alliance. Yet due to one of the unique rules of the alliance, a secretary general to NATO had to be unanimously elected, and Turkey refused to support the nominee.

Back in 2005, some political cartoons depicting the Prophet Muhammad had appeared in a Danish newspaper, and Turkish prime minister Recep Tayyip Erdoğan felt that Rasmussen's response had been unacceptable and thus that he was unsuitable for the position.

Uncharacteristically, Merkel prematurely insisted on Friday afternoon that Rasmussen should be appointed new NATO chief by the evening of April 4. However, on Saturday an agreement still had not been reached. As a host of the summit, it would have been disastrous for Merkel if an agreement was not reached. Perhaps recognizing an opportunity to solidify US–Germany relations, Obama telephoned Erdoğan directly and offered him certain unnamed guarantees—including top NATO posts for Turkey and some unknown promise regarding Denmark-based Kurdish broadcaster Roj TV. As one *Der Spiegel* article declared, "The US president, whose initial goal had been to soothe trans-Atlantic relations, seemed at times like a marriage counselor."[48]

Even though Obama stepped in and saved Merkel from humiliation in her own country, the chancellor said little to the president about his actions. There was a photo of her smiling with French president Sarkozy on the cover of *Der Spiegel*, but no public acknowledgment of gratitude toward the American leader. Perhaps this "oversight" was more a matter of cultural protocol than unfriendliness. But as Merkel had indicated in her *New York Times* interview prior to the G20 summit in London, she had concerns about the new president—particularly with respect to the economic crisis.

Nevertheless, between Obama's astonishing admission at the G20 summit, his willingness to take responsibility for the economic crisis, and his efforts to personally call Erdoğan and avert a disaster at the NATO summit, his actions indicated to Merkel that perhaps there was substance to his promises. A promising foundation had been laid, but it would be challenged in the ensuing months.

3

"WILD SPECULATIONS"

JUNE 2009

To commemorate the sixty-fifth anniversary of the Allies landing on the beaches of Normandy during World War II, President Obama scheduled a quick visit to Germany in June 2009 in between meetings in Egypt and France. While in Cairo, he gave his inspirational "A New Beginning" speech at Cairo University. Among the myriad topics Obama discussed, he emphasized certain policies for his upcoming meeting with Chancellor Merkel—notably, the need for a two-state solution in Israel and the issue of nuclear weapons in Iran. He argued passionately for a new beginning between the United States and Muslims around the world,

> *one based on mutual interest and mutual respect, and one based upon the truth that America and Islam are not exclusive and need not be in competition. Instead, they overlap, and share common principles—principles of justice and progress; tolerance and the dignity of all human beings.*[1]

Obama understood that one speech would not erase years of mistrust, but he urged people "to listen to each other, to learn from each other, to respect one another, and to seek common ground."[2]

Obama also reminded the audience that the United States and Israel share an unbreakable bond based on historical and cultural ties, and indicated that he understood the desire of the Jewish people to have their own homeland after centuries of anti-Semitism.[3] At the same time, Obama also asserted the importance of diplomacy when he encouraged people to examine the conflict from both sides. He argued that the failure of the Israelis to see the number of Palestinians forced to live in refugee camps for decades created a problematic moral dilemma, and that the only reasonable solution to this decades-old crisis would be the creation of a two-state solution where both Palestinians and Israelis could live in peace and security.[4]

This compromise, Obama proclaimed, would benefit not only the Israelis and the Palestinians but the United States and the rest of the world.[5] He emphatically stated that while the United States could not force peace among the two parties, it could provide the necessary support to help both parties achieve these goals.[6] Then he outlined a list of steps he thought both Israel and Palestine should take to help facilitate the change that, he believed, needed to come about sooner rather than later.[7]

Obama argued that the Palestinians needed to abandon violence, and the Israelis needed to stop denying the right of a Palestinian state to exist.[8] The president confessed his belief that privately Israelis understood the need for a Palestinian state, and that privately Muslims realized the state of Israel was here to stay. Therefore, he reasoned, "It is time for us to act on what everyone knows to be true."[9]

The conflict between Israel and Palestine was not the only pressing issue in the Middle East, and Obama knew he also had to comment on the public's fear that Iran would obtain nuclear weapons. When Obama addressed the issue of nuclear weapons, he placed the subject in a historical context. He admitted that the United States and Iran had a tenuous relationship going back to the Cold War, when the United States played a role in the overthrow of a democratically elected Iranian government. But Obama made it clear that he wanted the United States and Iran to move forward rather than dwell on the past, expressing his ambition to create a world free of nuclear weapons because "no single nation should pick and choose which nations hold nuclear weapons."[10]

As Obama recognized, the Nonproliferation Treaty (NPT) was an international treaty whose primary goal was to prevent the spread of nuclear weapons and technology. Participation in such a treaty would allow any country—including Iran—to access nuclear power if the government adhered to established guidelines.

Once again, Obama showed that he had the ability to see past his own nation's interests, a quality that Merkel valued. In particular, the need for a two-state solution in the Middle East was an issue very close to Merkel's heart, and something she and Obama agreed on. This contentious debate around nuclear weapons was yet another important foreign policy issue Merkel and Obama would be forced to address together, and another on which they agreed. So, as he prepared to meet with Merkel, Obama was in sync with his German counterpart.

The day immediately after Obama's speech in Cairo, he made a short trip to Germany. As part of his broader goal of visiting historic World War II landmarks on this anniversary trip, he opted to visit the city of Dresden, followed by a tour of the former concentration camp of Buchenwald. In the years that followed World War II, Dresden had become famous for the gruesome bombing campaign led by the British and American armies, a multiday military offensive that ultimately resulted in the deaths of between 18,000 and 25,000 Germans.[11] Reflecting Obama's tremendous popularity among the German people, the local citizens held a two-day welcoming party on the city's historical market square in anticipation of his visit. Mayor Helma Orosz saw the US president's visit as "an important event" in the city's history.[12]

While the citizens of Dresden were happy about the president's visit, his decision to go there in lieu of the traditional official state visit to Berlin caused controversy on both sides of the Atlantic. Some Germans viewed the decision as a slight to Merkel, while her foreign policy critics went so far as to blame Merkel for what they saw as a deteriorating relationship between the

United States and Germany since Obama had taken office.[13] On the other side of the Atlantic, one of Obama's critics, the conservative blog Power Line, ran the headline DRESDEN: NEXT STOP ON APOLOGY TOUR? and implied that the president's decision demonstrated an expression of regret for America's wartime behavior.[14]

Despite the criticism on both fronts, Obama and Merkel made valuable use of the president's time in Germany, which included a visit to a historic church and a trip to the former concentration camp of Buchenwald in between Obama's meeting and press conference with Merkel. The two began with a tour of Frauenkirche Dresden, the city's "Church of Our Lady," which had been recently rebuilt after World War II firebombing destroyed it. Their stopover at the church provided the two world leaders with an opportunity to spend time together in an informal yet educational capacity. At this point, the two were still strangers, but this visit allowed them to get to know one another without the challenges of the formality that accompanied traditional state visits.

The two then held a bilateral meeting and hosted a joint press conference, which followed the usual format: opening remarks by both leaders, followed by questions from the press corps. Apparently unbothered by the speculation around Obama's alleged refusal to visit Berlin, Merkel publicly welcomed Obama to Dresden and thanked him for his visit:

> *It is so important that the American president, Barack Obama, makes his first stop here in Dresden. This is a highly symbolic city [that was] almost completely destroyed during the Second World War, [and] then rebuilt after Germany [sic] unification. . . . [President Obama, this visit] shows that you also pay tribute to the tremendous efforts they made in those twenty years after the fall of the Wall.*[15]

If Merkel had been offended that Obama failed to visit Berlin, she did not let on publicly. By now, she recognized the president's enormous popularity in Germany, and she seized the opportunity to welcome him back. She refused to engage in the petty arguments of the media and instead saw the visit as an opportunity to show Obama the progress her country had made since World War II—progress that had occurred, in large part, because of the relationship between the United States and Germany. Following her welcoming remarks, Merkel listed the topics the two had discussed in their meeting, including some issues they agreed on as well as areas of disagreement. Her remarks indicated a fair amount of respect growing for the American president despite the disagreements. Accordingly, she made sure to reference her approval of Obama's speech in Cairo the previous day:

> *President Obama yesterday gave a very important speech in Cairo, which I think will be an ideal basis for a lot of action of a positive nature, particularly as regards speeding up the peace process in the Middle East. . . . I said on behalf of the Federal Republic of Germany that we would like to try and be helpful in this peace process to the extent that is possible to us. We need a two-state solution. . . . And whatever we can do in order to constructively accompany this along the way, we will gladly do.*[16]

The importance of Merkel's reference to Obama's speech was twofold: she made it known that she had attended his actions closely, and she indicated a solid sense of unity and alliance between the United States and Germany on this key issue. Furthermore, by employing the full name of "the Federal Republic of Germany" rather than simply "Germany," Merkel emphasized her passion to resolve this issue.

With respect to negotiations with Iran on its nuclear program, Merkel promised that Germany would work not only with the United States but with other close allies to ensure a satisfactory solution would be reached, saying, "Germany will try its utmost with its contacts, with its expert knowledge, to give a positive contribution to this issue."[17]

Merkel also addressed the controversial subject of the world markets amid the recession, and in her pragmatic manner, she hinted that there had been disagreement between her and Obama: "You have a very ambitious plan that you outlaid. So we will keep a close eye on developments."[18] She mentioned the need to implement the policies discussed during the G20 summit in London, and she expressed relief in the fact that both the United States and European countries were now doing so. Her statement on the fiscal crisis was significant because, reading between the lines of her comments, her apprehension about the plan was evident. She stopped short of completely criticizing the president's agenda outright, however—a very different tone than she took in the *New York Times* article where she detailed her plan to "resist" Obama just a few months earlier.

Before she gave Obama the opportunity to speak, Merkel also mentioned the importance of the United States passing legislation to help combat climate change. She also reminded the public of the upcoming 2009 United Nations Climate Change Conference in Copenhagen later that year, and she not-so-subtly emphasized how important it was for the United States to do its part:

> *We know that it's very much an uphill battle; we're very familiar with that from the debate that we have here in our country. And we are keeping a close eye on legislation that is passed.*[19]

The lack of climate change legislation was a point of contention between Merkel and the Obama administration. With these remarks, she alluded to the opinion that an unsympathetic US Congress was no excuse for Obama's inability to pass legislation of such global importance. She hinted that Germany and the EU would be watching for the United States to take action on climate change.

Obama began his remarks in his usual charming manner as he thanked Merkel and the German people for their hospitality and expressed his admiration for "the beautiful city of Dresden, which obviously is steeped in history."[20] He then underscored the importance of friendship between the two nations:

> *Germany is a close friend and a critical partner to the United States, and I believe that friendship is going to be essential not only for our two countries but for the world if we are to make progress on some of*

the critical issues that we face, whether it's national security issues, or economic issues or issues that affect the globe like climate change.[21]

Obama then summarized his account of the meeting with Merkel, and with respect to the economic crisis, he stated:

We've seen, I think on both sides of the Atlantic, some progress in stabilizing the economy, but we're far from done in the work that's required. . . . [W]e are working diligently to strengthen financial regulations to ensure that a crisis like this doesn't happen again, and it's going to be very important to coordinate between Europe and the United States as we move to strengthen our financial regulatory systems. We affirmed that we are not going to engage in protectionism. And as all of us do what's required to restart our economy, we have to make sure that we keep our borders open and that companies can move back and forth between the US and Europe in providing goods and services to our respective countries.[22]

In highlighting the security challenges that both countries faced, he stressed the importance of NATO and commented on how valuable a partner Germany had been.[23] He emphasized the collective commitment among all NATO partners to prevent terrorist attacks, and the need to maintain that commitment. When the president mentioned the need to avoid a nuclear arms race with Iran and to develop a two-state solution in Israel, he reaffirmed that these goals could only be achieved with the assistance of other nations.

Obama ended his opening remarks by expressing his admiration toward Merkel, whom he referred to again as his "friend" when he said, "It is a great pleasure to be with my friend once again, who I always seek out for intelligent analysis and straight talk."[24] Although Merkel still failed to be open about her personal relationship with or feelings toward the president, Obama made his affinity toward the chancellor public once again. Nevertheless, it was clear from the questions posed by the press corps that many remained skeptical of Obama's comments. Were they sincere or just a show for the media?

The first question directed to the president asked him to address the "wild speculations" over his brief trip to Germany and his reportedly strained relationship with the chancellor. The cameras focused on Merkel, whose serious expression turned into a small smile as Obama began to answer. He reaffirmed the journalist's characterization of their relationship as mere "wild speculations" and claimed that such conjectures failed to consider factors such as the coordination of traveling and tight schedules.[25] In other words, the president argued, the media was making too much out of his short visit to Germany.

Obama's next words captured the attention of the world and the amusement of those present. As he wagged his finger at the crowd, he scolded, "So stop it, all of you. I know you have to find something to report on, but we have more than enough problems out there without manufacturing problems."[26] Unfortunately, the cameras were focused on Obama as he professed those words, so viewers cannot see Merkel's response, but the laughter from the audience was thunderous.

Merkel politely waited for him to finish his answer before she insisted on replying:

> *Allow me, if I may, to . . . say that it's fun to work together with the American president because very serious, very thorough analytical discussions very often lead us to draw the same conclusions. And I think we proved that in London, we proved that on previous meetings. I think that's part of our job, isn't it, that you exchange views, different views that you may have also. And wherever it was necessary, we have come to common solutions. So I very much look forward to our future cooperation.*[27]

This was a bold statement from the normally reserved chancellor, who turned toward Obama as she spoke, and both her words and body language at that moment indicated that she had begun to see in Obama the promise of hope that her fellow citizens saw. At this point, the two had worked with each other enough that she slowly began to see the actions behind Obama's words.

When a reporter brought up the contentious subject of the Guantanamo detention center, which then-Senator Obama had promised to close should he win the presidency, he acknowledged the complexity of the problem and admitted he had spoken with Merkel and other EU leaders in an attempt to close the facility. The president made it clear that while the chancellor had not made any commitments on managing the closure, he had not asked for any:

> *Chancellor Merkel has been open to discussions with us. . . . I'm very appreciative of the openness, not only of Merkel but [of] other European countries, to work with us. . . . I very much appreciate the constructive manner in which Chancellor Merkel has approached the issue.*[28]

When Merkel answered the question, she admitted that Germany—and particularly her administration—strongly favored the closure of Guantanamo and that negotiations between Germany and the United States were underway. The closure of this facility was one issue that Obama and Merkel had agreed on from the beginning. It had dominated many of their early discussions, but unfortunately the lack of support from members of the US Congress had forced the issue onto the back burner in later meetings between the two leaders. In Dresden, however, Merkel stated, "I am absolutely confident that we will find a common solution."[29]

When another journalist asked about the ongoing crisis in the Middle East—especially after years of an impasse between the Israelis and the Palestinians—Obama reiterated that he believed progress toward peace would need the work of the entire international community. He especially called attention to Merkel's role in the negotiation process when he said,

> *I very much appreciate Chancellor Merkel's willingness to put the prestige and the resources of the German government behind that same effort. I think the entire international community is going to have a responsibility to help these parties achieve a hard-won peace that will ultimately be good for everybody's security interests.*[30]

Merkel responded by taking the opportunity to praise Obama, and she stated that both his words and his actions demonstrated a renewed sense of urgency on the issue—one that had been abandoned in the previous administrations:

> *Well, I believe that with the new American administration, with President Barack Obama, there is actually a unique opportunity now to see to it that this peace process—or let's perhaps be more careful—this negotiation process [can] be revived again.*[31]

She agreed that both Israel and the Palestinians had to be willing to take the steps Obama had outlined, and when they were willing to do so, both nations could depend on the help of Germany as well as the United States.[32]

On the topic of Israel, Merkel felt an overwhelming fear of guilt for the damage caused to the Jewish people during the Holocaust, and protecting them had become one of her signature foreign policy items.[33] She firmly believed that a two-state solution provided the safest way for Israelis and Palestinians to live side by side in peace. Merkel's deeply held belief in protecting peace and security in Israel was one of the cornerstones of her agenda. The fact that Obama, too, placed it at the top of his agenda and proposed solutions so early in his presidency could be another factor in the bond established between the two leaders.

In response to a question about Obama's next stop on that trip—Buchenwald concentration camp—the president explained that as part of his trip to commemorate the sixty-fifth anniversary of the Normandy landings, he felt he should visit a concentration camp, especially since he never had before. He added that he specifically chose Buchenwald because his grandmother's brother had been among the troops that liberated the camp.[34] Many politicians would have resisted a visiting leader's request to witness such a horrific part of their nation's history, but Merkel, not known for avoiding responsibility, encouraged the president's visit and in fact seemed to view it as an honor:

> *[T]his is for me deeply moving to see an American president, in this case President Barack Obama, as a visitor in Buchenwald. And he talked*

about his personal background as regards this question. Look at Buch-
enwald . . . one example of these horrible concentration camps, liberated
by American troops.[35]

Merkel's remarks illustrated that she understood the importance of Obama's visit to Buchenwald, not only for the US president personally but for the diplomatic relationship between their two nations.

The two leaders ended the press conference with a cordial handshake and smiles—and appeared significantly more relaxed than at the beginning of the meeting forty minutes earlier. Merkel had not yet gone so far as to refer to Obama as a friend, but for the first time, she had openly admitted her respect for the new president.

Immediately after their joint press conference, Merkel joined Obama for the 120-mile trip from Dresden to the Buchenwald Memorial, but not before she changed her clothes from the vibrant yellow she had worn earlier to an all-black outfit that visibly demonstrated the darkness of the site they were about to visit. For this appearance, two former camp detainees, Nobel laureate Elie Wiesel and Buchenwald Committee chairman Bertrand Herz joined the pair. Obama was the first US president to visit the former concentration camp, making it a historic event, and yet he had a personal connection with it. The president also wanted to witness firsthand the horror stories he had personally heard from his great-uncle Charles Payne, a young soldier who helped to liberate the Buchenwald subcamp Ohrdruf in April 1945.

As *Der Spiegel* reported on the day of their tour, "It's March weather in June"[36]—a scene appropriately melancholy for a visit to a place with such a bleak history. As they began their tour, Obama, Merkel, Wiesel, and Herz paused to place a white rose on the plaque to honor the 50,000-plus people who had perished there. Afterwards, Merkel, Obama, and Wiesel each spoke about the horror and historical importance of Buchenwald.

An emotional Merkel explained that Germans have a duty and respon-sibility to work toward a world free of xenophobia, racism, anti-Semitism, and right-wing extremism to ensure nothing like the atrocities of World War II ever happens again.[37] Then, just as Obama had taken responsibility for the fiscal crisis at the London G20 Summit, Merkel took ownership for the brutality and atrocities of World War II: "This appeal of the survivors defines the very special responsibility we Germans have to shoulder with regard to our history."[38] Merkel concluded by expressing gratitude to the United States for their help over the years, and to Obama in particular for his visit:

> *It gives me an opportunity to align [sic] yet again that we Germans shall never forget, and we owe the fact we were given the opportunity after the war to start anew, to enjoy peace and freedom, to the resolve, the strenuous efforts, and indeed to a sacrifice made in blood of the United States of America and of all those who stood by [America's] side as allies or fighters in resistance.*[39]

A visibly emotional Obama stumbled uncharacteristically over his words as he began to speak to the audience, and he proclaimed, "These sights have not lost their horror with the passage of time."[40] He further argued that memorials such as Buchenwald remind people that they must "reject the false comfort that others' suffering is not our problem and commit ourselves to resisting those who would subjugate others to serve their own interests."[41] As Merkel stood next to Obama and listened to him speak, her body language demonstrated her obvious discomfort. She shifted her weight uncomfortably from side to side and moved her hands and arms restlessly, but one thing remained constant—the tears in her eyes.

Obama emphasized the prisoners' resilience, and as he addressed the audi-ence, he pointed out that those who had suffered on those grounds all those years ago had no way of knowing that someday a museum and memorials would be there for future generations to see, including a tower clock set perma-nently to 3:15, the moment of liberation.[42] He continued to claim that people *could not have known how the nation of Israel would rise out of the destruction of the Holocaust and the strong, enduring bonds between that great nation and my own. And they could not have known that one day an American president would visit this place and speak of them, and that he would do so standing side by side with the German chancellor, in a Germany that is now a vibrant democracy and a valued American ally.*[43]

Obama's firm but uncharacteristically emotional demeanor illustrated his gratitude for being in a position where he could stand in solidarity next to the leader of a nation that was formerly an adversary.

Obama shared Merkel's sentiment that it was the obligation of the living and future generations to ensure nothing so inhumane and unthinkable ever happened again. He argued that

it is now up to us, the living, in our work, wherever we are, to resist injustice and intolerance and indifference ... and ensure that those who were lost here did not go in vain. It is up to us to redeem that faith. It is up to us to bear witness ... to remember all those who survived and all those who perished, and to remember them not as victims, but also as individuals who hoped and loved and dreamed just like us.[44]

And finally, he thanked Merkel for her ownership of one of the darkest periods in modern history, adding, "I want to express particular thanks to Chancellor Merkel and the German people, because it is not easy to look into the past in this way and acknowledge it and make something of it, make a determination that they will stand guard against acts like this happening again."[45]

Touring a former concentration camp may not have been as exciting as the traditional state visit to Berlin, but it proved to be equally educational—if not more so—for the two leaders. On a personal note, Obama finally witnessed firsthand the place that caused his great-uncle such horror all those years ago. On a professional level, Obama saw a more human side of Merkel, who let down her guard and showed an emotional aspect of her normally reserved character. Moreover, Obama had an opportunity to see in action some of the traits he admired in Merkel—namely, her honesty and her willingness to take responsibility.

Just as Obama had taken responsibility for the Great Recession at the London summit, Merkel took ownership of the atrocities of the Holocaust. The experience may have been eye-opening for Merkel as well. Many of her early reservations about the new American president came from a concern that he was all talk and no action. However, Obama's insistence on touring Buchenwald indicated that he was, in fact, a man of action as well as words. If anything, this visit demonstrated that alliances can be reaffirmed, policy can be discussed, and partnerships can be fortified in the absence of more traditional state visits. Indeed, the lesson seemed to be that two willing parties are more important than location and tradition.

4

"SEA CHANGE"

JUNE 2009

On June 26, 2009, Chancellor Merkel made her first official trip to Washington, DC, since President Obama had taken office. Ahead of her visit, news articles on the upcoming meetings continued to focus on the potential strain between the two—particularly with regard to climate change, Afghanistan, and the economic crisis. According to a *Der Spiegel* article earlier that month, Merkel had shared her skepticism toward the policies implemented by the US Federal Reserve and told an audience in Berlin that she called for a "return to rational policies."[1] Although the article did not elaborate on what Merkel meant by that phrase, her colleagues both within and outside the EU understood her reluctance toward excessive governmental stimulus spending, meaning her comments were most likely directed at the economic policies Obama had thus far supported.

If members of the press corps or the public expected a controversial or combative meeting between Merkel and Obama, however, it is safe to say they were disappointed. Indeed, the press conference that followed their one-on-one meeting showed a growing friendship, with Obama praising Merkel and her returning the compliment.[2]

In their encounters it had now become common, if not expected, for Obama to begin by expressing his admiration for Merkel. Indeed, this time he mentioned her "leadership," "candor," and "wisdom" and her "pragmatic approach to getting things done."[3] But in the early stages of Obama and Merkel's working relationship, as the two learned how to interact with each other, the content of their public statements generally focused on the strength of the relationship between the two countries. This encounter was no exception, as the president added his appreciation for the alliance between Germany and the United States:

> *Chancellor Merkel's visit is the latest chapter in the long partnership between our two countries: the service of our men and women in uniform who stood together through a long Cold War and who serve today in Afghanistan; the innovation of our entrepreneurs, who helped to sustain our economies; and the bonds of friendship and trust between our people, which are unbreakable.*[4]

Obama emphasized the importance of allied nations working together rather than in isolation when he claimed that

> *Chancellor Merkel shares my belief that no single nation can meet the challenges of our time alone. Today we reaffirmed that the United States and Germany, one of our closest allies and an indispensable partner, will continue to play a leadership role across the range of challenges.*[5]

When Obama addressed the controversy that surrounded solutions to the fiscal crisis, he highlighted the solutions important to Merkel, notably strengthening financial regulations and avoiding protectionism, and he complimented "Merkel's commitment to reform."[6] With these remarks, Obama not only emphasized his admiration for Merkel but reassured both the chancellor and the German people that the United States—under his administration—valued the ties between the two countries and wanted to undo the isolationist policies of his predecessor.

In addition to discussing the unsettled economic crisis, the two leaders also needed to address the challenge of global warming. Germany and the other EU countries had set a target of a 20 percent reduction from 1990 CO_2

emissions levels by 2020. Moreover, the EU promised to increase that target to 30 percent if other major polluters joined the effort.[7] Yet despite the fact that a panel of United Nations scientists claimed that a 25 percent to 40 percent reduction by industrial countries was necessary to avoid the devastating effects of global warming, the United States had been reluctant to support such ambitious targets. In fact, US climate delegate Todd Stern dismissed calls for higher reduction commitments, stating firmly, "The 40 percent below 1990 (levels) is something which in our judgment is not necessary and not feasible given where we're starting from."[8] Stern's comments illustrated the US government's profound stubbornness with respect to environmental policy and its unwillingness to consider the environmental policy changes that experts around the world had argued were necessary.

In light of the difficult subjects that awaited the two leaders, people on both sides of the Atlantic waited in anticipation. What would become of Merkel's first trip to Washington? Understandably, Merkel remained skeptical of any influence she might have in urging the president to raise awareness of this issue among the American people and to ask them to take more responsibility for altering their environmentally hazardous ways. Nevertheless, given the worldwide crisis climate change created, and the pressure she faced not just from her fellow citizens but from other world leaders, she knew she must try. Environmentalists in Germany expected Merkel to use her influence to convince Obama of the necessity of stricter emissions reduction goals.[9] One Greenpeace climate expert told *Der Spiegel*:

> *We have the impression that the American G-8 negotiator is slowing the discussion. It is important that Merkel makes it clear to Obama that something substantial must come out of the G-8 summit.*[10]

Coincidently, the US House of Representatives had scheduled a vote on an energy-saving bill known as the Waxman–Markey Bill during Merkel's Washington visit. If the 1,200-page bill were to pass, it would bind the United States to reduce greenhouse gas emissions 17 percent from 2005 levels by 2020, and more than 80 percent by 2050.[11] According to a report by the US

Environmental Protection Agency (EPA), 2005 greenhouse gas emissions levels totaled 7,320.28 million metric tons, and by 2015 that number had decreased by 9.3 percent to 6,638.1 million metric tons—indicating that the United States was on its way to reaching the targeted goal.[12] The legislation also called for measures to promote clean energy technology, including goals to expand the use of wind and solar power as well as develop technology for greener building codes.[13] As Suzanne Goldenberg argued in the British newspaper the *Guardian*:

> *The stakes could not be higher. A defeat would destroy the last chances of enacting crucial energy legislation before the UN treaty negotiations at Copenhagen.*[14]

Yet not a single Republican House member supported the bill; they viewed it as nothing more than a "hidden energy tax."[15] Although the preliminary voter totals taken by House Speaker Nancy Pelosi indicated that the Democrats had enough votes to pass the bill anyway, Democratic leadership refused to take anything for granted. Obama, too, understood the significance of this vote and realized that nothing could be assumed, so he actively lobbied Congress for its passage. In a speech given in the White House Rose Garden, Obama passionately argued about the importance of the vote, declaring that reforms were overdue and represented a crucial step toward illustrating US leadership on the international stage. "We have been talking about this issue for decades and now it's time to act," he said.[16]

Despite Obama's plea and the efforts in Congress to pass environmental reform legislation, the Germans remained unimpressed. The legislation failed to meet the ambitious targets on emissions reduction that the EU had already pledged.[17] German minister of the environment Sigmar Gabriel criticized the legislation and argued that, when it came to environmental awareness, the US and EU "live in two different worlds."[18]

Even so, Obama reiterated the United States' commitment to combating climate change—particularly with respect to energy consumption. He pointedly mentioned the upcoming House of Representatives' vote on the Waxman–Markey Bill and quickly complimented Merkel and the German government on how they had addressed the issue of climate change:

> *And let me say, Chancellor, that I've been very impressed by Germany's foresight and commitment to clean energy. . . . And it's my hope that the United States will match that commitment today when our House of Representatives votes on a critical energy bill that will promote a new generation of clean, renewable energy in our country.*[19]

Obama's remarks were not simply empty campaign promises; he truly wanted to improve the US record on climate control, and by linking his hopes for better legislation back to Germany's efforts, he hoped to also improve the strained relationship with Germany.

During their press conference, when Merkel addressed the issue of climate change, she referred to the bill before the House of Representatives as "a sea change" that indicated "the United States is very serious on climate."[20] The chancellor mentioned that she had gone through similar debates in her own country and understood the difficulty of coming to consensus on reduction targets.[21] Although Merkel did not mention Obama by name in her remarks about the progress the United States had made on climate change, there is no doubt that she was referencing Obama and his administration:

> *I think it's so important that we are at one in saying, if we want a success in Copenhagen, we need to talk to the emerging countries and the emerging economies as to their possible contribution. But the fact that with the United States we stand where we stand today is an enormous success, which I would have not . . . have thought possible a year ago—let me be very serious.*[22]

Merkel clearly felt optimistic that the change in policy—the move toward better environmental legislation—resulted from the efforts of Obama.

In the weeks prior to Merkel's trip to Washington, conflict arose in Iran when Ayatollah Khamenei and Mahmoud Ahmadinejad formed a coup d'état and overthrew the results of the country's June 13 election. Against the votes, and, ultimately, the will of the people, Ahmadinejad seized control over the government from reform candidate Mir-Hossein Mousavi. As Oxford Scholar and Iranian author and expert Farhang Jahanpour wrote at the time:

> *The issue at stake has indeed moved beyond the election and its outcome. The epic protests by Iranian citizens have been met by a disproportionate degree of force from government agents and revolutionary militia.*[23]

Citizens rebelled against what appeared to be a fraudulent election, which caused the Iranian government to retaliate against the protesters. Things had grown so out of control, so quickly, that by the time of Jahanpour's June 18 article, atrocities had already occurred: eight citizens had been murdered at a peaceful demonstration in the city of Tehran on June 15; more than three hundred reformist journalists and politicians had been arrested; gruesome attacks on college campuses throughout the country had resulted in large numbers of injuries and deaths; methods of communication such as SMS messages, social media, and internet access had been blocked; and foreign reporters had been banned from reporting unauthorized protests or from traveling outside of the city of Tehran.[24]

Since these activities violated the very nature of democratic institutions, both Obama and Merkel felt compelled to address the situation in Iran during their meeting in Washington. Obama emphasized that both the United States and Germany stood united in condemning the acts of Iranian authorities:

> *Today we speak with one voice. The rights of the Iranian people to assemble, to speak freely, to have their voices heard—those are universal aspirations. The violence perpetuated against them is outrageous. And*

despite the government's efforts to keep the world from bearing witness
to that violence, we see it and we condemn it.[25]

Furthermore, the president reiterated his plan to prevent Iran from developing its nuclear weapons capacity, thus preventing a nuclear arms race in the Middle East. He declared that coordination between China, Russia, Germany, and the other EU nations would be required in order to successfully urge the Iranian government to engage in activities that would lead to greater security and prosperity for the Iranian people without violating international protocols.[26]

Obama once again discussed his position on the need for a two-state solution to one of the biggest problems in the Middle East—whether Israel and Palestine were capable of "living side by side in peace and security."[27] Then he tied his comments back to his trip to Germany earlier that month:

> *And during our recent visit to Buchenwald, Chancellor Merkel spoke elo-*
> *quently of Germany's everlasting responsibility to the safety and security*
> *of Israel. Going forward, Germany will remain a critical partner in our*
> *efforts to bring safety and security to Israelis, the Arab states, and Pales-*
> *tinians, who must reject violence and recognize Israel's right to exist.*[28]

Once again, by shining the spotlight on Germany and Merkel, Obama demonstrated the strong alliance and partnership between the two nations.

Merkel, too, felt the need to address the crisis in Iran and expressed her support for the Iranian people when she said:

> *I would like to underline that the Iranian people need to be given the*
> *right to peaceful demonstrations . . . the right to have votes be counted*
> *and the election results substantiated; that the rights of human beings, of*
> *individuals, of citizens are indivisible of the world over and also apply,*
> *therefore, to the Iranian people.*[29]

Like Obama, she indicated the need to prevent the Iranian government from developing a nuclear weapon when she added that

we have to work to [ensure] that the Iranian nuclear program is stopped,
that Iran does not get possession of a nuclear weapon. . . . Germany and
America will work closely together on this, just as on questions related to
arms reduction and disarmament.[30]

Merkel then wished Obama good luck with his upcoming visit to Moscow. She understood the importance of the United States having a good relationship with Russia, especially since Russia provided valuable support with the crisis in Iran:

We need Russia, for example. We need it, looking at the problems we have
with Iran. And we want to forge a common position wherever possible
with Russia, but also with China. We've done that over the years in the
format of the United Nations with a number of resolutions, and that
needs to be continued.[31]

Merkel's words portrayed the importance of nations working with one another to forge partnerships whenever possible. The global complexities of the twenty-first century meant nations needed to be able to rely on one another in times of crisis.

Next, Merkel mentioned the fiscal crisis and praised the progress that leaders had made:

We're on a good path here. I think there's been progress. You have made
very important steps here in the United States as regards financial reg-
ulation. . . . We are very grateful that we are also able, together with the
United States, to work on principles as to how matters are to be taken
into the future after this crisis. But we now have to emerge, obviously,
from this crisis—and recovery of our economies is a great precondition
for further progress.[32]

Obama also referred to his upcoming trip to Moscow and stated that he and Merkel had reaffirmed their commitment to a better working relationship with Russia. In doing so, he once again managed to work his recent trip to Dresden into his comments:

> *Meeting these challenges will be neither quick nor easy, but I'm reminded of the lesson from my recent visit to Dresden. Chancellor Merkel took me to a timeless Baroque church devastated in the Second World War. For decades, it lay in ruin, a symbol of war. But thanks to the donations of Germans and Americans and people around the world, it was rebuilt, and its glory was restored. And today, it stands as a stunning symbol of what's possible when countries and friends work together.*[33]

It is unclear whether referencing his recent visit to Dresden was a deliberate political move aimed at emphasizing his budding relationship with the chancellor, or simply a way to demonstrate what he thought possible when allied nations worked toward a common goal.

Either way, Merkel then thanked Obama and the United States for their friendship and partnership. She pointed out that Germany had recently celebrated its sixtieth anniversary, and declared, "And we're more than aware of the fact that Germany would not stand as it stands today had not our American friends and partners helped us after the end of the Second World War."[34]

Just as Obama seemed to take any opportunity to compliment Merkel and the German people, Merkel in turn complimented the United States. Although she remained reluctant to refer to Obama as her "friend" or "partner," it became increasingly evident that she had begun to admire her counterpart.

Often, the question-and-answer session of a press conference is the most challenging part of talks between world leaders. Journalists frequently press dignitaries on key issues in an effort to get a head of state to make an official comment on the record, particularly with regard to controversial subjects. This press conference, as it turned out, proved to be the exact opposite. The atmosphere for both the leaders and the journalists appeared to be much more relaxed and laid-back than in previous encounters.

At one point, when a journalist began to ask a question, the translator intervened to apologize—the microphone was not functioning, so the translation was delayed.[35] As the translator apologized, Merkel looked over at Obama and rolled her eyes. The two exchanged wide smiles as if to say, *Technology is great . . . when it works.*

When a German reporter questioned Obama on why he had failed to grant the customary interview with the media of the host country in his two previous trips to Germany, Obama avoided an explanation but smiled widely and joked with the reporter, asking whether he still wanted that interview.

The journalist answered, amid a room full of laughter, "If this is a commitment, I would appreciate that very, very much."[36]

Obama turned to Merkel as if to obtain her permission, and in a rare move, she responded in English, "We have to talk about that," as she and Obama once more shared a smile.[37]

Later, when asked by a German reporter about his feelings toward Germany, both Obama and Merkel took the opportunity to weigh in. Obama described his affection toward both the nation and its leader:

> *I will always have, I think, a warm spot in my heart for Germany, in part because of the response and the reaction that I've received from the German people. I will tell you that part of the warmth I feel toward Germany is because I like Chancellor Merkel a lot. You know, I've now dealt with a lot of world leaders, and I think that Chancellor Merkel is smart, practical, and I trust her when she says something. And so that kind of approach is exactly what you want from an international partner. And I very much enjoyed my interactions with her and her team.*[38]

True to character, Obama had no problem publicly disclosing his feelings toward Merkel. On the other hand, Merkel remained quiet. She did not directly express her feelings about the president, though her indirect responses and body language, including her break from her typical "poker face" with a smile and laughter, throughout the press conference indicated a gradual shift in opinion had occurred.

One final illustration of the relaxed nature of the press conference came in the form of Obama's reaction to a question raised with regard to his half sister's experience as an African woman living in Germany, which he described in his autobiography *Dreams from My Father*. Obama, very light-heartedly, replied:

> *My sister, she obviously had a great time in Heidelberg. . . . [S]he was going out with a German guy. And I don't want to comment on how that played itself out. That may have an impact on how she views Germany right now, but that's, I think, a little too personal for a press conference.*[39]

At that, he received a roar of laughter from the audience. Despite the serious issues the two had discussed during their meeting and at the press conference, it was clear that the US president and the German chancellor enjoyed their interaction with one another and the press.

Although the question about Obama's sister and her life in Germany had been directed toward the president, Merkel quickly piped in with a response, if for no other reason than to demonstrate she had read Obama's book:

> *Let me perhaps say something on Auma in Heidelberg. [In] the book,* Dreams from My Father, *she is telling us a little about her own impressions in Heidelberg. . . . I found this very interesting because, on the one hand, she describes us as a country where quite quickly you have the impression that each and every one needs to fend for his or herself. . . . [But] it was also something good, maybe, because it strengthens people's own sort of awareness of their own self, of their own responsibility. . . . So it was, for me, a very enriching experience to read this book.*[40]

Merkel's refusal to permit Obama to speak at the Brandenburg Gate and her perception of Obama as arrogant appeared to be ancient history. The fact that she went out of her way to answer a question posed to Obama about his book, simply to demonstrate that she had read the book, indicated the friendly yet competitive spirit that would develop between them over the years as part of their normal working relationship.

Later that evening, the House narrowly voted in favor of the passage of the Waxman–Markey American Clean Energy and Security Act by a vote of 219–212.[41] Obama responded with a statement that displayed his gratitude:

> *Today, the House of Representatives took historic action with the passage of the American Clean Energy and Security Act. It's a bold and necessary step that holds the promise of creating new industries and millions of new jobs; decreasing our dangerous dependence on foreign oil; and strictly limiting the release of pollutants that threaten the health of families and communities and the planet itself. Now it's up to the Senate to take the next step. And I'm confident that in the coming weeks and months the Senate will demonstrate the same commitment to addressing what is a tremendous challenge and an extraordinary opportunity. . . .*
>
> *So I look forward to continuing this work with the Senate so that Congress can send me a bill that I can sign into law—and so that we can say, at long last, that this was the moment when we decided to confront America's energy challenge and reclaim America's future.*[42]

Despite the historic House of Representatives vote, however, intense lobbying ensured that the bill never made it to the Senate floor.

Merkel's next trip to Washington, DC, would be nearly five months later, in November 2009, when she would present an iconic speech before a joint session of Congress, a rare honor for a foreign leader. Because this next visit aligned with two important historical events, Merkel ensured she catered her remarks.

5

"WE HAVE NO TIME TO LOSE!"

NOVEMBER-DECEMBER 2009

On November 3, 2009, Chancellor Merkel made her second trip to Washington—this time to speak before a joint session of the US Congress in honor of the twentieth anniversary of the fall of the Berlin Wall.

According to Germany-based American foreign policy expert John Hulsman:

> *The US is a republic and a relatively new country, that doesn't have a lot of symbolism. To speak before a joint session of Congress is about as big an honor as can be bestowed on a foreign leader.*[1]

Although Konrad Adenauer, the first chancellor of the new Federal Republic of Germany, had spoken before Congress in 1957, he had not addressed a joint session but rather one chamber and then the other. Merkel would address both houses simultaneously—a first for a German head of government—in addition to meeting with President Obama to discuss the foreign policy issues of Afghanistan, climate change, Iran, and of course, the ongoing financial crisis.[2] Even though the invitation had come from House Speaker Nancy Pelosi rather than Obama, the German chancellor's appearance still demonstrated an important milestone in the relationship between Merkel and Obama.

In their usual manner, the media and various pundits characterized Merkel's upcoming speech as a political ploy as much as an honor. The headline for one article on the German public international news website DW— **HONOR, YES, BUT TOUGH QUESTIONS ALSO AWAIT MERKEL IN WASHINGTON**—demonstrated this point.[3]

Merkel's visit aligned with the twentieth anniversary of the fall of the Berlin Wall, but it also came shortly after her successful reelection for a second term as chancellor. The Obama administration had waited until after the distraction of Merkel's reelection campaign before confronting Germany on the amount of support the United States could expect on important policy decisions. As Hulsman characterized the visit, "Beneath all the symbolism and niceness there is an insistent push that now it's time for Germany to step up to the plate."[4] The DW article argued that despite the good "chemistry" between Merkel and Obama, they tended to shy away from subjects that could cause disagreements; any truly detailed and frank discussions with Germany about foreign policy had been missing from their encounters thus far.[5]

Other topics that still required joint cooperation included the ongoing crisis in Iran, the economic crisis, and global warming. But the precarious situation in Afghanistan remained of primary importance. Obama was considering sending 40,000 additional troops, and he needed to know what kind of commitment he could expect from Merkel—if not in soldiers, then in other matters. Merkel and Obama needed to address tough issues this time, and such candid talks would be difficult. But even though the two leaders had just begun to forge a working relationship, others could see that many of their characteristics balanced one another. As DW reported:

> *Now when practical policies are key, Obama can't find a more suitable partner than Merkel. . . . "She's intellectually capable of having this nuts-and-bolts policy discussion that's so desperately needed," [Hulsman] said. . . . If the planned meeting between Merkel and Obama does in fact signal the start of a new phase of open and honest exchange between Washington and Berlin, then Merkel's trip will have been not only symbolic, but also a sustainable success.*[6]

Prior to Merkel's momentous speech before Congress, she and Obama held their fourth bilateral meeting. Although they did not follow with their usual press conference, the two spoke to the media to summarize their talk. Both made brief comments but did not give reporters the opportunity to ask questions.

In his usual charming manner, Obama welcomed Merkel, congratulated her on her recent reelection victory, and expressed his delight about her upcoming congressional speech when he said:

> *She is going to be the first German chancellor in fifty years to address Congress—the first chancellor ever to address a joint session of Congress. And it is, I think, a very appropriate honor that's been bestowed on Chancellor Merkel.*[7]

At this point, the cameras shifted their attention from Obama toward the chancellor, who, seated to his right, nodded hesitantly and smiled modestly as she listened to the president.

One of the key reasons that the relationship between Merkel and Obama became so strong is that Obama admired Merkel, who—despite her upbringing in a communist dictatorship—had risen to become the leader of a free and united Germany. As he stated:

> *We are now moving towards the twentieth anniversary of the Berlin Wall coming down and Germany being reunified after so many painful years. And this is a special moment for Chancellor Merkel, as somebody who grew up in East Germany, who understands what it's like to be under the shadow of a dictatorial regime, and to see how freedom has bloomed in Germany, how it has become the centerpiece for [an] extraordinarily strong European Union.*[8]

Although Obama never stated it directly, one can surmise that he drew a comparison between Merkel's rise from her upbringing in a communist-controlled country to her position as the leader of Germany and the archetypal story of an American who pulls themselves up by their bootstraps—he equated political oppression with economic oppression.

Obama confirmed the two had discussed the ongoing foreign policy issues of Afghanistan, climate change, and the financial crisis. When he summarized their discussion, he emphasized his gratitude for the sacrifices of the German soldiers stationed in Afghanistan, as well as the "common work" between the two nations to bring "peace and stability" to the region.[9] Contrary to media speculation, Obama neither requested nor mentioned any request that Germany send additional troops to Afghanistan.

Ahead of the United Nations Climate Change Conference planned for later that year, global warming was a crucial topic. Through the president's statements it became clear that even if some of his fellow citizens had failed so far to see the imminent threat of climate change, Obama himself saw and understood this threat:

> *Chancellor Merkel has been an extraordinary leader on the issue of climate change. And the United States, Germany, and countries around the world, I think, are beginning to recognize why it is so important that we work in common in order to stem the potential catastrophe that could result if we continue to see global warming continuing unabated.*[10]

Then the president mentioned the economic crisis, and one would never know that the two had had such a difference of opinion on the subject just a few months before. "And on economic issues, on issues like proliferation," Obama said, "consistently I found Chancellor Merkel to be thoughtful, to be energetic, and to have a strong vision of how we can move forward in the future."[11] The fact that the two had begun to form such a close bond despite the inherent disagreements between them is an indication that both parties approached their relationship in a practical way and understood the importance of working together. It also demonstrated that they had a fair amount of respect for each other; they could agree to disagree, not hold it against each other, and move on.

Before Obama handed the floor over to Merkel, he expressed his gratitude and pleasure in "working with her as a partner. We are thankful, Chancellor, for your leadership not just in Europe but around the world."[12] Once again, the president acknowledged Merkel not only as a partner or an allied leader but as a particularly valuable world leader. The two exchanged a cordial handshake before Merkel began to speak.

Merkel first mentioned her anticipation over her scheduled speech at the US Capitol when she claimed, "I would also like to say that it is obviously a very great honor for me to address today the joint session of Congress, both houses of Congress as it were."[13] Surprisingly, despite that passing acknowledgment of her gratitude for the honor of speaking before Congress, Merkel spent most of her time discussing her enthusiasm about working with the president:

> *I am also very much looking forward to having an exchange of view with the president again. We have always had very intensive discussions, and we're going to have those today again on issues that are of mutual interest to us and that we have been working on almost daily. We are working and discussing issues, for example, related to climate change, Afghanistan, Iran, and obviously also the world economic situation.*[14]

In her usual manner, Merkel spoke in German. It is worth pointing out, however, that before the translator had an opportunity to convert her statements to English, Obama gave the chancellor and the press a big smile, saying, "I think what she said was good. I'm teasing."[15] The laughter in the room drowned out the sounds of the cameras clicking and flashing, with Merkel's giggle and smile among the loudest. Merkel's amusement at Obama's joke was a significant change from her usual reserved demeanor—a clear break from her past conduct in appearances with the US president or other world leaders. As the translator spoke, Merkel and Obama continued to laugh and joke among themselves.

Merkel gave her historic speech before Congress just one week shy of the twentieth anniversary of the official collapse of the Berlin Wall. In it, she provided a firsthand account of the physical and emotional challenges associated with a life under an oppressive government dictatorship when she said, "The Wall, barbed wire, and the order to shoot those who tried to leave limited my access to the free world."[16] She explained that from smuggled books and magazines, she learned and fantasized about America, and most specifically the American Dream.

Merkel was not known for her public speaking skills, although one never would have known that based on her presentation before Congress that day. In fact, some pundits argued that this thirty-minute presentation was the speech of her political career. Gabor Steingart of *Der Spiegel* declared, "This speech was bigger than her entire chancellorship to date."[17]

The passion and gratitude Merkel felt toward America during her first visit there, soon after the Wall fell, could still be felt by those in Congress who witnessed and listened to her fervent description of that trip nearly twenty years later. As Steingart argued in *Der Spiegel*, Merkel articulated the concept of the American Dream "more clearly than any other head of state. For Merkel," the article asserted, "it was like going to confession."[18]

Merkel went on to mention both President Kennedy's and President Reagan's monumental speeches, which served as bookends to the Cold War and have since become the subject of academic study, political acclaim, and pop culture fascination. Merkel thanked all of the American people, and not just politicians, for her freedom when she said:

> *Ladies and gentlemen, to sum it up in one sentence: I know, we Germans know, how much we owe to you, our American friends. We as a nation, and I personally, will never forget that.*[19]

For those interested in history, international relations, political science, or public policy, it would not be surprising if that statement one day became as impactful and ubiquitous as Kennedy's and Reagan's famous words.

Not only did the chancellor express her gratitude for the American people and for the strong partnership between the United States and Germany, but she also highlighted this tie between the two countries when she talked about many of the important issues she had discussed with Obama earlier that day.

In touching on the pressing foreign policy issues of the time, Merkel proudly stated that since 2002, Germany had provided the third-largest troop contingent in Afghanistan because "we had to do everything we could to prevent Afghanistan from ever again harboring a threat to security."[20] She avoided the issue of whether or not Germany would send additional troops to Afghanistan but stated that civilian engagement and military involvement were "inextricably linked." With her comments, she insinuated that even if Germany were not providing military support to Afghanistan, it provided civilian support, which, in her opinion, was equally important.

Although it remained unclear whether Merkel would provide the additional military support in Afghanistan that Obama had hoped for, she publicly recognized Germany's obligation to help fellow NATO members in their time of need. She argued that given the tremendous toll that monitoring the Afghan crisis had placed on the international community, she hoped a new Afghan government would be in place by the beginning of 2010. She promised that allied nations would be successful if they worked together, and guaranteed Germany's support where needed.[21]

Merkel began her speech by quoting the Basic Law, or *Grundgesetz*, of the German Constitution, which proclaims, "Human dignity shall be inviolable."[22] In fact, the statement was important enough that Merkel felt the need to repeat it. Perhaps that helps to explain why she expressed such outrage in response to reports that Iran was developing nuclear weapons:

> *Zero tolerance must also be shown if, for example, weapons of mass destruction fall into the hands of Iran and possibly threaten our security. Iran must be aware of this. Iran knows our offer, but Iran also knows where we draw the line. A nuclear bomb in the hands of an Iranian president who denies the Holocaust, threatens Israel, and denies Israel the right to exist, is not acceptable.*[23]

To Merkel, the actions of the Iranian government violated this basic principle of human dignity. And she had a second concern over Iran's nuclear program: the potential threat to Israel.

For me, Israel's security will never be open to negotiation. Not only
Israel is threatened but the entire free world. Whoever threatens Israel
also threatens us! This is why the free world meets this threat head-on,
if necessary with tough economic sanctions.[24]

Even when she discussed the economic crisis, Merkel did so in the context of freedom. She argued that as important as freedom is, it cannot come without order.[25] She emphasized that without universally binding rules for economic transparency and supervision, there would be widespread instability and abuse of that freedom. Overall, Merkel expressed a firm but nonjudgmental balance on the economic crisis. The combativeness and reluctance she had conveyed in earlier encounters had been replaced with cautious optimism. She articulated her appreciation of the efforts taken by the United States to alleviate the situation while at the same time striving to ensure the world never found itself in a comparable position again. Finally, she insisted that the economic crisis had started because of too much short-term thinking, and she stressed the "need to resist the pressure of those who almost led the nations of this world into the abyss."[26]

Merkel very much supported the idea of a free trade agreement between the United States and the EU, a concept that became even more important in the latter years of Obama's presidency. In her November 3 speech, Merkel argued that nations had an obligation to prevent an economic disaster from happening again, which included rejecting the temptation of protectionism. She envisioned using such a trade agreement "to prevent competing subsidies and give incentives to reduce trade barriers between Europe and America."[27] The fact that she mentioned it here indicated her belief that if the world had already enacted such an agreement, perhaps many of the problems of the financial crisis could have been avoided.

Merkel saved the issue of climate change as the last policy item to discuss in her speech. According to one DW article, the primary purpose of Merkel's visit was "to prepare for the United Nations summit on climate change in Copenhagen in December."[28] Indeed, based on her harsh, passionate warning about the importance of finding a solution to combat global warming, she accomplished her objective.

Merkel compared the crisis of global warming with

> *a wall . . . separating the present from the future. That wall prevents us from seeing the needs of future generations; it prevents us from taking the measures urgently needed to protect the very basis of our life and climate.*[29]

She passionately argued that the evidence of global warming could already be seen: "In the Arctic icebergs are melting, in Africa people are becoming refugees due to environmental damage, and global sea levels are rising."[30]

In the middle of her emotional plea, Merkel took a moment to praise Obama and the US Congress for shifting their focus to ensure climate neutral policies would be a priority.

> *I am pleased that you in your work together with President Obama attach such significance to protecting our climate. For we all know: We have no time to lose!*[31]

As Merkel spoke those words, the camera showed the reactions of various congressional members in the gallery, and while many leading Democrats like Speaker Pelosi and Vice President Joe Biden stood and cheered at her remarks, Republican members such as Representative Paul Ryan and Representative John Boehner sat quietly instead.[32] The different reactions between the two parties demonstrated the clear split in opinion over the issue, illuminating the challenges the Obama administration faced as it attempted to pass any proposed climate change legislation.

Understanding that members of one hundred nations would meet in Copenhagen later that year to combat climate change, Merkel spent a large portion of her speech emphasizing the importance of ratifying the Copenhagen Accord. With the force in her voice, Merkel attempted to use every ounce of influence she had to pressure American politicians on the importance of the Copenhagen Accord. Just as Merkel had set out to do, she emphasized the need for nations to come together and form an acceptable policy to combat the biggest worldwide threat of modern times: global warning. In her passionate plea, she insisted that nations

> *agree on one objective—global warming must not exceed two degrees*
> *Celsius. To achieve this we need the readiness of all nations to assume*
> *internationally binding obligations. . . . [I]n December the world will*
> *look to us, to Europe and America. It is true that there can be no agreement without China and India accepting obligations, but I am convinced that if we in Europe and America show that we are ready to*
> *accept binding obligations, we will also be able to persuade China and*
> *India to join in. And then, in Copenhagen, we will be able to tear down*
> *the wall between the present and the future—in the interests of our children and grandchildren and of sustainable development worldwide.*[33]

Merkel concluded her speech in a manner she seldom did—she made her closing remarks in English. She educated the audience about the history of the Freedom Bell in Schöneberg Town Hall in Berlin and explained that the bell, modeled after America's Liberty Bell in Philadelphia, had been given to the residents of Berlin in 1950. As she said:

> *A gift from American citizens, it is a symbol of the promise of freedom, a*
> *promise that has been fulfilled. On October 3, 1990, the Freedom Bell rang*
> *again, signaling the reunification of Germany—the greatest moment of*
> *joy for the German people. On September 13, 2001, it tolled again, two*
> *days after 9/11, the greatest day of mourning for the American people.*
> *The Freedom Bell in Berlin is like the Liberty Bell in Philadelphia, a*
> *symbol which reminds us that freedom does not come about of itself. It*
> *must be struggled for and then defended anew every day of our lives.*
> *In this endeavor, Germany and Europe will also in [the] future remain*
> *strong and dependable partners for America. That I promise you.*[34]

Pundits, critics, and even Merkel often acknowledged that public speaking was not Merkel's forte. She reportedly lacked charisma and, for quite a long time in her political career, often fidgeted with her notes and her hands when she spoke.[35] None of that occurred during this speech. Merkel spoke eloquently, confidently, reflectively, and passionately. Perhaps the change in delivery was a result of years of experience and practice. Possibly it was because of her comfort with the subject matter and her audience. More likely, it was a combination of the two. Ironically enough, one of Merkel's initial reservations about Obama had concerned his ability to bring a crowd to its feet with his speeches, and now, after working with him for only a short period of time, it appeared that—even if subconsciously—Merkel had begun to learn the important skill of public speaking from the president.

Whatever the reason, it was a moving and inspirational speech—one that might be expected from someone who lived such an extraordinary life. As Steingart argued:

> *With this speech, the German chancellor did her generation a service that cannot be underestimated. The symbols of the renewed German–American friendship are no longer the soldiers posted at Checkpoint Charlie, but . . . politicians like Barack Obama and, now, Merkel. Bravo, Madam Chancellor!*[36]

Merkel's opportunity to speak before Congress at a time that coincided with the twentieth anniversary of the fall of the Berlin Wall would have happened regardless of who was in the White House. Nevertheless, it was still another "first" these two leaders shared: Just as Obama had been the first US president to visit Buchenwald, Merkel was the first German chancellor to address a joint session of Congress.

Yet Merkel's primary reason for her historical congressional address—an attempt to encourage the United States to support the Copenhagen Accord—was not lost on the American media. The press vividly described Merkel's account of the importance of an agreement while simultaneously educating the American public about the division between politicians with regard to the necessary measure. As one journalist wrote:

> *The USA's role at the conference is seen as crucial to its success; however, opposition within the US Senate to a domestic climate bill sponsored by the Democrats is a big hurdle. Should the Senate be unable to agree on legislation to cut greenhouse-gas emissions before the summit, the Obama administration will have its hands tied in Copenhagen.*[37]

When scientists, policy makers, and world leaders from over one hundred countries met in Copenhagen in December 2009, their goal was to discuss the future of the Kyoto Protocol, which was scheduled to expire in 2012. Negotiated in 1997 in Kyoto, Japan, it was the first and only international treaty to impose binding limits on the greenhouse gas emissions from some signatory nations. The treaty distinguished between industrialized nations, which were to reduce their emissions, and developing countries, so that China, Brazil, and India could continue to release carbon dioxide into the atmosphere without restrictions. Thus, the Kyoto Protocol was based on the principle of joint but differentiated responsibility. [38]

The United States had signed the treaty but refused to ratify it as a rejection of terms that seemed to favor developing nations and a protest against the possible economic repercussions. Since China, as an emerging world economy, had been exempted from the treaty, both countries continued to pollute without any diplomatic consequences.[39] Meanwhile, in 2008, Germany had managed to meet its Kyoto obligation, and

> *remain[ed] an international frontrunner in the area of climate protection. Greenhouse gas emissions in 2008 sank by 22.2 percent over 1990 levels, a volume equivalent to nearly 280 million tons.*[40]

Because other EU nations also managed to reduce their greenhouse gas emissions, key European nations argued for a new, binding treaty to hold the United States, China, Brazil, and India accountable for their future emissions.

Initially, the United States had used China as justification for its refusal to comply with the treaty. Technically, China had been excluded from the Kyoto Protocol, but because of the rapid growth and industrialization occurring in the country, the United States believed the Chinese should be forced to comply—and refused to comply until they did. Even before Obama took office, however, he ran on an environmentally friendly platform that included a European public relations campaign. Diplomats affiliated with the US State Department targeted European embassies and other governmental institutions in order to reassure the Europeans of his platform and to illustrate to the rest of the world that, under the Obama administration, the United States was in fact serious about tackling climate change.

"Obama is taking the United States in a new direction in the fight against climate change" was the line promoted by the diplomats (according to *Der Spiegel*), and the president wanted a decisive 17 percent cut in greenhouse gas emissions.[41] However, the Europeans feared that the numbers Washington used were based on 2005 figures as opposed to the 1990 figures Europeans used. Despite the Europeans' apprehension, however, the Americans argued that their government's targets were "consistent with keeping the increase in global temperature to 2 degrees Celsius."[42]

Obama enthusiastically expressed his hope for the United States—as well as the rest of the world—to actively commit to combating the issue of climate change when he insisted, "The time has come for us to get off the sidelines and shape the future that we seek. That is why I came to Copenhagen."[43] Obama's optimism notwithstanding, the Copenhagen Climate Conference did not prove as successful as many had hoped.

The key components of the Copenhagen Accord included a goal of limiting the global temperature increase to 2 degrees Celsius, as well as a

> collective commitment by developed countries for $30 billion in "new and additional" resources in 2010–2012 to help developing countries reduce emissions, preserve forests, and adapt to climate change; and a goal of mobilizing $100 billion a year in public and private finance by 2020 to address developing country needs.[44]

However, while the Climate Conference provided for emissions pledges by all major economies—most notably China—it did not provide for a treaty with a legally binding commitment, but, rather, a decision on the UN's part to "take note of" the Copenhagen Accord, officially recognizing the existence of the agreement while neither approving nor disapproving of it.

There is much speculation as to what went wrong and why world leaders failed to obtain the legally binding treaty for which they had hoped. There are no easy answers, though in a press conference Obama hinted that China's refusal to look toward the past rather than the future was a cause. A BBC News article named other factors, suggesting that key governments not wanting a global deal, bad timing, the US political system, a twenty-four-hour news culture, EU politics, and ineffective political strategies all played important roles in the failure to create a binding treaty on climate change.[45]

To say that attendees were disappointed in the outcome is a major understatement. According to Lumumba Di-Aping, the chief negotiator for the G77 group of 130 developing countries, the deal ultimately offered:

> the lowest level of ambition you can imagine. It's nothing short of climate change skepticism in action. It locks countries into a cycle of poverty forever. Obama has eliminated any difference between him and Bush.[46]

Although the summit in Copenhagen did not prove to be the success that many had hoped for, no one can say that Merkel failed to try. Indeed, many environmental ministers and scientists blamed the United States for the failure of nations to come to an agreement in Copenhagen. If Merkel blamed Obama for the failure of this signature agreement, however, she did not let on. Moreover, given the importance Germany and other EU nations placed on environmental reform, the fact that this setback had no obvious negative impact on the budding Obama–Merkel connection testifies to the strength of their relationship on other matters. And as if to reaffirm that relationship, the next time Merkel and Obama would meet in Washington, the American president would bestow another honor on his European partner.

6

"DEAR BARACK"

JUNE-DECEMBER 2011

On June 9, 2011, Chancellor Merkel made her third visit to Washington, DC, during Obama's presidency—this time to accept the prestigious Presidential Medal of Freedom award from President Obama, making her the second German, after former chancellor Helmut Kohl, to receive the award. However, just before Merkel's visit, her government cast an extremely controversial vote when it abstained on the UN Security Council Resolution 1973, which authorized military intervention in Libya. For the first time in modern history, Germany had voted against the West, including France, the UK, and the United States.[1]

Because of this questionable move, the press on both sides of the Atlantic debated the sincerity of the upcoming ceremony. The issue quickly became politicized when media outlets with different political leanings placed their own spin on the ceremony. Conservative blogger Russell Berman stated:

> *When German Chancellor Angela Merkel meets with President Obama this week in Washington, symbols will outweigh substance, even more than they usually do in international politics. The rationale for the visit is explicitly symbolic: the president will bestow the Medal of Freedom on the chancellor.*[2]

On the other side of the Atlantic, European news outlets viewed the United States' gesture with suspicion as well. The weekly German newspaper *Die Zeit* claimed, "Sometimes praise is harder to bear than criticism. . . . Those who give praise expect something in return."[3] Similarly, the financial German daily *Handelsblatt* argued that

> the excessive American hospitality this week comes with a crystal-clear agenda. The US wants Germany to take responsibility on a number of points—as financier of reconstruction in the Arab world, as an anchor of stability in the euro turbulence and as a political heavy lifter in the Middle East.[4]

The crisis in Libya was only one of the pressing issues on which Merkel and Obama disagreed—another, which the two leaders would inevitably address, involved the deepening financial crisis that Greece faced. Obama had urged European countries and their creditors to come together and prevent disaster in Greece, promising US support in heading off the country's debt woes. With US unemployment still high at 9.1 percent, Obama blamed outside forces—including rising fuel prices, the recent earthquake in Japan, and the eurozone crisis—for impeding the economy. Meanwhile, the EU was in the middle of finalizing the details for a Greek bailout package worth the enormous sum of somewhere between €80 billion and €100 billion over a three-year period, a deal Merkel had trouble justifying to the German citizens, Bundestag, and even the German courts.[5]

Despite the disagreements and dubious press on the conservative side, the liberal newspapers saw Merkel's visit as the honor it was intended to be. The left-leaning papers viewed the relationship between the president and the chancellor with higher regard and less suspicion than the more conservative news outlets, and as such were less skeptical of the president's motives. Media outlets like the center-left *Süddeutsche Zeitung* claimed that in today's world, friendships arise as a result of open communications and deliverable actions based on said conversations, rather than the traditional friendships that resulted mainly out of loyalty to alliances.[6]

Despite early reports of a troublesome relationship between Obama and Merkel, the rumors of discord proved to be unfounded—if for no other reason than the two leaders were more alike than even they wanted to accept. Nevertheless, the relationship transformed as Obama discovered that having a reliable ally whom he trusted proved to be more beneficial than having one who simply admired him, and Merkel proved to be that person.

In his own book, *A Promised Land*, Obama acknowledged the traits he saw in Merkel and described why he appreciated them when he stated, ". . . her stolid appearance reflected her no-nonsense, analytical sensibility. She was famously suspicious of emotional outbursts or overblown rhetoric." From the very origins of their working relationship, the media and political analysts had argued that both Obama and Merkel had reservations about one another. However, Obama continued, " . . . her team would later confess that she'd been initially skeptical of me precisely because of my oratorical skills. I took no offense, figuring that in a German leader, an aversion to possible demagoguery was probably a healthy thing."[7] Obama's own admission illustrates that he held no ill feelings toward Merkel—despite the reports. On the contrary, she held skills that he found beneficial. Moreover, he liked the idea that Merkel had not been one of his biggest fans initially but proved to be someone with whom he could share the work and responsibility.

Merkel's unusual move to vote against the West on the question of Libya had caused quite a bit of controversy within other allied nations—including the United States. Nevertheless, Obama did not allow his disappointment to impact his overall impression of her leadership. Despite their differences of opinion, the president still willingly and publicly recognized Merkel with the highest honor he could bestow.

The president's actions seemed to indicate that his respect for Merkel went much further than one vote on a single, albeit important, foreign policy issue. According to the financial daily paper *Handelsblatt*:

> *The pragmatic Americans quickly realized the advantages that arose from Germany's surprising abstention on the Libya vote . . . Washington*

has avoided public criticism of Germany's decision to go its own way, instead building bridges.[8]

After more than two years, Obama and Merkel had developed an awareness of their shared values and a history of commonality with regard to other policies that far outweighed their differences of opinion. After all, such moments are typical among even the best of friends.

The opening ceremony for Merkel's historic celebration began on the South Lawn of the White House at approximately 9:30 a.m. on June 9, 2011. The sun shone brightly as President Obama, First Lady Michelle Obama, Vice President Joe Biden and his wife, Dr. Jill Biden, Secretary of State Hillary Clinton, and other key members of the administration greeted the German chancellor and high-ranking members of the German delegation with a full military ceremony. The United States flag flew high next to the German and EU flags, while the military band played the national anthems of both countries.

Such pomp and circumstance is typical of state affairs, designed to demonstrate the respectful relationship between two nations. But this event was different, because Obama also used it to demonstrate his respect for Merkel as an individual. And indeed, following the presentation, Obama and Merkel shared the podium once again to discuss their partnership and friendship— both as leaders and as individuals.

In Obama's brief remarks, he referred to the partnership between the United States and Germany as "the most successful alliance in human history" and stated that "our commitment to our common defense is also a pillar of global security, from completing our mission in Afghanistan to preventing terrorist attacks to achieving our vision of a world without nuclear weapons."[9] Obama also articulated his relationship with the German chancellor when he referred to Merkel as "one of my closest global partners."[10]

These remarks point to Obama's personal affinity with Merkel while also emphasizing the importance of the allegiance between Germany and the

United States. Moreover, the fact that the president mentioned the subjects of global security and Afghanistan showed the closeness of the partnership between the two nations and the trust between the two leaders. By stating this at an event to honor Merkel, it seemed that Obama believed her actions, as well as her government's actions, were paramount in keeping the world safe from future global attacks.

In a very moving closing statement, Obama used Germany as an example to demonstrate that with willing participants, even the most adverse of enemies can overcome differences in order to start again and form new bonds with one another. Obama even argued that the strong bond between the United States and Germany could be used as an example for other feuding countries to follow in their quests for peace and democracy.

> *As people around the world imagine a different future, the story of Germany and our alliance in the twentieth century shows what is possible in the twenty-first. Wars can end. Adversaries can become allies. Walls can come down. At long last, nations can be whole and can be free.*[11]

Throughout Obama's remarks, Merkel stood next to him and looked straight ahead as if she were concentrating on understanding his English words. But as the president turned toward Merkel and uttered the words "Madam Chancellor," she too turned toward him.

"It's obvious neither of us looks exactly like the leaders who preceded us," Obama continued, "but the fact that we can stand here today as president of the United States and as chancellor of a united Germany is a testament to the progress, the freedom, that is possible in our world."[12]

At this, Merkel uncharacteristically smiled broadly, and as the translators repeated those same words into German, her smile widened. Merkel's body language demonstrated her appreciation of the significance of Obama's remarks—and as it turned out, she would reiterate that same thought later that day.

When Obama turned the podium over to the German chancellor, Merkel began her remarks rather more formally:

Dear Sir Mr. President, Dear Madame Michelle Obama, Mr. Vice President, members of both cabinets, guests of honor . . . thank you very much for this very warm and very moving reception that is overwhelming. I am indeed delighted.[13]

Greeted by applause from the audience, Merkel used her time at the podium to forcefully and passionately remind the audience of the core values shared between the United States and Germany—the universality of human rights, freedom, and democracy. It is difficult to come out with just one takeaway from her powerful words, but in her remarks she boasted about how the relationship between the United States and Germany "is just as much part and parcel of Germany's *raison d'être* as is European integration. Both belong together. Both are and remain the pillars of German foreign policy."[14] This bold statement was arguably the most important component of her remarks.

Much like President Kennedy's historic speech in Berlin at the height of the Cold War had emphasized the importance of the relationship between the United States and Germany, Merkel's remarks on the White House lawn accomplished the same goal. Just as Kennedy argued, "*Ich bin ein Berliner*," so Merkel declared that her nation's partnership with the United States was an essential component of Germany's existence. In a sense, Kennedy offered the opening remarks in the case regarding the strength of this relationship, while Merkel's statement forty-eight years later served as the closing argument.

In her final remarks, Merkel acknowledged the complexity of the current world and the many difficult challenges that needed to be addressed. Then, she again employed the extremely rare approach she had used before Congress in 2009 and once again addressed the crowd in English:

Mr. President, dear Barack, in Berlin in 2008 you spoke to more than 200,000 people. And in your address, you said America has no better partner than Europe. And now it's my turn to say Europe and Germany have no better partner than America.[15]

This statement demonstrated how far the relationship between the two of them had come.

For the first time, Merkel discussed the support Obama had received from her citizens—despite her own opposition to him in Berlin in 2008. Not only that, but she addressed the president by his first name and even went further when she again called him "*lieber* Barack" or dear Barack. In light of the extraordinary lengths to which the Obama administration had gone to welcome the German chancellor, it would not have been unusual for someone to express their gratitude in a less formal manner such as this. Yet Germans, as a general rule, are normally very reserved in paying compliments or showing any form of affection, and the fact that the chancellor used the president's first name spoke volumes about their relationship.

Even though Merkel's English is considered to be good, she travels with a translator and seldom speaks English in public or in an official capacity.[16] That she did so here was a further sign of her warming relationship with both the president and the American people. More importantly, Merkel's words and demeanor alike illustrated that the initial rumored discord between the two leaders was all but forgotten, something for the history books.

Following a military opening ceremony on the South Lawn, Obama and Merkel held a bilateral meeting, followed by their usual press conference. Obama began his welcoming remarks in the East Room of the White House with his usual charm, but for the first time he addressed the German chancellor publicly as "Angela," rather than the more formal "Chancellor Merkel."

As usual, Obama complimented Merkel and tied these compliments to the theme of their meetings. This time, Obama chose Merkel's superb English skills as the source of his praise when he said, "We had a wonderful dinner last night—one on one—although, as you saw again this morning, Angela's English is much better than my German."[17] At this, Merkel smiled modestly and raised her eyebrows in response.

Obama expressed his gratitude toward both Merkel personally and her citizens for their assistance in Afghanistan. He acknowledged the alliance between the two nations remained strong, with soldiers standing "shoulder to shoulder"—American troops serving under German leadership and vice versa—and with diplomats working together as partners to "stand up for democracy in Europe and beyond."[18] These remarks were telling because here the president insinuated that the universal goal was to protect allied nations from attacks against their democratic principles. In his eyes, upholding the shared values between countries was more important than focusing solely on one's nationality, and if that meant Americans taking orders from Germans, then so be it.

Alliances like these were possible because of ongoing trust and relationship building between countries, particularly through the establishment of organizations such as NATO. Obama hinted that because of the partnership between the two countries, significant progress had been made in Afghanistan—including breaking Taliban momentum, training Afghan forces, and preparing to reduce the presence of American forces—as Germany and NATO allies supported Afghans in their political and economic efforts to forge a lasting peace.

Obama then changed focus from the conflict in Afghanistan to the alliance between the United States and Germany. He emphasized the "essence" of that alliance: "two peoples, bound by common values and committed to the security, the prosperity, and the dignity not just of our own citizens, but far beyond our borders. . . . And that's also the essence of my partnership with Chancellor Merkel."[19]

He then turned toward Merkel, at the matching podium to his right, and said:

> *Angela, I believe this is our tenth meeting together. That doesn't include the many phone calls and video conferences that we seem to have at all hours of the day and night. There's hardly any global issue where we don't consult one another. I've said before, I always value Angela's pragmatic approach to complex issues, her intelligence, her frankness. I trust her.*

And as she's said herself, it's just fun to work together. And it has been,
again, fun today, even as we've addressed some very urgent challenges.[20]

In light of the complex issues that faced the two leaders, it would take a certain amount of personal chemistry between the two parties for them to characterize their working relationship as "fun."

Obama went on to mention that he and Merkel had discussed their hope to create a free trade agreement between the United States and the EU. Although this had been an important goal for Merkel since the beginning of Obama's presidency, here Obama broached it publicly for the first time:

> *Germany is one of our largest trading partners, and we discussed how*
> *to keep our economies growing and create the jobs that our people need.*
> *. . . The Chancellor and I discussed the need to eliminate regulations and*
> *barriers so we can unleash even more trade and investment, including*
> *in the area of electric vehicles, where both our countries are leaders and*
> *where the possibilities of American–German cooperation are enormous.*[21]

Here the president took the opportunity to acknowledge the need and the opportunity for a cooperative trade relationship—one free of what some viewed as burdensome regulations between the two nations. Obama's choice of words was interesting. Rather than argue about the disagreements between him and Merkel over economic policies, he chose to concentrate on what they *did* agree on. As world leaders, they both understood that their own nations, as well as the rest of the world, depended on them to bridge their differences and put forth acceptable solutions. When the subject of Libya arose, for example, Obama addressed the issue without mentioning the controversial vote Germany had just taken. Instead, he emphasized that the United States and Germany spoke with one voice:

> *The chancellor and I have been clear—Gaddafi must step down and*
> *hand power to the Libyan people, and the pressure will only continue to*
> *increase until he does.*[22]

One area where the two did agree was Iran. If Iran continued to invest in its nuclear program while it refused to engage with the international community, Obama asserted, then members of the International Atomic Energy Agency—including both the United States and Germany—could be left with no alternative but to consider ramping up their punishment against the Iranian regime, including additional sanctions.

Finally, Obama acknowledged his profound respect for Merkel and her "own remarkable life story, and her experience helping to heal the wounds of the past and build a united Germany"—before he finished his remarks, he confessed, "I very much appreciate the personal friendship that I enjoy with the chancellor."[23]

No one can doubt that at this point, Obama had developed the utmost admiration for Merkel on both a professional and a personal level. Whenever the opportunity presented itself, Obama vocalized this respect for her leadership, her wisdom, and her candor. It was also apparent that Obama respected Merkel because of where she came from and what she had become. Perhaps, more than that, as the first Black president he may have felt that his life's voyage had unfolded in parallel with Merkel's—that he understood the difficulties and obstacles each of them had overcome to get where they were. He had a tremendous amount of respect for someone who had accomplished so much.

To begin her comments in response, Merkel referred to Obama once again as "Mr. President, dear Barack." She listed the challenges that faced the world but assured the public that these challenges would be met together "in this spirit of freedom, of shared values."[24]

She linked the past to the future with respect to the work that needed to be done in North Africa and the Middle East. She mentioned that Germany was able to get back on its feet following World War II because of the assistance granted by the United States with the passage of the Marshall Plan, and indicated that she saw a similar role for Germany with regard to Egypt and Tunisia. So, just as there had been discussion that Germany had not held up its end of the bargain with respect to Libya, Merkel knew her country had an obligation to help.

Both the United States and the EU realized that the unilateral decisions on the part of either the Israelis or the Palestinians had accomplished nothing.

Therefore, Merkel emphasized that both Europeans and Americans believed that a two-state solution where a Jewish state of Israel peacefully coexisted with an independent Palestinian state would be the easiest and most effective way to ensure peace in the Middle East. Merkel indicated that this compromise was so important to others around the world that she promised support from the EU and the United States to ensure this transition happened and happened in a timely manner.

The chancellor ended her speech by stating:

> *Barack, thank you very much again for the very friendly talks, for this very warm atmosphere, for making it possible to have this exchange of views in a very candid manner. I think even though we may look differently than our predecessors we have a lot in common, I think, and we have a lot to discuss.*[25]

Once again, she referred to the president by his first name—a level of intimacy that is unusual for Germans—and expressed her gratitude for their relationship and friendship. Additionally, it's clear she held his earlier remarks in high enough regard that she felt compelled to repeat them.

During the question-and-answer session that followed, the two leaders fielded numerous questions from the media about the overall health of the economy. Obama summarized steps the United States had taken to decrease unemployment nationally, which included the extension of unemployment insurance, a cut in the payroll tax, and tax breaks for certain business investments.[26] These steps had helped put the country on a path to recovery, he said, and "the overall trend that we've seen over the last fifteen months, [with] over two million jobs created . . . indicates that we have set a path that will lead us to long-term economic growth."[27] However, Obama admitted that while things were going well in the United States, they could be going better elsewhere. He and Merkel had discussed the difficult economic situation in Europe—particularly with respect to Greece, which, since spring 2010, had caused a great deal of stress and turmoil for the other, stronger European Union economies. The government of Greece had managed to find itself in a tremendous amount of debt and on the verge of economic collapse. After more than fourteen hours of negotiations in May 2010, Merkel, President Nicolas Sarkozy of France, and other European leaders had agreed that Germany would contribute €123 billion.[28]

Despite this loan, by 2011 Greece found itself once again in dire financial straits. In the June 7 press conference, Merkel and Obama displayed a difference of opinion on how to address this predicament. Obama stated:

> We are on the path of recovery, but it's got to accelerate. . . . I have had extensive discussions with Angela about the situation there. It's a tough situation, and I think we all acknowledge it.[29]

Although he admitted the situation was complicated, Obama's mention of "extensive discussions" and "a tough situation" only hinted at the disagreement between him and the chancellor with regard to the best way to address the problem.

When Merkel discussed the economic crisis, she reassured the audience that Germany and the EU understood their obligation to get the economy back on track and said:

> We are very well aware of our responsibility for the global economy. Barack just outlined what the Americans are doing in order to generate growth and combat unemployment, which is what we're doing in Europe as well.[30]

Merkel also emphasized that the economic crisis served as a reminder of how globalized and interconnected the world had become. She admitted that she understood the entire stability of the euro as a whole became questionable when one eurozone country was in trouble, and because of this, assistance from stronger economies to help endangered countries was not only necessary but expected:

> We've seen how interdependent we are. And the stability of the eurozone is therefore an important factor of stability for the whole of the global economy. So we do see clearly our European responsibility, and we're shouldering that responsibility together with the IMF.[31]

Her remarks implied that in their talks, she and Obama may not have been in total agreement on how to keep the path to recovery growing. Yet the fact that she still referred to him as "Barack" indicated that their personal disagreement over the issue did not impact her personal relationship with him.

Obama acknowledged that the debt in Greece significantly negatively impacted other international markets. In a direct way, he explained that Greece, as a member of the eurozone, could turn to other countries for assistance with the problem. He pointedly mentioned Germany:

> Germany is going to be a key leader in that process. And the politics of it are tough. . . . But I am confident that Germany's leadership, along with other key actors in Europe, will help us arrive at a path for Greece to return to growth, for this debt to become more manageable. But it's going to require some patience and some time, and we have pledged to cooperate fully in working through these issues both on a bilateral basis [and] also through international and financial institutions like the IMF.[32]

Although Obama did not mention it explicitly, if one reads between the lines, he indicated clearly that he hoped under Merkel's leadership, Germany would contribute the funds necessary to help revive Greece's struggling economy.

Despite whatever had passed between the two during their private talks, any conflict of perspective did not seem to undermine their strong connection. Obama reiterated, this time in regard to the ongoing crisis in the Middle East, not only the significance of America's relationship with Germany but also the significance of his personal relationship with Merkel:

> On the international stage, [there are] no issues that we don't coordinate closely with Germany. And our work in Afghanistan, our work together with NATO, the approach that we've taken with respect to the Middle East and the Arab Spring, our approaches to development issues and how we help the poorest countries find their place in the international economy—these are all going to be areas where I think Angela's leadership

will be welcomed and will be absolutely critical for us to be able to achieve
the kind of more peaceful and prosperous world that we want to see.[33]

And for her part, Merkel not-so-subtly told the United States to mind its own business with respect to the Greek crisis:

As far as the situation in the United States is concerned, I think each and every one ought to deal with his or her own problems. We in Europe have our hands full already with what we need to do, and I'm absolutely convinced that as we shoulder our responsibility and meet our responsibility, so will the United States of America.[34]

Yet clearly, any disagreement between Merkel and Obama did not impact their positive interaction in general. On the contrary, Merkel believed that the complicated world in which twenty-first-century leaders found themselves required trust and collaboration from as many friends and allies as they could have. Merkel admitted she and Obama shared a strategy with regard to their "international responsibilities":

[W]hat's also important in this context—and that's an approach that we both share, Barack and I—is that we need to combine military and civil engagement. And so I think we live up to our international responsibilities. The world is full of problems that we need to address. That's a reality, and you cannot have enough partners that work together with you in a coordinated way, and this is why this cooperation is so extremely important for our common future.[35]

When Obama responded to a question from the media about how to handle the financial crisis in Greece, he acknowledged that it was "a tough and complicated piece of business"—and that "ultimately, Europeans are going to have to make decisions about how they proceed."[36] He stressed the need to recognize

*Greece has to grow, and that means that there has to be private invest-
ment there. [But] it also means that other countries in the eurozone are
going to have to provide them a backstop and support. And frankly,
people who are holding Greek debt are going to have to make some
decisions, working with the European countries in the eurozone about
how that debt is managed.*[37]

Yet Obama then affirmed that because the growth of America's economy
was contingent on a solution to the problem, America would do what it could
to assist EU members with their recovery. To Germany and the other eurozone countries, he promised,

*[W]e will be there for you; we are interested in being supportive. We
think that America's economic growth depends on a sensible resolution
of this issue; we think it would be disastrous for us to see an uncontrolled
spiral and default in Europe, because that could trigger a whole range of
other events. And I think Angela shares that same view.*[38]

Aware of the interconnectivity of the world markets, Obama firmly held
that the problems that faced Greece and other EU nations also impacted the
United States. Although he believed that the Europeans needed to take a
more prominent role to help with Greece, he understood he could not directly
tell the Europeans what to do. Hence, the president's remarks served to push
them to take whatever actions necessary, and, since the health of the United
States economy rested with success in Europe, Obama offered EU nations
any support they needed in their efforts.

Merkel then added her answer to the journalist's question about the
economy, when she admitted that because of the success of the G20, they
were able to "ward off the worst that could have happened" as a result of
the Great Recession.[39] Merkel admitted that the G20 had proved to be
an effective format for establishing rules for financial markets and finding
"credible solutions" to ongoing problems,[40] and argued that the controversial

subjects debated at G20 summits—from how much stimulus was needed to the nature of structural programs to the number of savings and cuts programs—had helped them to succeed:

> *I think that shows great openness because we're all breaking new ground. These are uncharted waters, and we cannot . . . rely completely on the financial business community to give us good advice every day. So we were dependent on our own good and sound judgment.*[41]

Merkel's remarks indicated that one of the main reasons the financial crisis became as problematic as it did was because countries did not communicate effectively with one another. But, because of the formation of the G20 in 1999, these same countries could now serve as checks and balances on one another—something that had not truly been tried before. In other words, Merkel believed that, thanks to the G20, the crisis was resolved before it became an even bigger problem.

She revealed a similar position on the value of NATO, which now provided a much broader spectrum of support despite having military intervention as its initial focus. Because of the trust, alliances, and partnerships among NATO allies, Merkel believed, world leaders had successfully worked together to divert another Great Depression. In response to a question about Libya and her country's controversial vote, she reiterated her position that she believed Gaddafi needed to step down. And she mirrored Obama's insistence that Germany supported the NATO operation—mainly by having a presence there and by stepping up its commitment in Afghanistan, thus freeing American resources to focus on Libya.[42]

Merkel argued that often in a friendship and partnership there may be differences of opinion, but she professed, "What's important is that we wish each other every success."[43] Her important words illustrated how she believed true world leaders and partners should address and handle conflict.

In the course of their press conference, Obama and Merkel discussed a myriad of topics, including the upcoming Medal of Freedom ceremony, Afghanistan, and the economic crisis. But perhaps nothing illustrates the new, more familiar level of their personal friendship so much as the following behind-the-scenes story.

Before they addressed the press corps, Merkel and Obama strolled from the Oval Office to the East Room of the White House, and Merkel joked with Obama that media would most certainly question him about why he had not made the traditional state visit to Berlin. After the two leaders had answered numerous crucial policy and foreign relations questions, a German reporter stood up, presumably having saved the most "pressing" question of the day for last. And just as Merkel had predicted, the journalist asked Obama why he had not visited Berlin.[44]

As the journalist spoke, Merkel's normally stoic expression turned to a grin. She glanced sheepishly at Obama, who stood at the podium to her left. Obama caught her smile and returned it. Given the timing of the question, the fact that it came from a German reporter, and Merkel's response, one is left to wonder whether the chancellor had in fact persuaded the journalist to ask the question. Merkel's response, as translated, was:

> *Berlin opens its arms to him every day, but Berliners can also wait. They have proved this throughout their history.*[45]

Obama's smile grew wide as Merkel spoke. He gave an amiable response and then began to dismiss the press when he said, "Thank you very much, everybody." Merkel, however, clearly had not finished her answer. "And I can promise that the Brandenburg Gate will be standing for some more time," she concluded, and she walked over to the president's podium, where the two of them exchanged a cordial handshake.[46]

The change in protocol did not go unnoticed by the media. The *Washington Post* outlined this metamorphosis between the two leaders: "Soooo, it's Angela and Barack now," wrote Manuel Roig-Franzia. "This Angela and this Barack—better known as German Chancellor Merkel and President Obama—haven't always appeared to be the best of buds." He added that during the thirty-nine-minute press conference, Obama referred to Merkel as "Angela" no fewer than eleven times, while Merkel returned the compliment four times, even referring to him as "*lieber* Barack" or "dear Barack."[47] Roig-Franzia then noted:

> *That's quite a leap in coziness. During two joint news conferences back in 2009, for instance, the leaders referred to each other by their first names exactly, well, zero times, according to transcripts.*[48]

As author Hans W. Gatzke wrote in his book on German–US relations, an old German saying indicates that "for a true and lasting *Freundschaft* to develop, the prospective friends must first consume at least a bushel of salt together to give them time to get to know each other."[49] Perhaps this press conference was the end of Merkel and Obama's joint consumption of a bushel of salt.

The press conference that afternoon set the tone for the ceremony later that evening, during a formal state dinner in the Rose Garden. The guest list comprised 208 dignitaries, including Eric Schmidt of Google, Bob McDonald of Procter & Gamble, US Supreme Court chief justice John Roberts, and orchestra conductor Christoph Eschenbach.[50] As noted earlier, Merkel's husband, Professor Joachim Sauer, typically avoided his wife's public appearances. Nevertheless, understanding the importance of this event, Germany's "Phantom of the Opera" made yet another public appearance with his wife at an event with Obama.[51]

Michelle Obama sat next to Merkel's husband. At one point during the course of dinner, Michelle, who normally steered clear of foreign affairs, made a point of telling Merkel, "He really treasures you, Angela," referring to Obama's respect for the chancellor.[52] Like Professor Sauer's attendance at the evening's festivities, the first lady's decision to intervene where she normally remained silent speaks volumes about the significance of the event.

Prior to the presentation of the award, Obama explained that the Presidential Medal of Freedom is "the highest honor a president can bestow on a

*President Obama presents Chancellor Merkel with the
Presidential Medal of Freedom in the White House Rose Garden.
Merkel was only the second German to receive the award,
which is the United States' highest civilian honor.
(Official White House photo by Pete Souza)*

civilian"—and that by receiving this honor, Merkel joined the ranks of only a handful of other non-Americans, including Nelson Mandela, Pope John Paul II, and her fellow German, former chancellor Helmut Kohl.[53] He also took the opportunity to say a few words on behalf of Merkel and her achievements: "We want to pay tribute to an extraordinary leader who embodies these values and who's inspired millions around the world—including me—and that's my friend, Chancellor Merkel."[54]

Obama then described Merkel's first political experience as a young child who saw her country divided the day the Soviet government built the Berlin Wall, and emphasized the integrity she displayed when she refused to spy for the Stasi.[55] He declared that the intent of the evening's festivities was to focus on Merkel's achievements once she had obtained her freedom, adding, "Determined to finally have her say, she entered politics—rising to become the first East German to lead a united Germany, the first woman chancellor in German history, and an eloquent voice for human rights and dignity around the world."[56]

From the president's remarks, it is clear he found Merkel's journey, from her childhood under the oppressive East German government to her role as the first East German, first female chancellor of a united Germany, nothing short of remarkable. While he appreciated the journey Merkel's life had taken, he seemed even more impressed with what she had done for herself and others once she obtained her freedom.

The president concluded with a practice that had become common over the course of their working relationship: revisiting their counterpart's important declarations of the past, as if to reiterate the value of those statements. This time, Obama repeated the words Merkel had spoken at her speech before Congress in 2009, saying that those words "spoke not only to the dreams of that young girl in the East, but to the dreams of all who still yearn for their rights and dignity today: to freedom, which 'must be struggled for, and then defended anew, every day of our lives.'"[57]

When Merkel addressed the guests, she began with her now-standard greeting: "Mr. President, dear Barack."[58] She emotionally described the impact the building of the Berlin Wall had had on her as a young child: "Seeing the grownups around me, even my parents, so stunned that they actually broke out in tears, was something that shook me to the core."[59] Merkel also expressed humility as a recipient of the Medal of Freedom:

> *But imagining that I would one day stand in the Rose Garden of the White House and receive the Medal of Freedom from an American President, was certainly beyond even my wildest dreams. And believe me, receiving this prestigious award moves me deeply.*[60]

Merkel then personally thanked all Americans as well as Obama:

> *My thanks go to the American people, first and foremost, for this extraordinary honor, knowing full well how much you have done for us Germans. And I thank you personally, Mr. President, because you are a man of strong convictions. You touch people with your passion and your visions for a good future for these people, also in Germany.*[61]

Those sentiments are important because they indicated the profound respect Merkel had developed for Obama over the years. To the public, it appeared the two had gotten off to a difficult start in their relationship because Merkel thought that Obama was all talk and no substance; she had been reluctant to embrace the charisma and vision that her fellow citizens had seen in him. After more than two years of working with the president, however, she saw for herself that Obama held true to his words and his actions. Despite the fact that the two politicians did not agree on every single policy issue, they had established a respectful working relationship and personal chemistry between them.

Merkel exhibited the grace of a true leader and acknowledged that the award granted to her was also being granted, in effect, to the rest of the German people and to everyone who still fought for freedom. With these remarks, she demonstrated passion and conviction with respect to standing up for the fundamental principles of freedom:

Also today, the yearning for freedom may well make totalitarian regimes tremble and fall. . . . Freedom is indivisible. Each and every one has the same right to freedom, be it in North Africa or Belarus, in Myanmar or Iran. . . . We see that living in freedom and defending freedom are two sides of one and the same coin, for the precious gift of freedom doesn't come naturally, but has to be fought for, nurtured, and defended time and time again.[62]

Then, for the second time in the course of her visit, she addressed the guests in English, predicting that this prestigious award would encourage her in facing ongoing dilemmas:

Neither the chains of dictatorship nor the fetters of oppression can keep down the forces of freedom for long. This is my firm conviction that shall continue to guide me. In this, the Presidential Medal of Freedom shall serve to spur me on and to encourage me.[63]

In the later years of her chancellorship, Merkel would face obstacles that would force her to remember and even question this conviction. One can only wonder whether these words or this medal entered her mind as she made the challenging decisions.

Author Stefan Kornelius points out that "the finale to such occasions is traditionally provided by a big name from American show business or pop music"—in this case, James Taylor, "the most American of American singer-songwriters." According to Kornelius, Taylor "later declared that the White House had specifically requested his song 'You've Got a Friend.'"[64]

Despite all of the ceremonial activities of the visit, the festivities ended fairly anti-climatically, with a firm handshake from both parties. Merkel, after all, had her straitlaced and stern reputation to uphold.[65] She had already let her guard down when she referred to Obama as "*lieber* Barack." If she had shown any more emotion, she might have damaged her "poker face" reputation that had taken her so long to acquire.

Obama staffers had specifically requested James Taylor perform at the state dinner because of the highly symbolic nature of his famous song "You've Got a Friend." The sentiments certainly had not been lost on the night of the state dinner, but never would James Taylor's words be truer than when Obama and Merkel would meet again, later that year in Cannes, France, to discuss the global economy, most notably the Greece situation, at the G20 summit.

In October 2011, Greece caused trouble again. Despite receiving an astronomical second bailout of €240 billion—the equivalent of the nation's entire annual budget—Greek leaders remained unhappy. Merkel called Charles Dallara, who at the time was the managing director of the Institute of International Finance, the organization representing the world's leading financial institutions. She told the financier that investment banks had to accept losses of 50 percent on Greek government debt held in private hands.[66]

Dallara grudgingly accepted Merkel's terms, and everything appeared to be resolved. Merkel addressed the international media on October 27 in a manner author Matthew Qvortrup classes as "almost jubilant."[67] She happily reflected on the success of the deal, saying:

> *I am very aware that the world's attention was on these talks. We Europeans showed tonight that we reached the right conclusions.*[68]

Merkel's comments previewed not just the opinion of EU members but the markets as well. When the stock markets opened, every relevant index rose after what economists described as a "breakthrough."[69]

However, Merkel's relief was short-lived. On October 31, she received a telephone call from Greek prime minister George Papandreou, who informed her that their agreement of four days earlier would have to be submitted to a referendum among the people of Greece. Papandreou's move was unexpected and had not been coordinated with anyone outside his inner circle.[70]

*President Obama and Chancellor Merkel share a brief conversation
at the G20 summit in Cannes, France. While at the summit,
Obama publicly expressed his support of the chancellor, who was
facing enormous pressure from her European colleagues.
(Official White House photo by Pete Souza)*

But the response from the markets was unequivocal: the German DAX 30 Index, made up of the thirty largest companies listed on the Frankfurt Stock Exchange, lost 5 percent. Speculation was rife that Greece would leave the eurozone and in the process inflict serious damage on the European currency, if not cause its collapse.[71]

In early November, amid discussions over the global economy at the Cannes G20 summit in France, Merkel, President Sarkozy of France, and Christine Lagarde, the newly elected president of the IMF, told Prime Minister Papandreou that he would receive no money whatsoever until after a different referendum had been held: one on Greece's continued membership in the eurozone. Papandreou returned to Greece and resigned, and the referendum was canceled—the bailout would go ahead as planned.[72]

In remarks made ahead of the G20 summit, Obama commented to the press:

> It's wonderful to be back together with my good friend, Angela Merkel. I think that the last time we were in Washington, DC, together, we presented her with the Medal of Freedom, and that indicated the high esteem [in which] not only I, but the United States, hold her and her leadership.[73]
>
> This is going to be a very busy two days. Central to our discussions at the G20 is how do we achieve greater global growth and put people back to work. That means we're going to have to resolve the situation here in Europe. And without Angela's leadership we would not have already made the progress that we've seen at the EU meeting on October 27.... But I just want to say, once again, how much I enjoy working with Angela. She exhibits the kind of practical common sense that, I think, has made her a leader not only in Germany but around the world.[74]

With these remarks, Obama reiterated his profound support for Merkel and his admiration of her leadership. Apparently, Obama's praise of the German chancellor was not only for the cameras and the media but something he expressed behind the closed doors of the summit meetings as well.

Kornelius's account of the G20 summit in Cannes indicated that the other European leaders placed an enormous amount of pressure on Merkel to use the Bundesbank gold reserves to help resolve the eurozone crisis, and that Obama stopped the discussions when he believed the other participants had gone too far in their attacks on Merkel. In Obama's opinion, Angela Merkel should not have to undergo "political execution."[75] Just as Obama had stepped in to defend his partner from humiliation during the 2009 NATO summit in Germany early in their relationship, he employed the same tactic here. While Obama may have intellectually agreed with the other EU leaders about the use of Bundesbank funds, he did not take kindly to Merkel being bullied into such a decision.

The political attack that Merkel underwent during the Cannes summit was similar to the one that President Ronald Reagan had experienced at a 1981 G7 summit in Ottawa, Canada. Canadian prime minister Pierre Trudeau and the French president François Mitterrand had disagreed with many of Reagan's economic and foreign policy ideas, and, as Richard Aldous argued in his book *Reagan and Thatcher: The Difficult Relationship*, Reagan had been under constant attack from Trudeau and Mitterrand throughout the summit, setting the tone for future meetings.[76] Although British prime minister Margaret Thatcher happened to agree with the two world leaders on multiple issues—saving her reservations with regard to Reagan's policies for her one-on-one meetings with the US president—publicly she appeared to be the president's staunchest supporter. At one point during the discussions, Thatcher even scolded the Canadian prime minister when she stated, "Pierre, you're being obnoxious. Stop acting like a naughty schoolboy!"[77]

Trudeau himself recognized the closeness of their relationship when he later proclaimed, "She and Reagan formed a very solid team."[78] Just as Obama had come to Merkel's defense during the Cannes G20 summit, Thatcher had come to Reagan's. Both examples are telling of the strength of the relationship between the pairs of leaders. Even when the two counterparts had differences of opinion, they came to one another's defense regardless.

Despite Papandreou's sudden resignation and the cancelation of the original referendum, the markets remained unstable. So in December 2011, the

European Council—the EU's heads of state and government—agreed to the European Fiscal Compact, which introduced automatic sanctions, tightened the rules for national budget deficits, and empowered set targets for individual countries. The problem remained unresolved, but the danger of a complete meltdown had been reduced.[79] Once again, Germany was in the driver's seat and dictating the rules—and the plan stopped the relentless run on the euro.

Between the state dinner that Obama hosted in Merkel's honor when she received the Presidential Medal of Freedom, and the summit in Cannes where Obama defended his friend and partner, 2011 proved to be a turning point in the relationship between the two world leaders. The next time the two would meet, it would be Merkel's turn to return the favor: Obama would finally deliver a speech in front of the Brandenburg Gate.

7

"WE HAVE HISTORY
TO MAKE"

JUNE 2013

A year and a half after the confrontation at the G20 summit in Cannes, on June 19, 2013, Chancellor Merkel extended an official invitation to President Obama to give a speech in front of Berlin's historic Brandenburg Gate. The timing was notable: the invitation provided Obama the opportunity to deliver his address two weeks shy of the fiftieth anniversary of President Kennedy's famous "*Ich bin ein Berliner*" speech.

With limited time together and many issues for the two world leaders to discuss, Obama gave his much-anticipated speech in between a press conference with Merkel and a formal state dinner that she held in Obama's honor. In all three encounters together, their fondness for and rapport with each other was evident. They continued to refer to each other as friends and allies. Additionally, Merkel used the more familiar pronoun *du*, rather than the formal and polite *Sie*, when she introduced Obama to the spectators in front of the Brandenburg Gate.[1] It is extremely rare for non-English-speaking world leaders to address one another in this less formal manner—especially in such a public forum—and thus this gesture spoke volumes about their relationship.

In their joint press conference early in the afternoon, Merkel welcomed the American president on his first visit to Berlin after his election to the Oval Office. She, as usual, emphasized the many years of friendship between the two nations, rooted in shared values.[2] When Merkel mentioned Obama's upcoming speech, she stressed it would be before an open gate—the Brandenburg Gate, which had been closed during the Cold War until opened with the assistance of "our American partners and friends."[3]

Merkel linked the past to the future when she mentioned the challenges that faced the world of the twenty-first century:

> But we also see that the world is changing and changing at a very rapid pace, so new challenges come to the fore. And we want to tackle them with resolve, and we want to tackle them together.[4]

Merkel's statement reiterated the alliance between the United States and Germany and indicated the importance of this ongoing relationship as the two nations addressed problems that modern world leaders now faced—problems such as the economic crisis, global warming, and issues in the Middle East.

First, Merkel addressed her support of a free trade agreement between the EU and the United States and told reporters, "We will throw our effort behind this fully and squarely because we think that the economies on both sides of the Atlantic will very much benefit from it . . . both politically and economically."[5] Although Merkel had discussed the agreement with Obama in some of their earliest conversations, her support of free trade between the two parties became more important through the course of their working relationship. In previous encounters, if the subject were mentioned at all, it was only in passing. In this press conference, however, her decision to select it as the first item illustrated the growing importance of this subject for Merkel and her global agenda.

When Merkel summarized the progress in Afghanistan, she again emphasized the "transition of responsibility" that had occurred as she described the activities involved in moving from a military operation to a civil one. The chancellor emphatically declared her standing with the United States: "This is a process that we are going to tackle together, just as we tackled the greater military challenges of the past together—building up the security forces in Afghanistan together."[6] Merkel's remarks clearly demonstrated that she had no intention of abandoning her obligation to an allied nation, or her obligation to a reliable friend and ally.

In what had become her usual manner, as Merkel turned the floor to Obama, she thanked him for the open conversation they had just had, and once again welcomed him to Berlin.

As part of his opening remarks, the president thanked the German chancellor for the invitation to speak in front of the Brandenburg Gate and expressed his appreciation for

> *the humbling privilege that I'll have to address the people of Berlin from Pariser Platz on the Eastern side of the Brandenburg Gate—the other side of the wall that once stood there, the wall that President Reagan insisted be torn down. A quarter century since then has been one of extraordinary progress. We can witness this in the incredible vibrancy and prosperity of Berlin.*[7]

Obama's speech before the Brandenburg Gate was not the first one given there by a US president, but it would be the first given on the Eastern side, thereby making it yet another "first" that Merkel and Obama shared during their working relationship.

It is worth noting that neither the chancellor nor the president publicly mentioned Obama's previous trip to Berlin as a presidential candidate in 2008 or his speech in front of the Victory Column rather than the Brandenburg Gate. Perhaps both viewed any mention of the subject as counterproductive, but more likely, they considered the incident something that belonged in the past. Or, even more probable, the media had in fact made too much of the initial request in the first place. As Ben Rhodes argued in *The World as It Is: A Memoir of the Obama White House*, Merkel had rejected Obama's 2008 request

> *saying that the venue should be reserved for an actual president. When he learned about this, Obama was embarrassed and annoyed. "I never said I wanted to give a speech in front of the Brandenburg Gate," he snapped.*[8]

Whatever the reason, at this monumental event, the two looked forward rather than backward.

Obama fully understood the fondness the German people felt toward him, and he returned the affection. In his typical manner, he opened his remarks with a reference to his appreciation toward Germany and the German people. This time, however, the lighthearted comment came with a friendly jibe at the staggering ninety-degree temperature that greeted him. "I've always appreciated the warmth with which I've been greeted by the German people," Obama said, "and it's no different today, although I'm particularly impressed with the warmth of the weather here in Berlin."[9]

Obama reminded the press that he had presented Merkel with the Medal of Freedom during her last visit to Washington, DC, and emphasized the significance such a gesture had for the strength of the alliance between the two nations.[10] While critics could argue that Obama's continual mention of Merkel's award was further hyperbole overstating the gesture, there is another side of this argument—the Presidential Medal of Freedom is indeed the highest civilian honor a president can bestow on an individual. When he continued to emphasize it as an illustration of his respect and admiration for the German chancellor, the president made it exceedingly clear that he cherished and acknowledged the bond between the two of them.

Obama had heard rumors within the international community that members of the EU felt their alliance with the United States was being replaced by the US relationship with Asia and other countries in the Pacific.[11] Also present that day was the German president Joachim Gauck, who in his position, under Article 59 (1) of the German Constitution, represented his country with regard to international law. Crucially, the German president is also responsible for negotiating treaties with other nations and accrediting German diplomats.[12] So, in an effort to calm those fears, Obama spoke pointedly to Merkel, Gauck, and the German people about the alliance between the two nations as he saw it:

[S]ometimes there's been talk that the Transatlantic Alliance . . . is fading in importance, that the United States has turned its attention more

towards Asia and the Pacific. And in both conversations with Chancellor Merkel and earlier with your president, I reminded them that from our perspective, the relationship with Europe remains the cornerstone of our freedom and our security; that Europe is our partner in almost every- thing we do.[13]

In the spirit of illustrating his seriousness about maintaining that tie between Europe and the United States, Obama confirmed his support of the Transatlantic Trade and Investment Partnership (T-TIP) as well. Obama argued that the US–EU relationship was already the most substantial economic relationship in the world, and as it stood, thirteen million Europeans and Americans already had jobs directly supported by mutual trade and investment.[14] Obama and Merkel agreed that a successful trade agreement would help grow their economies, improve productivity, create jobs, improve efficiency, and boost competitiveness around the world—that it would benefit everyone, not just the United States and countries of the EU.[15]

However, even with the best of intentions, a free trade agreement can be contentious. Supporters argue it helps stimulate growth; opponents claim it kills jobs. Regardless of one's position, such agreements take years of negotiations and require a great deal of trust among those involved. The fact that Merkel and Obama were willingly engaged in such contentious discussions illustrated the trust they had in each other, as well as in the greater global economy. Clearly, they both agreed the benefits of such an arrangement outweighed the drawbacks.

When the US president discussed the issue of Afghanistan, he underscored the support Germany had provided in the mission:

Our men and women have been serving side-by-side in Afghanistan. Germany is the third-largest troop-contributing nation there. We're both grateful for the sacrifices that our servicemen and -women and their families have made in this common effort. And because of those efforts, Afghanistan now has the opportunity to secure itself and determine its own destiny.[16]

Obama made it clear that the Afghan people would not be in a place to determine their own fate had it not been for the assistance of German troops serving alongside Americans. He indicated that more work remained, however. He applauded Merkel's commitment to seeing it completed, and said, "And I appreciate Germany's interest in making sure that even after our troops are no longer involved in combat operations . . . we can continue to see progress in Afghanistan."[17]

Obama next affirmed that the two had discussed the ongoing crisis in Syria:

> We are united [in our desire] to see a negotiated political settlement to that conflict. We want to see a Syria that's unified, democratic, and at peace. Right now, we need to see an end to the bloodshed, and we have to make sure that chemical weapons are not used on the ground.[18]

This topic was a point of discontent between the two leaders, as Obama was willing to approve military engagement to assist the Syrian people, whereas Merkel adamantly opposed any kind of military involvement. Nonetheless, the two remained united in their belief that President Bashar al-Assad needed to step down in order to restore peace to the Syrian people.

When a journalist asked Merkel and Obama about the ongoing crisis in Syria, each implied that they had a difference of opinion on the subject, although none was directly stated. Obama said:

> I cannot and will not comment on specifics around our programs related to the Syrian opposition. What I can say is that we have a steady, consistent policy, which is, we want a Syria that is peaceful, non-sectarian, democratic, legitimate, tolerant. And that is our overriding goal. . . . And so we've had a consistent view in our desired outcome in Syria. It's also been our view that the best way to get there is through a political transition.[19]

Since conflict had arisen in Syria, political and military analysts seemed to expect European allies such as Germany to play a more active role in attempts to secure peace. To them, that meant more military supplies or more combat troops. Here, Merkel made it clear she understood her country's role in the process, and her idea of providing the needed assistance involved matters besides active military support.

When Merkel answered a similar question on whether Germany should provide supplies to the Syrian people, she responded:

> *Germany has very clear, strict rules on this, legal rules, according to which we are not allowed to supply arms into areas where there is civil strife. And that is not specifically designed for the Syrian question; it is a general rule. But [we may play] a constructive role as regards the political process—for example, as regards humanitarian assistance; as regards also the debate on which is the right way to go about this.*[20]

The media already had reason to suspect Obama would approve drone strikes against the Assad regime as he had in past conflicts—one journalist asked, "Madam Chancellor, the Nobel Prize winner Obama is waging a drone war also via Germany. And is he allowed to do that, according to German law?"[21]

Obama answered:

> *One thing with respect to drone policy . . . we do not use Germany as a launching point for unmanned drones . . . as part of our counterterrorism activities. I know that there have been some reports here in Germany that that might be the case. That is not.*[22]

As it became clear that the media was on the warpath, Merkel came to Obama's defense with a very pointed response:

> *Let me complement [this] by saying that the United States of America have bases here, they have soldiers here. They fulfill a very important function; particularly in the fight against terrorism. . . . We as allies, as members of NATO, stand shoulder-to-shoulder here. And we provide bases for activities, and our work is based, also, on shared values. As I*

said, we have exchanges on values. And I think it's good. I think it's the
right thing to do for the United States of America to be present here with
military bases in Germany. It's a normal thing within an alliance, and
this is as it should be and as it will be, and [will] continue to be.[23]

Merkel's response indicated that she unquestionably supported the United
States' military activities on German soil, that she believed the United States
was well within its rights on the subject, and that she would not interfere. Her
statements further elaborated on remarks she had made on previous occasions—that she welcomed US military troops in her country, and if anyone
had any doubts as to her sincerity about that promise, Merkel reaffirmed it
here. And though Merkel was reluctant to assist militarily with the United
States on the question of how best to handle the ongoing crisis in Syria, the
two agreed that Assad needed to step down.

On that sweltering ninety-degree day, the sun shone brightly, and the sky was
crystal blue in the late afternoon as a crowd gathered for Obama's much anticipated speech. Berlin's mayor, Klaus Wowereit, who had been a proponent of
Obama speaking in front of Brandenburg Gate in 2008, sat alongside Merkel
in seats provided next to the podium. The crowd of approximately 8,000 citizens—including Germany's own "Phantom of the Opera," Professor Sauer—
cheered, clapped, and waved German and American flags. Wowereit spoke
briefly and then welcomed the American president, mentioned the ongoing
friendship and partnership between the two countries, and noted President
Kennedy's and President Reagan's famous words at the Brandenburg Gate in
years past.

Following the mayor's remarks, Merkel took the stage to say a few words.
She began with a more informal tone and again referred to the president as
"dear Barack Obama," then she welcomed him to Berlin and joked about the
weather: "We have chosen the best possible weather for this historic visit."[24]
Merkel then discussed the history of the Brandenburg Gate and the Berlin

Wall. She talked about the importance of Germany being able to rely on the United States as a strong partner and friend—even after the horror of enduring two wars as enemies.

At one point, approximately halfway through her remarks, Merkel stated in German something about being "able to greet the president of the United States of America, Barack Obama," and an overly ambitious Obama, who perhaps thought that was his cue, headed toward the podium.[25] Perhaps catching the president's movement out of the corner of her eye, Merkel thought quickly, and without even looking up from her notes, she told the excited American president, in English, "Not yet, dear Mr. President, dear Barack Obama."[26] Obama sheepishly returned to his seat to allow the chancellor to finish her speech.

Merkel continued by reflecting on the shock of the 9/11 terrorist attack in the United States and the lessons learned from the global financial crisis of 2008. Her final words were:

> [A]lso in the twenty-first century, one thing holds true: there can be no better partners for each other than America and Europe. Dear Mr. President, dear Barack, I welcome you to this city, and welcome you to the Brandenburg Gate. I welcome you among friends.[27]

It was at this point, as Merkel turned the stage over to Obama, that she referred to him with the informal *du* instead of the more formal *Sie*.

Obama embraced her with an affectionate, European-style kiss on both cheeks as he took the stage. He expressed his admiration for Merkel and for both her friendship and her leadership, as well as for the example she had set with her journey "from a child of the East to the leader of a free and united Germany."[28]

He then reiterated one of his and Merkel's favorite remarks:

> As I've said, Angela and I don't exactly look like previous German and American leaders. But the fact that we can stand here today, along the fault line where a city was divided, speaks to an eternal truth: no wall

DEAR BARACK

*can stand against the yearning of justice, the yearning for freedom, and
the yearning for peace that burns in the human heart.*[29]

As Obama spoke those words, the cameras shifted their attention to
Merkel, who laughed joyously.[30] Obama enthusiastically reflected on the symbols of a reborn Germany that surrounded him:

> *A rebuilt Reichstag and its glistening glass dome. An American
> embassy back at its historic home on Pariser Platz. And this square
> itself, once a desolate no man's land, is now open to all.*[31]

Obama proudly acknowledged that he was not the first US president to
speak in front of the Brandenburg Gate, but he was the first "to stand on the
Eastern side to pay tribute to the past"[32]—representing yet another "first"
the two leaders afforded one another during their working relationship.
Obama declared the purpose of his speech in Berlin that day was

> *to say complacency is not the character of great nations. Today's
> threats are not as stark as they were half a century ago, but the
> struggle for freedom and security and human dignity—that struggle goes on. And I've come here, to this city of hope, because the tests
> of our time demand the same fighting spirit that defined Berlin a
> half-century ago.*[33]

The president, as he usually did, catered his message to his audience,
and specifically pointed to the characteristics of the Berliners. Through his
remarks, in fact, Obama gave Berliners a stern warning about the dangers of
complacency. He wanted people to understand that modern threats—such as
global warming, terrorism, and civil wars—might not be as dire as the dangers
of the Cold War, but, nevertheless, he believed democracy to be a continuum
and that it was undemocratic for people in free countries to sit back and do
nothing while other societies still suffered and struggled for equality. He urged
the citizens of Berlin to use the same fighting spirit they had used to obtain

120

their freedom during the Cold War to help others obtain their freedom today. Obama's unique ability to apply any message or take any speech and make it relevant to his audience was one of the reasons many people were drawn to him and his words. Obama had a gift of personalizing and identifying with people on their terms, and the Germans appreciated that.

As if to illustrate his point of democracy being a continuum, Obama spoke Kennedy's famous words "*Ich bin ein Berliner*"—and as he uttered that phrase, applause erupted from the audience, and from the stage Merkel and Wowereit looked at each other and smiled.[34] Obama reminded the crowd that Kennedy had instructed people to look around and

> *lift our eyes, [and] then we'll recognize that our work is not done. For we are not only citizens of America or Germany—we are also citizens of the world. And our fates and fortunes are linked like never before.*[35]

Obama argued that citizens in free and democratic countries would never be completely free as long as people in other countries suffered or lacked basic rights. Therefore, people in free countries had a responsibility to fight for the rights of people under oppressive regimes. Obama's remarks implored all citizens of democratic countries to fight on behalf of the shared values of everyone—including those who were strangers. As the world becomes smaller and smaller, he explained, people needed to fight for the rights of all now more than ever. He added that

> *When Europe and America lead with our hopes instead of our fears, we do things that no other nations can do, no other nations will do. So we have to lift up our eyes today and consider the day of peace with justice that our generation wants for this world.*[36]

This theme of "peace with justice" was at the heart of his speech. He indicated that it began with the "example we set here at home, for we know from our own histories that intolerance breeds injustice"—and repeating that phrase each time, he continued:

Peace with justice means extending a hand to those who reach for free-dom, wherever they live. . . . Peace with justice means pursuing the security of a world without nuclear weapons, no matter how distant that dream may be. . . . Peace with justice means refusing to condemn our children to a harsher, less hospitable planet. . . . Peace with justice means meeting our moral obligations. . . . And finally, let's remember that peace with justice depends on our ability to sustain both the security of our societies and openness that defines them. Threats to freedom don't merely come from the outside. They can emerge from within—from our own fears, from the disengagement of our citizens.[37]

In closing, the president referred to the Berlin Wall:

The Wall belongs to history. But we have history to make as well. And the heroes that came before us now call to us to live up to those highest ideals. . . . This is the lesson of the ages. This is the spirit of Berlin. And the greatest tribute we can pay to those who came before us is . . . carrying on their work to pursue peace and justice, not only in our countries but for all mankind.[38]

Obama's final remarks were a call to action—his effort to encourage his audience to engage in political activities that could help others around the world achieve a bigger form of democracy. Just as the Germans had fought for freedom during the Cold War, Obama urged today's generation to embark on a similar form of activism based on the same valuable ideals.

Following Obama's speech, the chancellor, Professor Sauer, and members of the delegation hosted the president and the first lady at a state dinner at the Schloss Charlottenburg, a Baroque palace in Berlin. In many ways, the dinner that evening demonstrated the friendship between the two leaders more firmly than either the press conference or the remarks at the Brandenburg

Gate. In their exchange of toasts, Merkel and Obama expressed perhaps the most telling sentiments of the affection they felt toward each other.

Merkel again shared her gratitude for the Medal of Freedom ceremony and the fond memories she had from that event:

> *I'm able to say this also on behalf of the whole Federal Republic of Germany, because I am aware that this was an honor that was granted to me on behalf of my country. . . . Now we still have very fond memories. This was indeed a very moving moment, and we greatly appreciated the warmth of your hospitality and also the friendship that you showed.*[39]

In a sentiment unspoken since Obama's inauguration, Merkel articulated her admiration for Obama as the first Black president of the United States, saying, "Barack Obama, I think what was possible today, was to show you how many people here in Germany feel a great sense of admiration toward you— because, in many ways, you personally embody the image of the United States as a country of unlimited possibility."[40] On occasion, Merkel had referenced Obama's comments about how neither of them resembled their respective predecessors, but until now she had stayed away from public remarks that even remotely expressed her personal admiration toward Obama in light of the challenges he had faced on his journey.

Merkel reiterated her respect for the unlikely friendship that had emerged between the United States and Germany, given the difficult history between them:

> *We've come a long way. Again, it is not a matter of natural course, but a long way that has brought us to this place where we can finally celebrate, can meet together and celebrate our freedom together. All the way leading up to German unity, to the unification of our country, you have demonstrated that you trust us, that the United States places great trust in our country . . . that you support us . . . and that is something for which we are grateful.*[41]

At this point in their working relationship, not much was surprising about the chancellor's remarks. She had made no secret of her gratitude toward the United States. What was unusual, however, was the level of emotion and sentimentality expressed by the normally reserved chancellor. True, she had shown her emotions in previous encounters with the American president, such as when they toured Buchenwald together, or when Obama presented her with the Medal of Freedom. Yet her demeanor on this night, and the emotions she showed alongside the words she spoke, indicated that her respect and esteem for the US president had reached a new high point.

After Merkel's supportive remarks toward Obama, he followed with equally supportive words. He began by thanking "Angela" and Professor Sauer for their hospitality and kind words, and joked about the "warm welcome" he and the first family received in Berlin—"both literally and figuratively."[42] To illustrate the interconnectedness of the two cultures, Obama emphasized the gratitude Americans have toward German immigrants such as Chrysler, Guggenheim, Heinz, and Hershey. To the amusement of the audience, Obama added that young Americans will be grateful to Levi Strauss for their blue jeans, "and Americans will always be grateful for some important German immigrants—Anheuser-Busch"—at which point even the translators laughed and lost their place.[43]

Once again, Obama mentioned his admiration for Merkel and her aspirations and accomplishments:

> Now, on a very personal level, I'm thankful to Angela. [German poet] Friedrich Schiller once said, "Keep true to the dreams of your youth." Angela, you've spoken often of the dreams of your youth. . . . And you've not only kept to those dreams, but you've also helped those dreams become real for millions of your countrymen. I'm extraordinarily grateful to our partnership and our friendship. As I've said before, you're an inspiration to me and the people around the world.[44]

Obama then took the opportunity to build upon the remarks about the Freedom Bell that Merkel had made during her congressional speech in 2009:

Here in Berlin, that bell tolled after President Kennedy's speech. It rang after German unification. It rang after 9/11, which obviously meant so much to us as a symbol of the freedom and friendship that binds [sic] us together. What you may not know is that before the bell was given to our German friends, it traveled all around the United States. Millions of Americans joined the effort, lending their support and signing their names to a declaration of freedom.

Here, Obama professed his intention to echo that effort,

by borrowing the words that those millions of Americans once expressed to their German friends as part of this gift, the [Freedom] Bell. We believe in the sacredness and dignity of the individual. We believe that all men derive the right of freedom equally from God. And we are proud to join with millions of men and women throughout the world who hold the cause of freedom sacred.[45]

Just as Merkel's visit to Washington to receive the Presidential Medal of Freedom in 2011 came at a turbulent time in the relationship between Merkel and Obama because of Germany's vote on Libya, another scandal would soon break out—the leak of classified United States National Security Agency (NSA) information—that would cause an equally disruptive conflict given the timing of Obama's speech in Berlin. Through their shared admiration and respect for one another, the two leaders had moved past the disappointing vote on the use of military forces in Libya two years earlier. Perhaps with the same work and patience, they could move past the problems caused by the NSA scandal to come.

8

"FRIENDS SPYING ON EACH OTHER IS NOT ACCEPTABLE"

JUNE 2013-JULY 2014

L ess than two weeks after Chancellor Merkel and President Obama appeared together in Berlin—where the world observed them displaying their friendliest interactions to date—European headlines sang a different tune, with *Der Spiegel* asking, FRIENDS OR FOES? BERLIN MUST PROTECT GERMANS FROM US SPYING. This latest controversy arose on June 29, 2013, when claims emerged that the NSA had spied on EU offices in both the United States and Europe. The *Guardian* broke the scandal and reported that the highly secretive intelligence agency had monitored thirty-eight embassies and the phones of thirty-five world leaders.[1]

This revelation followed controversial leaks provided by former US Central Intelligence Agency (CIA) contractor Edward Snowden in early June 2013 that the NSA was collecting the telephone records of tens of millions of Americans.[2] Later articles published in both the *Guardian* and the *Washington Post* revealed that the NSA—along with Britain's electronic eavesdropping agency, Government Communications Headquarters (GCHQ)—directly tapped into the servers of nine internet firms, including Google, Microsoft, Yahoo, and Facebook, to track online communication in a surveillance program known as PRISM.[3] According to these reports, the NSA used a myriad of spying methods to intercept messages, including bugs, specialized antennae, and wiretaps.[4] This angered Americans, since many, if not all, of these tactics seemed to violate Fourth Amendment protections from undue search and seizure of citizens and their effects.

Furthermore, a follow-up report by Snowden revealed that the NSA's actions had worldwide implications, not just consequences within the borders of the United States. In fact, the NSA's questionable activities began to cause a considerable amount of discord between the United States and many of its supposed closest allies. *Der Spiegel* reported that the NSA had exempted only a few select countries from surveillance—countries that the agency defined as close friends, or "2nd party partners": the UK, Australia, Canada, and New Zealand. A document classified as "top secret" stated, "The NSA does NOT target its 2nd party partners, nor request that 2nd parties do anything that is inherently illegal for NSA to do."[5]

It is unclear what criteria the US government used to determine which countries fell into the second-party partner category—but Germany, along with many other EU nations, fell into the group of third-party partners the NSA targeted for surveillance.[6] According to *Der Spiegel*, "The Americans are collecting metadata from up to half a billion communications a month in Germany—making the country one of the biggest sources of streams of information" flowing into the NSA's data pool.[7] NSA expert and American journalist James Bamford said, "We probably put more listening posts in Germany than anyplace because of its proximity to the Soviet Union."[8]

Much like some Americans believed the NSA had violated the spirit of the Fourth Amendment, the agency had also offended Germans on a basic level—Article 10 of the German Constitution states that the "privacy of letters, posts, and telecommunications shall be inviolable." Given all the statements both US and German leaders made about the important alliance between the two countries, Snowden's revelations came as a major shock to the Germans. And given how frequently Obama had emphasized that partnership, it's understandable that these actions immediately insulted German citizens. As *Der Spiegel* recounted, Germans viewed the spy activities as a direct violation and a betrayal of their civil liberties.

> *The NSA's totalitarian ambition regarding information-gathering does not affect just states and authorities. It does not affect just businesses. It affects us all. It even affects those who think they have nothing to hide. A constitutional state cannot allow it. None of us can allow it.*[9]

In the early days which followed the news, the public outcry was louder than that of the German government. Germans demanded action from Merkel, but much to their dismay, she remained silent for several days after the story broke.

The German press viewed the inaction of the German government and politicians as unacceptable, and promised to replace them with leaders who would take the NSA scandal seriously and act on it.

Merkel had given only a brief statement as the scandal broke, saying through spokesman Steffen Seibert, "The monitoring of friends—this is unacceptable. It can't be tolerated. We're no longer in the Cold War."[10] When she finally broke her silence in an interview with the weekly *Die Zeit* the next week, she defended the actions of the NSA and stated it was impossible to prevent terrorist attacks without the information that telecommunications monitoring provided. In fact, Merkel argued, democracies frequently relied on intelligence agencies to protect the safety of citizens.[11] While Merkel argued that the accusations against the NSA needed to be clarified, she continued to defend America to her citizens and affirmed that "America is and has been our truest ally throughout the decades and remains so."[12]

It would seem reasonable that Merkel—both as Germany's leader and as someone who had come to trust the American president—would be the first to criticize the United States' actions. Yet the pragmatic Merkel knew spying occurred on a regular basis and to be angered by expected actions was a waste of time and resources.[13] She may have privately been disturbed by the spying, but she knew all too well that the United States was one of Germany's strongest allies. As interconnected as the world had become, she would have to work with Obama again in the future, and holding a personal grudge against him would pose a threat to the security of both nations.

In their outrage over the NSA actions, many Germans compared the actions of the NSA to those of the Stasi during the Cold War, but Merkel shut down the argument immediately:

> *For me, there is absolutely no comparison between the Stasi in East Germany and the work of intelligence services in democratic states. These are two totally different things, and such comparisons only lead to a trivialization of what the Stasi did to the people in East Germany.*[14]

It may have seemed unusual for Merkel to defend the actions of the United States against her own country, but because of her East German roots and the assistance the United States had provided during Germany's quest for freedom and unity, Merkel was willing to give the United States the benefit of the doubt—more so than any of her predecessors and European counterparts. In her mind, her freedom was linked to the United States, and it would take much more than spying allegations to damage that relationship.

As word spread across the world of the allegations of surveillance, countries across the world began to conduct their own investigations. According to an article written in Reuters, in October 2013, many European allies, including Germany and France, had mixed feelings about the allegations.[15] French president François Hollande cautioned the United States in July 2013 that such a breach in trust between the United States and the European Union could negatively impact the upcoming talks on a free trade agreement if the US did not explain its actions to the satisfaction of the EU leaders.[16] Additionally he implored the United States to alter its behavior:

We cannot accept this kind of behavior between partners and allies. . . .
We ask that this immediately stop. . . . There can be no negotiations or
transactions in all areas until we have obtained these guarantees, for
France but also for all of the European Union.[17]

On the other hand, the Reuters article pointed out that despite the German people's heightened sensitivity to government surveillance because of the Cold War, Merkel had been relatively quiet about the whole affair. As one journalist wrote, "Chancellor Angela Merkel has not been particularly outspoken in her criticism of the programs, although she did ask US President Barack Obama for explanations during his July visit to Germany."[18] Nevertheless, despite the varying levels of concern over the allegations, at a European Council Meeting in Brussels on October 24 and 25, 2013, leaders of all twenty-eight EU countries emphasized in a statement that they understood the necessity of intelligence gathering in efforts to successfully combat terrorism. Additionally, they emphasized the close and valued partnership between the United States and Europe.[19] However, they added that such a partnership "must be based on respect and trust, a lack of which could prejudice the necessary cooperation in the field of intelligence gathering."[20] The statement issued by the EU Council clearly indicated that while they understood the importance of the partnership between the United States and the EU, that partnership was not limitless—when a government sacrificed the basic principles of freedom and democracy that all nations held dearly, said nation would be held accountable for its actions.

Obama had already defended the US government's actions in the joint press conference with Merkel before his speech at the Brandenburg Gate. At that point, Obama had assured the public that "the encroachment on privacy has been strictly limited by a court-approved process."[21] He promised that the NSA had not been "rifling through ordinary emails of German citizens or American citizens or French citizens or anybody else," and claimed the information had enabled the United States to avert at least fifty threats to both America and Germany.[22] The NSA's work saved lives, Obama argued, thus the surveillance was warranted—although he did admit that a balance was needed between keeping citizens safe and protecting personal privacy:

> *Free, liberal democracies live off people having a feeling of security. . . .*
> *[But] there needs to be proportionality. . . . And I'm confident that we*
> *can strike this right balance—keep our people safe, but preserve our civil*
> *liberties even in this Internet Age.*[23]

Tensions between Merkel and Obama escalated in October 2013, however, when reports indicated that Merkel's cell phone had been a target of the NSA. On October 23 Merkel called Obama personally to confront him on the issue.[24] Although Obama promised there would be no further tapping of Merkel's phone while he remained president, he neither confirmed nor denied any previous espionage.[25]

Then, in a rare event, German foreign minister Guido Westerwelle summoned US ambassador John B. Emerson on October 24 to explain Germany's displeasure with Merkel's cell phone being tapped.[26] In an interview with Fox News, German officials emphasized how unusual it was for the high-ranking foreign minister to hold such a meeting:

> *In any previous cases of displeasure with Washington, the session*
> *would have been handled at a lower level than the German foreign*
> *minister. One official said this kind of treatment usually is reserved*
> *for Syria and Iran.*[27]

Hence, the fact that the US ambassador had been called before Foreign Minister Westerwelle spoke to the level of discomfort and distrust that had surfaced between the two nations over the Snowden revelations.

Even though Merkel had not been disturbed by the initial reports of the NSA spying on German citizens, having her personal cell phone tapped took matters to a new level. Moreover, she faced continuing pressure from her citizens about the ongoing problem. In an October 25 interview before the EU summit in Brussels, Merkel stated:

> *Friends spying on each other is not acceptable.... This isn't about me or my*
> *issues, but for every German citizen. We need to trust in our allies, and this*
> *trust needs to be built, and this means thinking further about the kind of*
> *data privacy we need.... This goes for everyone, but as German chancellor*
> *it is my responsibility to ensure protection for German citizens.*[28]

Sources close to Merkel indicated that she was more bewildered by the United States' actions than angry, but as a national leader, she recognized her obligation to speak for her citizens.[29]

Several months later, the controversy surrounding the Snowden leaks still had not died down, so Obama had to implement reforms within the NSA—on both domestic and international matters. On January 17, 2014, he gave a speech that outlined the changes and emphasized the impact for citizens on foreign soil as well as US citizens: "Our efforts will only be effective if ordinary citizens in other countries have confidence that the United States respects their privacy too."[30]

Obama believed that in order to protect the world from the rising threat of terrorism, a balance had to be struck to safeguard individuals both in the United States and abroad. While the president knew that the risk of terrorism was a growing concern, maintaining the right to privacy against undue governmental interference was equally important in a democracy. He judged that the policies he outlined in his new presidential directive struck that balance—for foreign citizens as well as those in the United States—and said that, "Just as [we] balance security and privacy at home, our global leadership demands that we balance our security requirements against our need to maintain the trust and cooperation among people and leaders around the world."[31]

Under the directive, according to Obama, the United States only "uses signals intelligence for legitimate national security purposes and not for the purpose of indiscriminately reviewing the emails or phone calls of ordinary folks."[32] Additionally, he promised that the US intelligence agencies would use bulk collection of signals intelligence only to meet specific security requirements: the protection of troops and allies; the continuation of counter-terrorism, counterproliferation, and cybersecurity efforts; and the prevention of transnational crime (including evasion of sanctions).[33] Then Obama took the unprecedented action of "extending certain protections that we have for the American people to people overseas."[34]

Obama directed his attorney general and the director of national intelligence to develop safeguards that would limit both the amount of time the government can hold personal information and the use of this information.[35] With his executive order, he attempted to reassure the public that the United States would not spy on citizens anywhere in the world without cause. Obama took his policy one step further:

> *This applies to foreign leaders as well. Given the understandable attention that this issue has received, I've made clear to the intelligence community that unless there is a compelling national security purpose, we will not monitor the communications of heads of state and government of our close friends and allies.*[36]

Because of the rift caused between the United States and Germany over the Snowden allegations, Obama provided an interview on German television following his speech, with Claus Kleber of ZDF *heute journal plus*. Kleber told the president that the initial response from historically pro-American viewers was "skeptical, guarded, disappointed, and they expected more."[37]

Obama acknowledged that it would take time to restore trust, but he hoped the German people would remember the good partnership and history the two countries shared. He promised that the executive order was only the beginning of the conversation on the question of cybersecurity versus personal liberties, and that he would continue to hold conversations with Merkel and make changes as needed—all while keeping in mind the values, laws, and customs of the German people.[38]

Obama conceded that he and the chancellor may have had disagreements on foreign policy issues, but that was not a valid excuse to spy on her. The two of them enjoyed a good relationship based on friendship and trust, he explained, and one of the reasons for that was they were honest with each other. Obama also assured Kleber that under his presidential directive, Merkel's personal cell phone would not be tapped.[39]

Despite the new executive order and the promises, unfortunately, however, the spying issue between the United States and Germany did not end there.

In July 2014, Germany expelled America's top spy chief in Germany—an unnamed CIA officer stationed at the US embassy in Berlin—from the country. The German government asked the American to leave after two new possible US espionage cases broke back-to-back in a week's time: two Germans—one working at the Ministry of Defense and another at a German intelligence agency—were suspected of spying for the United States.[40] According to Ben Brumfield from CNN,

> *It's a punitive gesture usually reserved for adversarial nations in times of crisis and only very rarely for an ally, particularly a very close one. But allegations of American spying have seriously injured German trust.*[41]

Following the expulsion of the US spy, Merkel reportedly told Obama that she faced tremendous pressure from her country to address what many Germans viewed as "unconscionable provocations," according to *Politico*.[42] The two leaders agreed that their chiefs of staff should meet immediately—in Berlin, rather than Washington. According to *Politico*:

> *This last point was important for Merkel, since Germans well know that more familiar custom is for them to cross the Atlantic to come calling on Americans. That was how Obama's trusted retainer, Chief of Staff Denis McDonough, found himself in the office of Peter Altmaier, her chief of staff and longtime confidant, for a four-hour meeting.*[43]

Obama knew the situation between him and Merkel was fractured, and he understood the importance of sending his chief of staff to Berlin to address the issue. Though a relatively simple gesture, it was an important one. Undoubtably many policy and diplomatic issues are negotiated and addressed behind closed doors—not often does the public obtain full knowledge of said conversations. To assume that the simple fact of Obama sending his chief of staff to Berlin to meet with Merkel's chief of staff and mend the fences was the single act that repaired this serious break in trust is naïve. It is certain that much more took place behind the scenes between Merkel and Obama personally as well as among their staffs to repair the damage. This was an important and significant first step, but this breach in trust is one that would remain in the background throughout the rest of Obama's presidency.

Over a year later, in October 2015, an article published in *Der Spiegel* revealed that Germany's Federal Intelligence Service, the BND (*Bundesnachrichtendienst*), may have known about the NSA's activities long ago—and did nothing.[44]

Two years after that, *Der Spiegel* journalists uncovered documents proving that the BND had targeted many US businesses and governmental agencies with surveillance between 1998 and 2006. The BND used thousands of search terms, or "selectors," to surveil email addresses and telephone and fax numbers belonging to American organizations such as the NASA, the US Air Force, the Marine Corps, the Defense Intelligence Agency, government contractor Lockheed Martin, and even the Secret Service. The BND also targeted connection data from the International Monetary Fund, the Washington, DC, office of the Arab League, and over one hundred foreign embassies in Washington—not to mention the State Department, the US Treasury Department, and the White House.[45]

Another *Der Spiegel* report claimed that the BND spied on Poland, Austria, Great Britain, France, the Vatican, and even the International Committee of the Red Cross in Geneva as well as the United States.[46] Given all these facts, Merkel's comments about not spying among friends were revealed as nothing more than empty words.

Even so, these revelations about German surveillance efforts shed potential new light on why Merkel had remained so quiet about the Snowden allegations when they first surfaced. "People either knew or likely suspected that their own service had been just as unscrupulous in monitoring its closest partners," *Der Spiegel* claims. "The truth is that the Germans were snooping far more extensively than they ever wanted to admit."[47] But publicly, Merkel maintained that it was pointless to spy among allies:

> *From a common sense standpoint, in my opinion, spying on allies is, in the end, a waste of energy. We have so many problems, and we should, I find, concentrate on the essentials.*[48]

Merkel may have been annoyed at the president's actions—and may even have brushed her own government's actions under the rug—but all the same, the two world leaders knew they would have to find a way to move forward. Fortunately, the two still had a remarkable working relationship, and, given the crisis about to erupt on the international scene, they would need each other more than ever.

9

"A FEW DIFFICULTIES YET TO OVERCOME"

NOVEMBER 2013-MAY 2014

The trouble in Ukraine began on November 21, 2013, when—after pressure from Russia—Ukrainian president Viktor Yanukovych suspended discussions about signing a trade deal with the European Union. The Russians opposed Ukraine forming a closer relationship with the EU, and soon protests erupted, which illustrated the division between the pro-European West and Yanukovych's pro-Russian base, east of Ukraine.[1] The crisis reached new heights on February 20, 2014, after Ukrainian police killed several protesters in central Kiev. Yanukovych blamed oppositional leaders for provoking the violence; the protesters blamed government snipers.[2]

As a result, on February 22, under increased pressure from the people, Yanukovych fled Kiev, while former prime minister Yulia Tymoshenko was released from jail, where she had been held since 2011—for "abuse of office" charges people believed were politically motivated—and triumphantly addressed pro-Western protesters in Kiev.[3] In retaliation, on March 1, the Russian parliament authorized Russian president Vladimir Putin's request to send military forces into Crimea, an autonomous southern Ukraine region with strong Russian loyalties. Russian-speaking troops wearing unmarked uniforms poured into the area, and two weeks later, Russia annexed Crimea in a referendum that most of the world viewed as illegitimate.[4]

On April 15, Kiev's government launched military action against the pro-Russian rebels who had seized government buildings across eastern Ukraine. Putin argued that Ukraine was on the verge of a civil war, and less than a month later, separatists in the eastern regions of Donetsk and Luhansk declared independence from Ukraine after unrecognized referendums.[5] The United States and the European Union imposed two rounds of sanctions against Russia for destabilizing Ukraine by stoking the rebellion in eastern Ukraine—a charge Russia denied.[6]

Throughout the first months of 2014, Putin must have anxiously watched the discord between Merkel and Obama over surveillance while he planned his move to illegally annex Ukraine. As it turned out, however, Putin overcalculated the tensions between Merkel and Obama. Although angry at having her personal cell phone tapped, Merkel was first and foremost a pragmatist, and she realized that spying occurred regularly as part of international politics. The threat of Russia far outweighed any remaining personal negativity she felt toward Obama. Qvortrup characterized her response as follows:

> *To be sure, having your phone bugged is unacceptable, especially if you have grown up in a Communist dystopia. . . . But nothing would ever get done—and Merkel would not have succeeded in politics—if such personal issues could cloud everyday decision-making.*[7]

So, Merkel made her first trip back to Washington in over a year, and the first following the NSA scandal, to address the Ukraine crisis with Obama. The escalating Ukrainian crisis had provided the necessary opportunity for Germany and the United States to put their differences aside and jointly address Putin. The press on both sides of the Atlantic speculated on how the meeting would be received, considering the ongoing controversy between the two leaders.

The conflict had been escalating since February 2014, when Yanukovych fled to Russia, and as Qvortrup characterized the situation: "And then it kicked off." Undercover Russian soldiers infiltrated the Crimean Peninsula, which had been Ukrainian territory since the 1950s, and soon it seemed they were encroaching on eastern Ukraine. Although Putin had initially denied knowledge of the undercover soldiers infiltrating eastern Ukraine—known in Germany as "little green men"[8]—the Obama administration swiftly implemented a series of economic, diplomatic, defensive, and congressional penalties to show stern disapproval of his illegal actions.[9] In March, Obama banned or revoked the US visas of approximately a dozen unnamed Russian citizens; the president also signed an executive order that provided the foundation for additional sanctions, which included powerful economic sanctions on individuals and entities that were responsible for the situation in Ukraine.[10] The White House then canceled all prefatory meetings for the upcoming G8 summit to be held in the city of Sochi, Russia, in June, as well as all discussions on trade and all commercial ties with Russia. And, finally, the president refrained from sending a delegate to the 2014 Paralympic Games in Sochi.[11]

From a defense perspective, the US military canceled all military consultations with Russia and sent F-16 fighter jets to Poland to participate in expanded military activity there. As a reassurance measure, the Department of Defense expanded flights over all former Soviet states as well as the Baltic nations. In addition to these actions ordered by Obama, the US House of Representatives passed a measure for $1 billion in loan guarantees for Ukraine, and the Senate pushed for a measure to blacklist certain Russian individuals, companies, and banks. US lawmakers also called for an enhanced missile defense system in Poland and the Czech Republic.[12]

While the Obama administration and the US government engaged in aggressive retaliatory measures in a brisk fashion, the EU and Merkel—much to the annoyance of the Americans—stalled before they made any decisions on how to address the crisis. Merkel kept a low profile, perhaps while she pondered her options. To complicate the situation, while Merkel appeared to be paralyzed and unable to decide how to address the crisis, her foreign policy and security advisor reportedly admired the Russian's tactics and recognized the skill and intelligence behind Putin's strategy even if he did not care for the Russian president on a personal level.[13]

In a leaked document, American senior diplomat Victoria Nuland reportedly allowed her frustration about Europe's inactivity over the conflict to boil over, stating, "Fuck the EU."[14] Merkel's spokesperson responded by publicly calling the remarks "completely unacceptable"[15]—and the already tense situation between the United States and Germany over the NSA allegations suddenly became even more so.

Merkel, who speaks fluent Russian, could handle Putin better than any of her counterparts. To her, he was a known quantity—not someone she liked or agreed with, but the devil she knew.[16] According to Merkel, Putin's vanity was his soft spot, and he had an "almost desperate quest to be recognized as a great statesman by an equally great power."[17] She knew he wanted to show off the city of Sochi, where the next G8 meeting had been scheduled. The G8, or Group of Eight, was a prestigious, informal group of the world's eight leading industrial nations, with membership viewed as "symbolically significant."[18] She told him that until Russia complied with international law, there would be no G8 summit in Sochi.[19] But despite the humiliation, Putin still refused to comply.

Fortunately for Merkel and Obama, the other G8 leaders shared the United States' and Germany's concerns over Putin's illegal actions, and on March 24, they issued a joint statement known as the Hague Declaration.[20] Under the guidelines of the statement, nations pledged to boycott the G8 summit in Sochi but would convene without Russia in Brussels instead.[21] The foreign ministers also planned to boycott a G8 meeting in April in Moscow.[22] Finally, the statement argued, "We remain ready to intensify actions including coordinated sectoral sanctions that will have an increasingly significant impact on the Russian economy, if Russia continues to escalate this situation."[23]

The fact that the other G8 nations (which would soon become the G7) all banded together to retaliate and impose punishment on a fellow member who had violated rules of the NATO Treaty demonstrated the importance of the NATO alliance. The economic pressure of seven nations combined could certainly convince Putin to do the right thing more effectively than any one or two nations alone. Yet to Merkel's dismay, Putin appeared to be unbothered by his expulsion from the G8; according to Russian foreign minister Sergei Lavrov, one could not be expelled from the G8 since it was an informal club without official membership anyway.[24]

Because dismantling the G8 proved ineffective in discouraging Putin from violating international law, Merkel encouraged her European colleagues to impose economic sanctions on Russia. Since Germany was more dependent on Russia for nuclear power than other Western European countries, Putin assumed Merkel and her new foreign minister, Frank-Walter Steinmeier, would "plead, talk, and criticize" when they considered Russia's actions but would never carry out sanctions. Once again, he was wrong.[25]

Over the course of her career, Merkel had faced many men who tended to underestimate her, and she did not take kindly to it. Additionally, the German chancellor had demonstrated many times that she knew how to handle herself amid macho male behavior. For example, Merkel has a well-known fear of big, black dogs, and Putin knew this about his German counterpart. During their first encounter, to rattle her, he let his black lab roam about his office. Photos of the incident indicated that Merkel neither let down her guard nor showed Putin her uneasiness despite her discomfort with the situation.[26]

Although France, the United States, and Ukraine participated in negotiations with Russia, Qvortrup argued that the crisis over Ukraine was mainly between Putin and Merkel.[27] After all, the distance from Germany to the Ukrainian border is a scant four hundred miles. Despite the opposition from England and France, Merkel used her alliances with smaller EU countries to convince them that economic sanctions were the most effective way to contain the Ukraine crisis. Although European pharmaceutical manufacturers would reportedly lose approximately €2.1 billion and car manufacturers a similar amount, business leaders were reportedly happy to "make sacrifices."[28] In fact, Qvortrup reported that German companies held up well, while the UK worried that London's economy would suffer, and France feared to lose a lucrative helicopter carrier contract with Russia.[29]

Since the United States did not have as much to lose when it came to increased sanctions against Russia as European countries did, it would be easier to convince the United States to punish Russia. One important point to raise here, however, is that these sanctions could be addressed and ultimately implemented largely because of Merkel's good rapport with Obama and other EU leaders, such as President François Hollande of France and Prime Minister David Cameron of Britain. As the *Christian Science Monitor* argued:

> *Ever since the Ukraine crisis began last November, Ms. Merkel has emerged as the leading decider on Europe's foreign policy. Her preferred mix of hard diplomacy and soft sanctions on Russia over its actions in Ukraine has been the dominant position of the European Union, and one largely followed by Mr. Obama.*[30]

In addition to demonstrating to the world that the United States remained a reliable partner in the effort to keep Putin in check, Obama seized the ongoing crisis in Ukraine as an opportunity to mend ties with his friend and partner, Merkel. The Obama administration extended an invitation to Merkel to visit the White House to discuss the conflict in Ukraine, though support of the Transatlantic Trade and Investment Partnership (T-TIP) agreement and the lingering effects of the NSA scandal remained topics of discussion at the White House.

Following their discussion on that morning of May 2, 2014, the mood between Obama and Merkel at their news conference was cordial but more reserved than at previous encounters. Obama still referred to the chancellor as "Angela" when he welcomed her, and reiterated that she and Germany remained his—and the United States'—closest partners.[31] Nonetheless, even the normally charismatic and jocular president remained subdued, and he spoke only of the issues at hand rather than inserting flattering comments toward Merkel and the Germans as he usually did.

More dramatic was Merkel and her response to the American president. As at her last visit, she stood at a podium to the right of Obama, and while he made his opening remarks, she focused mainly straight ahead, and only occasionally looked to the president to acknowledge his remarks with a curt nod or a half smile. Their interaction with each other lacked the same chemistry that had been apparent in previous meetings.

Only in passing did Obama speak of the NSA controversy, when he revealed, "We agreed to continue the close security cooperation—including law enforcement, cyber, and intelligence—that keeps our citizens safe."[32] After all, there were more pressing matters the two needed to discuss, such as their commitment to completing T-TIP, which Obama labeled "critical to supporting jobs and boosting exports in both the United States and Europe," and the energy security that could come from greater diversity of energy sources in Europe—a partnership that would benefit the United States in terms of natural gas exports.[33]

The president acknowledged that they had spent much of their time that morning addressing the conflict in Ukraine, and made sure he publicly thanked Merkel for her leadership on the issue:

> *Angela, I want to thank you for being such a strong partner on this issue. You've spoken out forcefully against Russia's illegal actions in Ukraine. And you've been a leader in the EU, as well as an indispensable partner in the G7. And your presence here today is a reminder that our nations stand united.*[34]

Aside from demonstrating that he valued the partnership between the United States and Germany on the conflict in Ukraine, Obama also illustrated that the crisis was one that impacted both nations. He made it clear that he believed the stance and position Merkel took to combat the crisis had demonstrated bold leadership and that he respected her leadership skills. The fact that she stood beside him again showed the partnership of the two countries. Yet despite Merkel's bold leadership, she could not solve the crisis without the assistance of the United States—a reliance that demonstrated how linked the countries had become.

Obama noted the negative impact of the current sanctions on Russia:

> *The ruble has fallen to near all-time lows, Russian stocks this year have dropped sharply, and Russia has slipped into a recession. Investors are fleeing, and it's estimated that $100 billion in investment will exit Russia this year. Russian companies are finding it harder to access the capital they need, and Russia's credit rating has been downgraded to just above "junk" status.*[35]

Obama emphasized that NATO allies preferred to solve the crisis diplomatically, but they were prepared to employ additional sanctions and tools if the Russian government interfered with the election scheduled for later that month.[36]

Obama concluded his remarks with more kindness toward Merkel, and more references to their shared vision of a free and peaceful Europe: "So Angela, I want to thank you again for being here. . . . Just as our predecessors stood united in pursuit of that vision, so will we."[37]

From the very early stages of Obama and Merkel's working relationship, Obama had expressed his admiration for the German chancellor. He had worked hard to earn her trust, and she had reluctantly given it. Yet, for those present at this May 2014 meeting, a new uneasiness had settled between the two leaders. Judging by the humility with which Obama uttered his words, it seemed that the NSA scandal had wounded him the most—and that he was willing to do what was necessary to repair the relationship.

Although Merkel thanked "Barack" for his hospitality, the stressful atmosphere was hard to ignore.[38] When she discussed the continuing conflict with Ukraine, she acknowledged the importance of a strong transatlantic relationship in effectively addressing the conflicts currently facing them. She also discussed her relief that the measures being taken against Russian aggression had been taken together and that, based on their conversations that morning, this would remain the case—just as it had been in the past.

When she addressed the ongoing NSA scandal, Merkel said the work of the intelligence services was "indispensable" in combating problems of terrorism, but she admitted that there were still differences of opinion between the two countries on how to maintain the appropriate balance between protecting citizens against threats and protecting individual privacy and freedom.[39] She then acknowledged that it would take more than one meeting to resolve their differences, but the fact that the two countries could openly and honestly discuss the matter was important.

The German chancellor went on to emphasize her desire for an agreement on T-TIP. She admitted that despite the apprehensions people had, a free trade agreement was needed:

> *I think particularly in the overall context of further intensifying our trade relations, of global growth, but also in the context of diversification of our energy supply—this is a very important issue. It will be very important for us to bring the negotiations very quickly to a close on T-TIP.*[40]

One of the biggest challenges for the German economy was the country's heavy reliance on Russia for fuel and energy, so one of the main reasons Merkel wanted to see an agreement on T-TIP sooner rather than later was to address this complication. Merkel continued to claim that despite people's reservations about T-TIP, it needed to be implemented, and said "People have doubts. But these doubts, this skepticism can be overcome, and it needs to be overcome."[41]

A free trade agreement between the United States and the EU had been an important agenda item for Merkel since the beginning of Obama's presidency, and her insistence on its passage seemed to have reached a new level at this meeting. Perhaps Merkel saw this as a way to restore her relationship with the United States and Obama.

The German chancellor concluded by thanking "Barack" for his "gracious hospitality" and the opportunity for candid discussions.[42] Although Merkel appeared to be more reserved with the president than in previous encounters, she remained polite and cordial. If their interactions were less warm than before, one thing could be counted on consistently in their relationship: they could be open and honest with one another. When she thanked Obama for the frank discussions, Merkel may have also been expressing her hope that the two leaders could restore the honest and open discussions they had shared before the NSA scandal.

When the two opened the floor to questions from the media, the subjects of Ukraine and the NSA allegations were understandably of primary interest. Obama stressed that the goal of diplomatic and economic sanctions had been to encourage the Russians to choose "the better course" rather than to punish them.[43] He stated that if it appeared that the Russians interfered with the election planned for later that month, the United States and Germany would have no choice but to impose further sanctions. "The goal," he claimed, "is not to punish Russia; the goal is to give them an incentive to choose the better course, and that is to resolve these issues diplomatically. And I think we are united on that front."[44]

The president's remarks alluded to a united front and conveyed a sense that whatever actions were deemed necessary to take against Russia would be taken jointly by the United States and Germany. He continued:

> *But what has been remarkable is the degree to which all countries agree Russia has violated international law, violated territorial integrity and sovereignty of a country in Europe. And I think there's unanimity that there has to be consequences for that.*[45]

Indeed, the president seemed to express relief as well as gratitude that allied nations, under Merkel's guidance, felt the need to work with one another to pressure Russia into doing the right thing:

> *And I thank Chancellor Merkel's leadership on this front. She has been extraordinarily helpful not only in facilitating European unity, but she's also been very important in helping to shape a possible diplomatic resolution and reaching out to the Russians to encourage them to take that door while it's still open.*[46]

Was the president's excessive praise for the German chancellor merely an attempt to get back into her good graces? While there may be some truth to that, Obama sincerely respected Merkel and her policy decisions. Over the years it had become clear that when she spoke of her reasoning for policy decisions and actions, the American president listened thoughtfully and responded with admiration—and perhaps a little bit of awe.

This time, when Merkel weighed in on the possibility of additional sanctions, she reiterated that the United States and Europe had long been united in decisions and that would remain the case.[47] She expressed her utter accord with Obama regarding sanctions, saying that "they are not an end in itself, but combined with the offer that we want diplomatic solutions, [sanctions are] a very necessary second component to show that we're serious—we're serious about our principles."[48]

Also evident during this appearance by Merkel and Obama was the imperative to work together for greater global security. So when a journalist asked Merkel about the NSA issue, Obama insisted on answering too, saying:

> Germany is one of our closest allies and our closest friends, and that's true across the spectrum of issues—security, intelligence, economic, diplomatic. And Angela Merkel is one of my closest friends on the world stage, and somebody whose partnership I deeply value. And so it has pained me to see the degree to which the Snowden disclosures have created strains in the relationship.[49]

He then claimed that as important as it was to maintain personal liberties and privacy, legal structure needed to keep pace with rapidly changing technology as well. Obama listed the steps taken by the US intelligence community to always consider the privacy interests of non-US persons as well as citizens—"something that has not been done before and [that] most other countries in the world do not do."[50] He reiterated that ordinary Germans were not subject to continual surveillance or bulk data gathering. Instead, the focus had been to stop terrorists and criminals. "And in that," he said frankly, "we can only be successful if we're partnering with friends like Germany. We won't succeed if we're doing that on our own."[51]

Obama's words show that he felt the deep impact of the NSA scandal on his relationship with Merkel and the German people. More importantly, his remarks demonstrated that the fight against terror was a widespread problem, and without the trust and assistance of allied nations like Germany, it posed a security threat to everyone:

> *These are complicated issues and we're not perfectly aligned yet, but we share the same values and we share the same concerns. And this is something deeply important to me and I'm absolutely committed that by the time I leave this office, we're going to have a stronger legal footing and international framework for how we are doing business in the intelligence sphere.*[52]

When pressed, Obama claimed the United States did not have a blanket no-spy policy with any of their closest partners. "What we do have," he said, "are a series of partnerships and procedures and processes that are built between the various intelligence agencies."[53]

The president spent a fair amount of time describing the special relationship between the two countries, and his fondness for Merkel. In light of not only the bond between these countries but also the history of the United States as a protector of civil liberties, including privacy—a history the country prided itself on—it would not have been unreasonable for people to argue that it was right to implement a no-spy policy.

When Merkel addressed the question of intelligence, she emphasized the need for dialogue:

> *I think the whole debate has shown that . . . we have a few difficulties yet to overcome. So this is why there's going to be this cyber dialogue between our two countries. . . . [T]here needs to be, and will have to be, more than just business as usual. . . . But it's very good that we have taken these first steps, and what's still dividing us—issues, for example,*

of proportionality and the like—will be addressed. We will work on this,
and it's going to be on the agenda for the next few weeks to come.[54]

Merkel's comments with regard to "a few difficulties" and the need for more than just "business as usual" demonstrated her disappointment over the whole scandal, but because of the history and the strength of the relationship between the two countries, it made no sense to throw it away. Therefore, the leaders needed to reach a balance between personal privacy and the urgent task of protecting countries from terrorist attacks, and Merkel remained optimistic that a successful compromise would be reached.

After the meeting, most media reports emphasized the NSA controversy and how the two had addressed it, but at least one article also commented on the progress of the free trade agreement:

The two sides were closer on the issue of trade.... Europe and the United
States see free trade as a way to create more jobs. A deal could boost the
EU and US economies by more than $100 billion a year each.[55]

Although Merkel had spoken in generalities on overcoming "doubts" about the trade agreement, the article highlighted food safety and environmental standards as some of the controversial issues that still needed to be worked out.[56]

Other articles covered the NSA issue at length, such as one published in the *New York Times* that discussed both the good relationship between Merkel and Obama and the tension. The article emphasized Merkel's clear indications that fences had not been mended despite Obama calling her "one of my closest friends on the world stage." It was too soon to resume the "business as usual" relationship.[57]

Even so, Obama's comments clearly indicated that he wanted not just Merkel but the whole world to understand that he valued their friendship and regretted that the spying allegations had impacted their partnership. Even as the two world leaders came together on the question of Russia and Ukraine, the scope of surveillance remained the biggest point of contention between them. While Germany still hoped for a blanket no-spy agreement, the United States proved unwilling to promise that, and Obama argued that the United States did not have a blanket no-spy policy with any of its closest allies, including the UK, Australia, or Canada.[58] Additionally, German officials wanted the United States to refrain from any unsanctioned espionage in Germany, even from the US embassy in Berlin—but without such stipulations with other allies, US officials feared it would set a dangerous precedent.[59]

In the months to come, tensions in Ukraine would continue to increase. While Obama and Merkel understood the importance of mending ties with each other, once again the two leaders had a difference of opinion on how to address the escalating crisis. The world waited anxiously. What would happen in Ukraine as the United States and the EU resolved their differences?

While Obama still struggled with the fallout from the spying allegations, both the NSA scandal and the conflict in Ukraine had arrived at a particularly crucial moment for Merkel, who had just reached new heights of popularity in Germany, in part because of her leadership on the international stage. Back in September 2013, Merkel had won a historic reelection victory as her conservative CDU party won its best result since reunification in 1990—increasing its share of the vote by 7.7 points to 41.5 percent and placing Merkel on track for a third term as chancellor. As David Crossland argued in his article for *Der Spiegel*:

> *It was the best result for the conservatives since the heady days of 1990, when Germans handed the then-Chancellor Helmut Kohl, Merkel's former mentor, his third term in a wave of gratitude for his role in reunifying the nation. Germans are similarly grateful to Angela Merkel, it seems, for steering them through the euro crisis.[60]*

The German tabloid *Bild* professed that Merkel won so overwhelmingly because of one factor: "Who do people trust to rule calmly, sensibly and with strong nerves?" Indeed, as one political scientist pointed out, "Merkel has represented Germany at a difficult time and on all the red carpets and in her whole demeanor, she has given Germans the feeling that she's stood up for their interests."[61]

Merkel's decisive victory illustrated to the rest of the world that the German people clearly trusted Merkel and her leadership. They were relieved with how she and Obama managed to help the financial markets recover from the 2008 collapse. Her citizens respected how she had addressed the Greek financial crisis in the eurozone and how she effectively dealt with Putin. The foreign and domestic issues that Merkel would face next, however, would challenge her in ways she had not yet been challenged. And on more than one occasion, Obama would come to her rescue and help her to save face not just among her own people but as leader of the European Union.

10

"WHEN FREE PEOPLE STAND UNITED"

FEBRUARY 2015

After ousted former Ukrainian president Viktor Yanukovych fled to Russia, Ukraine's parliament scheduled a new presidential election for May 25, 2014, to select his replacement. President Vladimir Putin opposed it at first, because the Russian government viewed Yanukovych's removal as illegal. Remarkably, Putin had a sudden change of heart, and stated on May 7 that "the election is a step 'in the right direction' but that the vote would decide nothing unless the rights of 'all citizens' were protected."[1] Moreover, he appeared to reconfirm the need for a free and fair election on May 23, promising to respect the outcome and professing his willingness to work with whoever won the presidency.[2]

Despite Putin's promise, and despite the shared convictions of allied nations, President Obama, Chancellor Merkel, and other world leaders remained apprehensive. The United States and the European Union vowed that they would impose further sanctions if Russia disrupted the election; unlike previous sanctions, which were limited to individuals and companies, these would target entire sectors of the Russian economy.[3] On May 25, opposition supporter Petro Poroshenko declared victory in the Ukrainian presidential election.[4] And on June 27, President Poroshenko signed an EU

Association Agreement and warned Russia that Ukraine's determination to join the EU would not be thwarted.[5]

In September—at talks in Minsk, Belarus—Ukraine and pro-Russian separatists agreed to a total cease-fire and buffer zone, which required all sides to remove heavy weaponry from the front lines of the eastern conflict; two weeks later, they signed an initial truce, called the Minsk Protocol. In the meantime, a convoy of Russian trucks entered the border area without the Ukrainian government's approval, reportedly to deliver humanitarian aid to skeptical Ukranians.[6] Then, on November 12, a NATO commander indicated that Russian tanks and other weapons and troops had crossed Ukraine's border—actions that violated the September cease-fire.[7]

After months of fighting between pro-Russian separatists and the Ukrainian government, Donetsk International Airport fell to rebel forces on January 22, 2015.[8] Following days of increased violence, President Poroshenko declared he would ask the International Criminal Court at The Hague to investigate allegations of "crimes against humanity"[9]—and the United States indicated it was considering providing lethal aid to Ukraine.[10]

While the United States favored arming Ukraine, the European leaders opposed such actions because they feared it would only intensify the conflict, and they did not want to see the death toll climb higher than the 5,000 already killed.[11] World leaders had last met at the National Security Conference in Munich, Germany, on February 8. Since Obama had not attended the conference with Merkel and other important European leaders, Senator Bob Corker of Tennessee, Senator John McCain of Arizona, and Vice President Joe Biden represented the United States instead. Disagreement erupted between the United States and Germany when Senator McCain expressed support for providing weapons to Ukraine to assist the government's fight against the separatists, and insisted that the Ukrainian people had the right to defend themselves.[12]

Both Merkel and French president François Hollande firmly opposed the idea. "Look, I'm absolutely convinced there is no military solution to this conflict," Merkel countered. "A lot of weapons are already there and have done nothing to resolve the conflict."[13] Amid these clear differences of opinion on whether the Ukrainians should be armed, however, all believed that Russia needed to be stopped. And the clock was ticking.

Time was also running out on the question of Iranian nuclear power. In 2006, the UN Security Council's six world powers had formed the P5+1—the five permanent council members (China, France, Russia, the UK, and the United States) plus Germany—to diplomatically negotiate Iran's nuclear program. For the past eighteen months, the P5+1 had been negotiating a permanent nuclear deal while it worked under an interim agreement that lifted some of the economic sanctions on Iran in return for Iran converting some of its uranium stockpile to a form that is more difficult to refine to weapons grade. That agreement stipulated that no new sanctions would be implemented while negotiations continued.[14] Yet the US Senate planned to vote in favor of additional sanctions should talks with Iran fail to reach an agreement by March 24.

In January, Obama had threatened to veto any new sanctions bill passed by Congress; he feared new sanctions would interfere with ongoing negotiations.[15] Because Germany was a participant in the negotiations over the Iran nuclear deal, Obama and Merkel would have to address a change in course on the treatment of Iran as well as Ukraine.

So, while the level of discord and havoc Putin created in Ukraine proved to be unsettling, it presented an opportunity for Merkel and Obama to join forces and address the conflict. In mid-February, Merkel and France's president Hollande prepared to travel to Minsk, the capital of Belarus, seeking to broker a second cease-fire agreement between Russia and Ukraine. Although it had been less than a year since Merkel's last trip to Washington, DC, the intensifying international issues created an urgent need for the chancellor to meet with the US president—on February 9, just two days before Merkel Putin, Poroshenko, and Hollande's all-important meeting in Minsk.

In the days that led up to the Minsk meetings, in addition to the escalating crisis in Ukraine, the two leaders needed to address the ongoing nuclear negotiations with Iran, the rising influence of the Islamic State, and ending the conflict in Afghanistan.[16] Since the United States and Germany had a strong difference of opinion on the best solution to the Ukraine conflict, journalists assumed the meeting between Merkel and Obama would be tense. According to Berlin journalist Soraya Sarhaddi Nelson:

> *When Merkel visited President Obama in Washington last May, German relations with the US were at a low point over revelations the NSA had spied on German soil and tapped the Chancellor's cell phone. This time, it's the US that has hard feelings, and the reason is Germany's response to the crisis in Ukraine.*[17]

Much to the dismay of leading congressional members, Obama seemed to follow Merkel's lead rather than their own with respect to military force in Ukraine. According to Texas senator Ted Cruz:

> *It is long past time for us to step forward and provide defensive weapons to the people of Ukraine.... What we are seeing is when America doesn't lead, Europe cannot be expected to step into the breach. What is missing is the president of the United States.*[18]

Between pressure from his own government to send military support to Ukraine, and concern over whether the upcoming peace talks with Russia would lead to a successful cease-fire when the first Minsk agreement had failed, Obama had begun to shift his position on the crisis in favor of military intervention. He told his government to weigh all options. Lawmakers felt the decision was a long time coming, while the Germans and the other EU members remained concerned about any type of military action. The *Guardian* reported that "if there is no deal in sight by the time Merkel and Obama meet, then the two leaders will have to seek tougher alternatives"—and quoted the German ambassador to the United States, Peter Wittig, as saying, "A lot depends on whether these talks open up a new potential for diplomacy."[19]

Both countries understood that alternative penalties for Russia—mainly in terms of economic sanctions—had to be employed, as the current ones appeared to be ineffective. Many European leaders remained reluctant to engage in military activity with Putin, but Merkel, who reminded the others of her Eastern European roots to justify her resistance, proved to be the most vocal of these opponents. According to the *Guardian*, she argued that "Putin cannot be beaten militarily so there is no point in arming Ukraine" and raised "the precedent of the building of the Berlin Wall in 1961 and how it took thirty years to overcome the division of Germany."[20]

Having grown up behind the Iron Curtain, and with Germany still reliant on Russia for most of its natural resources, Merkel understood—above any other world leader—the ramifications of engaging militarily with Russia. Therefore, she would fight to her core to resolve the Ukraine crisis with diplomatic measures.

Notwithstanding the anticipated tension between Obama and Merkel before their February 9 press conference, the two appeared before the media, following their four-hour morning meeting, in relatively good spirits. In his welcoming comments, Obama once again referred to the German chancellor as "my close friend and partner, Chancellor Angela Merkel."[21] Obama congratulated Merkel on two impressive milestones:

> *Well into her third term, Angela is now one of Germany's longest-serving chancellors. Perhaps more importantly, this is my first opportunity to publicly congratulate Angela and Germany on their fourth World Cup title. As we all saw in Rio, Angela is one of her team's biggest fans. Our US team, however, gets better each World Cup, so watch out in 2018.*[22]

Despite the serious topics they had just discussed, the two world leaders could still joke with each other.

The president revealed that the morning's focus had been on global security issues—reaffirming their joint commitment to "supporting a secure, sovereign, and united Afghanistan," and enforcing sanctions to "prevent Iran from obtaining a nuclear weapon"—but remained focused on Russia's aggression in Ukraine and the international fight against ISIL.[23] He acknowledged that Russia and the separatists had violated almost every pledge established in the first Minsk agreement:

> *Instead of withdrawing from eastern Ukraine, Russian forces continue*
> *to operate there, training separatists and helping to coordinate attacks.*
> *Instead of withdrawing its arms, Russia has sent in more tanks and*
> *armored personnel carriers and heavy artillery. With Russian support,*
> *the separatists have seized more territory and shelled civilian areas,*
> *destroyed villages and driven more Ukrainians from their homes.*[24]

Obama stated the obvious here, yet he proposed no solutions. He surmised that Russia's combativeness with Western allies over Ukraine had only strengthened the unity among the United States, Germany, and other allied nations, and he complimented Merkel for the way she had handled the crisis so far.[25] He reiterated that the United States, along with other NATO allies, planned to continue with the current strategy to provide Ukraine the necessary financial support—including full enforcement of sanctions against Russia—until Russia complied with its obligations under the Minsk agreement.[26] But he did not elaborate on suggested plans for Ukraine's defense. Nor did he acknowledge the discord between the United States and Germany on this position.

On the subject of ISIL, Obama made it clear that the United States and Germany remained united in their efforts "to destroy this barbaric organization."[27] He commented on the important role of Germany in helping equip Kurdish forces in Iraq to defend against terrorist fighters, including training local forces, and explained that "under Angela's leadership" Germany "is working on enacting new legislation to stop fighters from traveling to and from Syria and Iraq."[28]

Obama and Merkel both recognized, he said, that young people in Muslim communities in both Germany and the United States were prime targets for recruitment by terrorist organizations like al Qaeda and ISIL. He

acknowledged that protecting those young people from the hateful rhetoric that made them susceptible to recruitment was the responsibility of local communities, and admitted that "we can help these communities, starting with the tone and the example that we set in our own countries."[29] These words set the tone for policies that allied Western nations would be forced to address more aggressively in the years to come, as the Syrian civil war continued to escalate and the flow of refugees began to cause unparalleled anxiety in Europe—especially within Germany.

Then Obama commended Merkel for "speaking out forcefully against xenophobia and prejudice and on behalf of pluralism and diversity," and continued with a very bold and direct statement: "She's made it clear that all religious communities have a place in Germany, just as they do here in the United States"—a show of solidarity with his European counterpart that few others had offered.[30] Obama saw the dilemma European leaders, especially Merkel, faced with the rapid influx of immigrants resulting from the Syrian civil war, and he felt compelled to offer his moral support. In fact, according to Obama's deputy national security advisor for strategic communications, Ben Rhodes:

> *Obama admired her pragmatism, her unflappability, and her stubborn streak. Over the previous year, he had battled his own bureaucracy to increase the number of refugees that America would welcome, telling us again and again, "We can't leave Angela hanging."*[31]

Obama not only supported Merkel's actions but also hoped they would serve as a push to encourage the American public and lawmakers to adopt a policy like that which Merkel had implemented in Germany. His comments further illustrated a bond between the two of them based on shared values.

In his final remarks, the president reminded the audience that 2015 marked the seventieth anniversary of the end of World War II, and the twenty-fifth anniversary of Germany's reunification. His understanding of those historic milestones gave him confidence that the challenges of the twenty-first century could be overcome:

*So in a time when conflicts around the world sometimes seem intrac-
table, when progress sometimes seems beyond grasp, Germany's story
gives us hope. We can end wars. Countries can rebuild. Adversaries can
become allies. Walls can come down. Divisions can be healed. Germany's story and the story of Angela's life remind us that when free people
stand united, our interests and our values will ultimately prevail.*[32]

Merkel began her address when she emphasized her pleasure to be in
Washington again, and updated the press on the issues she and Obama had
discussed; she reiterated her support of the free trade agreement between
the United States and the EU and indicated that she believed a free trade
agreement between the two nations would help boost growth substantially.[33]
The longer Merkel and Obama worked together, the more important the
free trade agreement became—particularly for Merkel, who believed it to
be important for improving the economy of not just the EU but also the
United States.

As Obama had done, Merkel linked Germany's past to the future when
she spoke of Afghanistan and the fight against terrorism:

*After we thought in the nineties maybe that things would turn out
somewhat more easily, somewhat less complicated, now we see ourselves
confronted with a whole wealth of conflicts, and very complex ones. We
worked together in Afghanistan—we talked about this as well. Germany has decided, in its fight against [ISIL], to give help to deliver
training missions, to deliver also weapons . . . if necessary. We work
together on the Iran nuclear program, where we also enter into a crucial
phase of negotiations.*[34]

Merkel's focus, as ever, was on preventing actions that threatened the
peace and integrity Europe had experienced since World War II. As such,
she viewed the lack of stability in Afghanistan and Iran as intolerable—and
likewise, she viewed Russia's actions in Ukraine as unacceptable:

We stand up for the same principles of inviolability of territorial integrity. [As] someone who comes from Europe, I can only say if we give up this principle of territorial integrity of countries, then we will not be able to maintain the peaceful order of Europe that we've been able to achieve. This is not just any old point; it's an essential, a crucial point, and we have to stand by it. And Russia has violated the territorial integrity of Ukraine in two respects: in Crimea, and also in Donetsk and Luhansk.[35]

Merkel then expressed her gratitude for the close cooperation with the United States and the rest of the EU community on both diplomatic initiatives and sanctions, but stated that she still unequivocally opposed more military conflict in Ukraine and encouraged a diplomatic resolution instead. Merkel knew Germany and the United States would continue to work closely as they had in the past, and she had faith that in doing so, they would resolve these conflicts.

She closed her remarks with her usual, "Thank you for your hospitality,"[36] and then the media chimed in. Journalists raised the issue of the differing opinions between the two leaders over military intervention in Ukraine—and a reporter from the *Washington Post* asked,

You've [stressed] that US and Europe need to have cohesion on the issue of sanctions and on dealing with Ukraine, and yet the administration is discussing sending lethal weapons to Ukraine, which is very different from what the chancellor has said over the weekend. So, I was wondering whether this was a good cop-bad cop act, or is this a real reflection of difference of views in the situation on the ground?[37]

Obama emphasized that both he and "Angela" believed the likelihood of "a military solution to this problem has always been low" and that he hoped the issue would be resolved diplomatically.[38] He even admitted that he asked his advisors to look at every possible option, even providing defensive weapons, but he reiterated that no decision had been reached.[39]

Merkel claimed that she and Hollande planned to make one further attempt to resolve the issue diplomatically:

> *We have the Minsk agreement—the Minsk agreement has never been implemented. Quite the contrary is true. The situation has actually worsened on the ground. So now there is a possibility to try and bring about a cease-fire and to also create conditions that are in place where you [don't have] everyday civilians dying, civilian victims that fall prey to this. And I'm absolutely confident that we will do this together. . . . I myself actually would not be able to live with not having made this attempt. I have to be very clear about this.*[40]

Unlike her US counterparts, Merkel remained unwilling to consider military intervention until Germany had given the Russians time to adhere to the policies agreed to in the first Minsk agreement. In other words, from her perspective, intervention before the upcoming second round of talks in Minsk would be premature.

Yet she seemed confident that this difference in perspective would not undermine US relations with Germany and the EU:

> *But you may rest assured that no matter what we decide, the alliance between the United States and Europe will continue to stand, will continue to be solid, even though on certain issues we may not always agree. But this partnership, be it Ukraine and Russia, be it on combating terrorism . . . is a partnership that has stood the test of time. . . . [T]his transatlantic partnership for Germany and for Europe is indispensable. And this will remain so. And I say this also on behalf of my colleagues in the European Union.*[41]

The next journalist wasted no time and asked a bombastic question with regard to whether military intervention "would make matters worse" and "what can the Nobel Laureate Obama do more to defuse this conflict? And, Madam Chancellor, . . . with looking at all of the big issues that you discussed, this breach of confidence due to the NSA affair, of the US–German relations, has that played a role today?"[42] Obama appeared slightly flustered and asked Merkel to respond first, which she "gladly" did.[43] She reiterated that Obama had not decided upon his course of action and that the two of them stood united in their hopes for a diplomatic effort:

> *We keep each other informed. We're in close touch. And nobody wishes more for a success than the two of us who stand here side by side.*[44]

Besides the conflict in Ukraine, the NSA scandal remained a topic of interest for the media. Merkel acknowledged the two leaders' different assessments on individual rights and privacy, but repeated that with ongoing terrorist threats, the two countries needed to work closely together. Then she said, more forcefully:

> *And I, as German chancellor, want to state here clearly that the institutions of the United States of America have provided us and still continue to provide us with a lot of very significant, very important information that also [ensures] our security. And we don't want to do without this.*[45]

This was not the first time Merkel indicated that some of the information the German government had obtained from the NSA's PRISM program was useful and necessary, but it was the first time she responded so emphatically, which showed that while all had not been necessarily forgiven, progress had been made.

Obama then responded, as he had done on numerous occasions, with an acknowledgment of the sensitivity of the issue given the experience of Germany's citizens with government surveillance during the Cold War.[46] He admitted that more work needed to be done, but he emphasized that his 2014 executive order had created greater transparency to help restore confidence in the United States among other worldwide allies—not just with the Germans.[47] Obama clearly regretted the divide in his friendship with Merkel that the Snowden revelations had created, and sent an emotional plea to the German people:

[T]he United States has always been on the forefront of trying to pro-
mote civil liberties. . . . [W]e have been a consistent partner of yours in
the course of the last seventy years, and certainly the last twenty-five
years, in reinforcing the values that we share. And so occasionally I
would like the German people to give us the benefit of the doubt, given
our history, as opposed to assuming the worst—assuming that we have
been consistently your strong partners and that we share a common set
of values.[48]

Obama further reminded the audience that differences of opinion undoubtedly occurred among even the best of allies, and that as long as the two nations trusted one another—and remained united on the core principles of dignity, respect for law, and democracy—the relationship would be able to withstand those differences. "And if we have that fundamental, underlying trust," he said, "there are going to be times where there are disagreements, and both sides may make mistakes, and there are going to be irritants like there are between friends, but the underlying foundation for the relationship remains sound."[49]

When she addressed their more recent disagreement over the Ukraine crisis, Merkel continued in the same vein:

I'm very glad that with the American president, I have always been able
to put all the cards on the table and discuss the pros and cons. In my speech
in Munich, I gave you clearly where I stand [on a military solution]. But
we'll continue to try [for an agreement]. I think that's why we are politi-
cians, that's why we chose this profession. . . . We never have a guarantee
that the policies we adopt will work.[50]

Merkel's remarks offered insight into why she had such a good working relationship with Obama: she knew she could always be completely honest with him and he would listen to her—even if they did not agree, they were able to engage in completely honest discussions. This is clear in how Obama echoed Merkel's sentiments:

The point Angela made, I think, is right—we never have any guarantees
that any particular course of action works. As I've said before, by the
time a decision reaches my desk, by definition, it's a hard problem with
no easy answers.[51]

Throughout his presidency, Obama frequently made the point that if the
problems of the world were not complicated, then someone else would have
solved them already.[52] The issue of Iranians and disarmament was one such
issue, and one reporter asked whether, after Iran had already missed two previous deadlines on disarmament, the March 24 deadline would be the last.[53]

Obama's response seemed to indicate an unwillingness to extend another
deadline to Iran, nor was he in a position to impose further sanctions as Congress had suggested:

I don't see a further extension being useful if they have not agreed to the
basic formulation and the bottom line that the world requires to have
confidence that they're not pursuing a nuclear weapon. . . . The issues are
now, does Iran have the political will and the desire to get a deal done?[54]

Obama used this opportunity to confess that progress on the Iran deal
would have been impossible were it not for the collaboration of the P5+1
partners and added that "there [have] been no cracks in this on the P5+1 side
of the table. And I think that's a testament to the degree to which we are acting reasonably in trying to actually solve a problem."[55] Surprisingly, Merkel
remained silent on this issue, and thus it is not known where she stood on
increasing sanctions or extending the March deadline.

As the press conference drew to a close, a reporter asked Obama about
Israeli prime minister Benjamin Netanyahu's desire to speak before the US
Congress about Iran. The president took the opportunity to tease Merkel
when he said, "As much as I love Angela, if she was two weeks away from
an election she probably would not have received an invitation to the White
House—and I suspect she wouldn't have asked for one."[56] He went out of his
way to bring Merkel into a conversation that had no immediate relevance to

her to indicate a readiness to express his affection toward the German chancellor—another example of the affinity between the two. And as he closed the press conference, Obama once again emphasized the importance of this transatlantic relationship:

> *What I do know is that we will not be able to succeed unless we maintain the strong transatlantic solidarity that's been the hallmark of our national security throughout the last seventy years. And I'm confident that I've got a great partner in Angela in maintaining that.*[57]

This statement set the stage for the international successes that would soon follow in the remaining months of 2015.

After a marathon sixteen-hour session on February 12, 2015—over a year after the events that first sparked the conflict—Putin, Poroshenko, Hollande, and Merkel reached a new cease-fire deal for eastern Ukraine. Under the terms and conditions of the so-called Minsk II agreement, both sides agreed to the following: an immediate and full bilateral cease-fire to take effect on February 15; withdrawal by both sides of all heavy weapons; dialogue on holding local elections; release of all hostages and illegally detained people; an effective monitoring and verification regime for the cease-fire; internationally supervised, unimpeded delivery of humanitarian aid; restoration of full economic and social links with affected areas; restoration of full Ukrainian government control over the state border through the conflict zone; and constitutional reform in Ukraine, including the adoption of a new constitution by the end of 2015.[58]

Despite the work Merkel and Hollande put forth to get both parties to agree, the United States and the EU remained doubtful that the Russians would comply. "The Ukrainian crisis was not caused by the Russian Federation," said Putin in remarks posted on the Kremlin website. "It emerged in response to the attempts of the US and its western allies—who consider themselves 'winners' of the Cold War—to impose their will everywhere." According to the *Guardian*, "The remarks reinforced western suspicions that Putin has never accepted the outcome of the collapse of Soviet and eastern European communism in 1989–1991 and is engaged in an attempt to revise the results of the post-Cold War order in Europe."[59] One could argue that the united front Obama and Merkel displayed here against Russia helped to bring the two leaders closer together again—not exactly the response for which Putin had hoped. One thing Putin had not counted on was that the shared belief in upholding democracy overshadowed personal disagreements between the two nations.

11

"THERE'S NEVER A BAD DAY
FOR A BEER"

JUNE–DECEMBER 2015

To demonstrate to the world that the fences had been mended between the United States and Germany after the NSA spying scandal, an event carefully orchestrated by both the German and US governments occurred on the morning of June 7, 2015, to promote President Obama and Chancellor Merkel's friendship. The two leaders met in the historic Bavarian village of Krün, where they shared a traditional breakfast with local residents before they headed to Schloss Elmau, the castle where Merkel planned to simultaneously host the annual G7 summit meetings. Government officials hoped that Obama's effort to travel to the small German town with Merkel to spend time with local residents would help to put an end to "almost two years of frosty public relations following a string of spying revelations."[1]

The encounter between the two was spirited and cheerful, and it appeared as if much of the animosity between them had been all but forgotten.[2] Moreover, the harmony demonstrated between the two leaders in Bavaria on that June morning cleared the way for two remarkable events later that year—the passage of the Iran nuclear deal in July and the Paris Agreement on climate change in December—that arguably came about much more easily because of the partnership and friendship between Obama and Merkel.

On the morning of June 7, 2015, the sun shone high in the clear blue sky, and with the Bavarian Alps visible across the horizon, the scene looked fresh out of a fairy tale. Obama greeted Merkel with an embrace and kisses on both cheeks, and the "Phantom of the Opera," Merkel's husband, Professor Sauer, made yet another rare appearance and offered a warm handshake. The two leaders greeted the locals and made their way to the podium as a local band—including a traditional alphorn group—played traditional Bavarian music.[3] They signed the visitor guestbook before they addressed the crowd of approximately 2,000 citizens, and the townspeople, dressed in customary Bavarian apparel, with men in *Lederhosen* and women in *Dirndls*, sat at long tables in a public square and sipped beer while they waited for the president and the chancellor to speak.[4]

Merkel addressed the crowd, and for the first time since the NSA scandal two years earlier, the warmth that had been missing from her voice returned as she introduced the president and once again referred to him as "dear Barack."[5] In her brief comments, Merkel acknowledged that the United States and Germany occasionally had differences of opinion but nevertheless remained important friends and partners. It was highly significant that, when she turned the floor over to the president, she said in German, "*Barack, du hast das Wort,*" or "Barack, you have the floor."[6] As she had done when she introduced the US president in Berlin, she addressed him publicly with the informal *du* for the first time since the NSA controversy in 2013.

On this day, the normally reserved, poker-faced Merkel seemed almost like a giddy schoolgirl. When Obama addressed the crowd with the standard Bavarian greeting "*Grüß Gott,*" or, translated, "Greetings from God," the crowd roared in laughter and applause, fully appreciating his attempt to speak the native dialect, with Merkel clapping and laughing the loudest.[7]

Although the mutual respect between the two was unquestionable, this breakfast provided the first public opportunity for Germans to witness first-hand how they interacted not just with one another but with average citizens. For approximately an hour among the townspeople, the two leaders smiled, laughed, and joked.[8] Merkel's mood had not even been as jovial for her Presidential Medal of Freedom ceremony. People had long criticized Merkel and argued that she had not taken the spying allegations seriously enough—that she acted only reluctantly and only under political pressure did she denounce the US government's actions. Nevertheless, the admiration the two leaders displayed for each other, and the affection the German people showed toward the American president, illustrated that both parties had placed the scandal behind them. In this more relaxed setting, Merkel witnessed firsthand how her citizens interacted with Obama and saw that they appeared to have forgiven him; it seemed she felt free to do so as well.

Not to be outdone by the chancellor's mood, Obama made sure his humor and allure were in full force. He expressed regret at forgetting his *Lederhosen*—to the great amusement of the townspeople, led by Merkel—and he suggested he would buy a pair before he returned to the United States.[9] When Obama expressed his disappointment that Merkel had not scheduled the G7 summit in Bavaria during Oktoberfest, the crowd—including Merkel—cheered.[10] "But then again," he said, "there's never a bad day for a beer and a *Weißwurst*."[11]

Given the lighthearted, carefree forum, one might never think twice about the difficult challenges that faced them at the upcoming G7 summit. But Obama did not allow the relaxed atmosphere of the morning to deter him from briefly commenting on more serious matters.[12] He quickly switched gears and gave a short overview of the issues the world leaders planned to discuss over the next two days.

Obama also showed the audience that he understood Germany and its history. He reminded the spectators that 2015 marked seventy years since the end of World War II, and twenty-five years since Germany reunified, boldly proclaiming that the alliance between the United States and Germany was "one of the strongest alliances the world has ever known.... We stand together as inseparable allies—in Europe and around the world."[13] Although Obama spoke those words among everyday citizens in a celebratory environment, the crowd listened intently as they snapped photos and then lined up to shake his hand and have their photos taken with the American leader.

Then Obama and Merkel joined locals for a traditional Bavarian breakfast, which included tall glasses of *Weißbier* (wheat beer), pretzels, and *Weißwurst* (white sausage). However, at the request of both American and German officials, the guests were given nonalcoholic beer, so everyone—including Merkel, Obama, and Professor Sauer—drank the alcohol-free beer.[14] Regardless of the choice of beverages, the purpose of the meeting had been to demonstrate the friendship between the two countries, and based upon the day's activities, it seemed that goal was achieved.

Ever since the president's initial visit to Berlin as a presidential candidate in the summer of 2008, a mutual love and respect had been evident between the president and the German people. From that crowd of many thousands at the Victory Column to the historic address in front of the Brandenburg Gate to the traditional Bavarian breakfast in the village of Krün, the American president's shared affinity with the German people was clear. The interaction between Merkel and Obama during their two-day visit demonstrated that the chancellor also shared her citizens' feelings toward the US president.

After their breakfast, Merkel and Obama held a private meeting during which they discussed the crisis in Ukraine. During their forty-five-minute meeting, neither raised the issue of the NSA surveillance controversy.[15] According to the *New York Times* and White House press secretary Josh Earnest, discussion about how to address Russia encompassed more than half of the session. Both agreed that sanctions against Russia should not be lifted until Moscow fully implemented the Minsk peace deal and respected Ukraine's sovereignty.[16] The article continued:

> There is little doubt that Mr. Obama, who tends to prioritize strategy and shared interests over personality in his relationships with world leaders, needs Ms. Merkel, and that she needs him. [She] has been important in rallying Europe to stay united against Russia's interference in Ukraine, even as the economic sanctions designed to pressure Mr. Putin have placed political strain on her and many of her counterparts.[17]

Following the meeting, former White House deputy national security advisor Julianne Smith indicated that the president "continues to reach out" to Merkel, and pronounced, "I think they still trust each other."[18] Agreeing on the importance of maintaining the Russian sanctions allowed them to work together despite the fact that other European nations—including Germany—had begun to pressure Merkel to lift the sanctions. With respect to the NSA controversy, according to the Associated Press, "Merkel seemed eager to move on. She said in interviews that she didn't bring up the spying controversy with Obama since they've already discussed what needed to be said in previous meetings."[19]

As both a pragmatist and a leader in the true sense of the word, Merkel knew that it was best to put her personal irritants aside for the greater good of not just her country but the entire EU. She understood that the situation in Ukraine required her to work successfully with Obama, and her manner during the breakfast in Krün conveyed a belief that the issue had been resolved. She was willing to move forward.

At the close of the two-day G7 summit, Obama held a solo press conference to update members of the American press corps with regard to the progress world leaders had made on key international issues. Although Merkel did not appear beside Obama for his press conference, he referenced her many times in his remarks, particularly noting his fondness for her and the German people:

> *Let me begin by once again thanking Chancellor Merkel and the people of Bavaria and Germany for their extraordinary hospitality here at the G7. My stay has been extraordinary. I wish I could stay longer. And one of the pleasures of being president is scouting out places that you want to come back to, where you don't have to spend all your time in a conference room. The setting is breathtaking. Our German friends have been absolutely wonderful, and the success of this summit is a tribute to their outstanding work.[20]*

Obama then discussed some of the key international issues that the G7 leaders had addressed during the summit—many of which affected the United States and Germany, and a couple of which would have important policy implications in the coming months. He argued how important a trade deal would be to help stimulate the economy, stating that the G7 leaders "agree that the best way to sustain the global economic recovery is by focusing on jobs and growth."[21] He reminded journalists that the unemployment rate was nearing its lowest level in seven years and that America remained "a major source of strength" in the global economy.[22] At the same time, he continued,

> *We recognize that the global economy, while growing, is still not performing at its full potential. And we agreed on a number of necessary steps.... I updated my partners on our effort with Congress to pass trade promotion authority so we can move ahead with TPP in the Asia Pacific region, and T-TIP here in Europe—agreements with high standards to protect workers, public safety and the environment.*[23]

Aware of the ever-growing world economy, the president acknowledged that the US economy had experienced tremendous growth, but that because of the interconnectivity of world markets and the value of long-established partnerships with allied nations, policies had to be implemented to ensure all nations did well, not just the United States—hence his willingness to endorse trade agreements with Asia and Europe.

Next, Obama addressed the subject of climate change. The G7 leaders understood the importance of reaching a global agreement at the United Nations Climate Change Conference in Paris, scheduled for December 2015. They realized the imminent threat that climate change poses for the planet—not just for one nation or even one continent; moreover, they recognized that the exorbitant cost of reducing emissions should not be the prohibitive factor in whether countries could reduce their carbon emissions. At his press conference, Obama stated that the other G7 leaders had offered their 2020 targets to reduce carbon emissions, and encouraged other high emitters to publicize their plans as well; he promised to abide by their climate financial commitments to help developing countries transition to low-carbon growth.[24] Obama's remarks seemed to demonstrate the world leaders' collective understanding that combating climate change is everyone's responsibility, and no excuses would be accepted.

Additionally, the president said something that one had not historically heard with respect to the United States and climate change—there was an area in which the United States had taken the lead:

> *As we've done in the US, the G7 agreed on the need to integrate climate risks into development assistance and investment programs across the board, and to increase access to risk insurance to help developing countries respond to and recover from climate-related disasters. And building on the Power Africa initiative I launched two years ago, the G7 will work to mobilize more financing for clean-energy projects in Africa.*[25]

In order to understand the significance of the G7 actually following the lead on climate change from the US government, one must remember the initial hesitance of Merkel and the German government about the position of the United States and the Obama administration on the subject. The fact that Obama had brought about a drastic change in the US's attitude toward and policy on climate change illustrated another important milestone in his relationship with the German chancellor.

Another important subject on which Obama reflected Merkel's point of view—one that was surprisingly not addressed often between the two of them or in government generally—is gender equality for women and girls. In his press conference, Obama commended Merkel for

> *ensuring that this summit included a focus on expanding educational and economic opportunities for women and girls. The G7 committed to expanding career training for women in our own countries, and to [increasing] technical and vocational training in developing countries, which will help all of our nations prosper.*[26]

Merkel understood the importance of fighting for more effective policies to help promote gender equality on an international stage. Over the course of her career, Merkel often experienced her male counterparts dismissing her because of her gender. On the other hand, Obama respected her rather than dismissed her—a fact that he stressed when he commended her in this regard. Both Obama and Merkel clearly saw education and vocational training for girls and women as an important global issue, further demonstrating the similarities and the bond between these two world leaders.

The G8 summit had returned to its original format, the G7, following Putin's illegal annexation of Crimea the previous year, with Merkel as the primary actor in that development. During the 2015 summit, therefore, that contentious subject naturally had an important role in discussions among the world leaders. In his post-summit remarks, Obama reminded the audience, "This is now the second year in a row that the G7 has met without Russia" and reiterated that the G7 partners remained "strongly united in support for Ukraine."[27] He promised the people of Ukraine that the partners would continue to assist them with any technical or economic support needed to help Ukraine establish its own government, and added that all seven member nations remained committed to maintaining sanctions in response to Russia's actions.[28]

Ongoing concern among allied nations about the economic impact the sanctions had on their economies made it imperative for Obama to emphasize to the Ukrainian people that world leaders would not abandon them in their time of need. Obama also emphasized that the sanctions had "seriously weakened" the Russian economy and added

> *The ruble and foreign investment are down; inflation is up. The Russian central bank has lost more than $150 billion in reserves. . . . Russia is in deep recession. So Russia's actions in Ukraine are hurting Russia and hurting the Russian people.*[29]

This remark provided concrete proof that the sacrifices of companies and individuals had not been in vain—that together they were working toward crippling the Russian economy enough that Putin would be faced with no choice but to surrender the Ukraine government back to the Ukrainian citizens.

Obama also emphasized that although the G7 leaders would prefer a diplomatic solution to the crisis, they would continue the sanctions as long as Russia refused to abide by the conditions of the Minsk agreement, and they were prepared to impose additional sanctions on Russia if necessary.[30] The president made it abundantly clear that all seven countries had come together as promised and would "stand ready" in solidarity with the Ukrainian people.[31]

The final hot-button issue that Obama spoke of was Iran's nuclear program. "Iran has a historic opportunity to resolve the international community's concerns about its nuclear program," he stated, "and we agreed that Iran needs to seize that opportunity,"[32] exhibiting optimism about the scheduled discussions to finalize the deal in Vienna, Austria, the following month. He reiterated that the seven partners remained united as they headed into the final stages of negotiations. Finally, Obama thanked

> *Angela and the people of Germany for their extraordinary hospitality. I leave here confident that when it comes to the key challenges of our time, America and our closest allies stand shoulder to shoulder.*[33]

Although Merkel had not been present for Obama's remarks, she was ever present in his comments, further evidence that he respected the German people and valued the partnership they provided in the challenging times facing the global community.

According to an article written in the *Jerusalem Post*, Iran had a nuclear program of one kind or another for over fifty years before it caught the international community's attention in 2002, when Western intelligence agencies discovered a uranium enrichment facility at Natanz and a heavy-water plutonium facility at Arak and revealed them to the world.[34] In 2003, diplomacy talks between France, Germany, and the UK proved unsuccessful, and in

2009, officials uncovered another covert facility inside the city of Qom, leading to the UN Security Council passing a total of eight sanctions against Iran the following year.[35] Meanwhile, Washington had already imposed sanctions against Iran for other activities, including "its violations of human rights and its sponsorship of terrorism worldwide."[36] Despite the sanctions the Western countries imposed on Iran, the country failed to adhere to the demands and continued with its nuclear program.

Additional negotiations seemed futile and thus ceased—until 2013, when the efforts of the Obama administration secretly helped reopen diplomatic discussions between Iran and the United States.[37] Obama then opened communication lines with the newly elected Iranian president, Hassan Rouhani— Iran's first contact with the Oval Office in more than three decades—and talks were soon scheduled in Vienna, Austria, a few weeks after the June 2015 G7 conference.[38]

Representatives of the allied nations from across the world met in Vienna, Austria, where they drafted a nuclear arms agreement with Iran known as the Joint Comprehensive Plan of Action (JCPOA), a 159-page document that "amounts to the most significant multilateral agreement reached in several decades."[39] The JCPOA permitted Iran to retain much of its nuclear infrastructure and granted it the right to enrich uranium on its own soil, but required Iran to partially roll back the infrastructure for ten to fifteen years while the International Atomic Energy Agency (the UN's nuclear watchdog) monitored the program with thorough inspections.[40] In exchange for these concessions, the governments of Germany, the United States, the United Kingdom, China, France, and Russia agreed to lift all UN sanctions on Iran—including access to $100 billion in frozen assets.[41] Obama, who vehemently supported the deal, faced significant challenges with the US Congress over the agreement—so to those reluctant to support the deal, he emphasized over and over that sanctions would be imposed immediately if Iran violated any part of the agreement.[42] "If Iran violates the deal," he warned, "the sanctions we imposed that have helped cripple the Iranian economy—the sanctions that helped make this deal possible— would snap back into place promptly."[43]

July 14, 2015, marked a tremendous diplomatic victory for the international community as key allies had worked together to create a deal that had been unreachable for a decade. Obama's perseverance—in addition to the relationships he had formed with other world leaders, including Merkel, helped to make this victory possible. Upon hearing that an agreement had been signed in Vienna, Obama announced:

> *Today, after two years of negotiations, the United States, together with our international partners, has achieved something that decades of animosity has not—a comprehensive, long-term deal with Iran that will prevent it from obtaining a nuclear weapon. This deal demonstrates that American diplomacy can bring about real and meaningful change—change that makes our country, and the world, safer and more secure. This deal is also in line with a tradition of American leadership. . . . Today, because America negotiated from a position of strength and principle, we have stopped the spread of nuclear weapons in this region. Because of this deal, the international community will be able to verify that the Islamic Republic of Iran will not develop a nuclear weapon.*[44]

Obama viewed the signing of the agreement as a tremendous diplomatic victory—not just for the United States but for all the Western allies. His remarks demonstrated that the success of the agreement came about only after a significant amount of work and dedication among all allied nations, illustrating the necessity of allied nations to work together for their own safety and security.

Five months after the members of the P5+1 signed the historic Iran nuclear deal in Vienna, representatives from 195 countries came together to make history yet again—this time in Le Bourget, France, to sign the Paris Agreement on December 11, 2015. Under the provisions of this climate agreement, which legally required essentially every country in the world to participate, countries would be mandated to reconvene every five years, beginning in 2020, with updated plans to further cut their greenhouse gas emissions.[45] Additionally, starting in 2023, countries would be legally obligated to reconvene every five years to publicly report on their progress compared with their plans, and to report their emissions levels and reductions, using a universal accounting system. "So the individual countries' plans are voluntary," the *New York Times* reported, "but the legal requirements that they publicly monitor, verify, and report what they are doing, as well as publicly put forth updated plans, are designed to create a 'name-and-shame' system of global peer pressure, in the hope that countries will not want to be seen as international laggards."[46]

Adoption of the historic agreement, which proved to be very similar to the Copenhagen Accord that had "collapsed in acrimonious failure" five years earlier, legally committed nations to efforts to keep the global temperature rise below 2 degrees Celsius.[47] According to a French foreign minister, the Paris Agreement passed after the disaster of Copenhagen simply because "the stars for this assembly were aligned."[48] In truth, a combination of factors—such as an increased commitment from US and Chinese government leaders, and further scientific research on the significance of climate change—helped increase the probability of a climate agreement in Paris.

In the years that followed the collapse of the Copenhagen Accord, scientific studies confirmed that the earliest impacts of climate change had already started—contradicting the initial speculations that the impact would be for future generations.[49] Flooding, droughts, and water shortages around the world had been linked to global warming—with the United States and China as the world's two largest emitters of greenhouse gas. This led scientists to a change of opinion on the severity of global warming. Instead of seeing it as a problem for future generations, more scientists argued that it was an urgent, imminent problem that needed to be addressed immediately—a sense of urgency unrealized in Copenhagen.[50]

In November 2014 in Beijing, Obama and President Xi Jinping of China had jointly announced that they would respectively explore options to cut domestic greenhouse gas emissions. "That breakthrough announcement," according to the *New York Times*, "was seen as paving the way to the Paris deal."[51] When the Paris deal was finally announced, Obama professed in a televised address:

> *This agreement sends a powerful signal that the world is fully committed to a low-carbon future. We've shown that the world has both the will and the ability to take on this challenge.*[52]

Obama viewed the task of addressing climate change as a vital component of his legacy, and although the subject had been one of the initial strains between Merkel and Obama, the two might easily have proclaimed December 11—like July 14—another perfect day for a beer. Where once Merkel had thought Obama had not done enough to combat climate change, now pundits suggested his actions may have been a turning point that helped to ensure the passage of the Paris Agreement.

It is possible that climate change may not have initially been one of Obama's most important policy items when he campaigned for and ultimately became president. Nevertheless, the fact that the topic came up during Obama and Merkel's first meeting together in Baden-Baden and continued to resurface with every subsequent meeting seemed to indicate to Obama he needed to take the subject as seriously as his colleagues. Fairly rapidly in his administration, curbing CO_2 emissions became a cornerstone of Obama's domestic policies. One can speculate whether the rise in importance of this ever-growing crisis on Obama's radar came as a result of his willingness to learn more about the dangers of climate change, the pressure Merkel placed on him to take the crisis more seriously, or, more than likely, a combination of the two. Whatever the truth was, from Merkel's first trip to Washington she realized the sudden and drastic shift or "sea change" in global environmental policies came from Obama's lead on the issue. While it is likely Obama would have gradually understood the importance and need for the United States to reverse its trend on environmental policies, the fact that the issue was so important to Merkel—a trained scientist whom he respected and admired—no doubt helped move the needle on the issue. And as a result, the passage of the Paris climate agreement became so important to Obama that many feel his support helped to put the agreement over the finish line.

The strong relationship between Merkel and Obama assisted them both in supporting several major successes for the international community in 2015. However, 2015 also proved to have some extremely challenging times for the German chancellor. Decisions Merkel made that year created tension among not just her country members but also her European colleagues. In the year that followed, she would turn to her American friend and partner for moral and political support, and to reaffirm the political decisions she had made.

12

"ON THE RIGHT SIDE OF HISTORY"

APRIL 2016

Leaders are tested only when people don't want to follow. For asking more of her country than most politicians would dare, for standing firm against tyranny as well as expedience and for providing steadfast moral leadership in a world where it is in short supply, Angela Merkel is Time's *Person of the Year.*[1]

"Every saga has its galvanizing moment," wrote Karl Vick and Simon Shuster in their article on Chancellor Merkel for *Time* magazine's annual Person of the Year award—and the publication of a photograph on September 2 of the body of three-year-old Alan Kurdi washed up on a Turkish beach proved to be the tipping point for the crisis in Syria.[2] Since war had begun in 2012, more than 250,000 people had been killed, but suddenly, with this heartrending photograph, the Syrian refugee crisis became a higher priority on the international scene. And just days later, when Hungary's prime minister refused to allow refugees to board trains toward Austria and Germany, Merkel took notice.

The standoff, which occurred in a Budapest train station, left hundreds stranded. Since that train station had been one of the few places the Soviet government had allowed East German residents to travel, Merkel knew it well. And as one article reported, those who know Merkel say her decision to grant asylum to those Syrian refugees "followed logically from the sight of Hungarian border guards holding back refugees at gunpoint in order to build a fence topped with razor wire."[3] Said Matthias Wissmann, who had been a member of Chancellor Helmut Kohl's cabinet along with Merkel:

> She does not want to see people surrounded by walls. . . . If you ask me what is her main principle belief, it's around this issue: Let us be free. From the station of a person, up to the free-trade pact of a nation.[4]

Much to the surprise, and even the dismay, of many of her colleagues, Merkel cast aside her typical hardnosed policies for a softer, more humane position with respect to the refugee crisis. In late summer 2015, Germany opened its doors to an unprecedented one million Syrian refugees—a decision that ultimately resulted in a decline in Merkel's poll numbers by more than 20 percentage points.[5] *Time* classified Merkel's policy as "an audacious act that, in a single motion, threatened both to redeem Europe and endanger it, testing the resilience of an alliance formed to avoid repeating the kind of violence tearing asunder the Middle East by working together."[6]

Nevertheless, Merkel reiterated her position on the migrant situation when she stated again and again, *"Wir schaffen das"* or "We can do this."[7] Her approach brought widespread admiration and recognition from certain sources, solidifying her role as the de facto leader of Europe. Yet despite positioning her as a true world leader, the refugee crisis certainly did not help Merkel in the eyes of her conservative colleagues any more than the ongoing crisis in Ukraine, which continued to plague the European Union throughout 2015. Merkel faced tremendous pressure, both from CEOs in her own country and from other world leaders, to lift the sanctions against Russia as they created an undue burden on EU businesses as well as Russian ones. In need of reinforcement, Merkel called upon her reliable friend and partner President Obama to provide her with much-needed moral support.

Following World War II, the German city of Hannover started an annual trade fair, and in 2016, Merkel asked Obama to cosponsor the event with her. Although Obama had initially been ambivalent, after he realized the importance his attendance had for Merkel, he instructed his team to build a presidential trip around it.[8] In many ways, the US president's two-day visit in Hannover captured the intimacy of his and Merkel's bond more than any other time in their eight-year working relationship.

After Air Force One landed in Hannover, Obama grinned widely as he greeted the chancellor. He then embraced her and kissed her on the cheek, and she returned with a quick hug. The two began Obama's visit with their usual format—a bilateral meeting followed by a press conference—and would continue with an additional feature: speeches at the trade show's opening ceremony.

When she addressed the press corps, Merkel welcomed Obama to Germany for his fifth visit as president, and she expressed "delight" not only to speak with him but also to share with him cosponsorship of the Hannover Messe.[9] She acknowledged that times were "turbulent," but because she and Obama had such "excellent" bilateral relations, they did not need to spend too much time discussing their meeting earlier that day.[10] The chancellor then conveyed to the audience her appreciation for the president in an informal way and said, "But let me tell you, Barack, that I very much value our candid, open talks that are always based on mutual trust."[11] Referring to the president as "Barack" had by that time become common practice and a sign of her closeness with him.

Merkel listed off the trouble areas they had just discussed, which included the ongoing crises in Syria, Ukraine, and Libya. She admitted that she was grateful for the support the United States provided toward the NATO mission in the Aegean Sea to support the refugee and migrant crisis, reiterating the united front she and Obama wished to put forth:

> *And this in many ways is also a joint European-American effort,*
> *a transatlantic mission, and we were at one in saying that all of the*

security issues on the very doorstep of Europe actually can only be solved,
can only be tackled by joint transatlantic efforts. And only in this way
can our common security be ensured.[12]

Merkel's words emphasized the partnership between the EU and the
United States and set the stage for Obama to voice his agreement and support later in the press conference. Her statement reflected a lesson familiar
to them both: that even though the crises in Ukraine and the Middle East
occurred in Europe's backyard, they could not be solved without the assistance of the United States.

Merkel continued:

But this also means—and here we were also in agreement—that a
European agreement is necessary, a German agreement is necessary in
many of these issues. And I think Germany over the past few months has
demonstrated that we are willing to make this additional effort to go
the extra mile, be it in Iraq fighting terrorism [or] in the Syrian issue.[13]

Although Merkel did not state it outright, her next remarks surely were
intended to insist to the world that Germany still planned to uphold its
responsibility under Article 5 of the NATO Treaty, which stated that an
attack on one was an attack on all. Merkel proclaimed:

We are ready and willing to be militarily engaged. We're grateful to the
United States of America for the very great responsibility that you are
willing to continue to shoulder. And I think the message to the Taliban
needs to be the international community will not leave Afghanistan in
this current predicament.[14]

Merkel, in effect, promised that the United States could count on Germany's support on the mission in Afghanistan until it was complete.

She promised the same solidarity with Obama and the United States with
respect to working toward a solution to the ongoing crisis in Ukraine:

We stand by the Minsk agreement. We attach the greatest possible
importance to the Minsk agreement being implemented as quickly
as possible. . . . Unfortunately we still don't have a stable cease-fire.
We need to bring the political process forward. And the next few steps
we've also discussed very thoroughly.[15]

This mutual commitment to the Minsk agreement was significant, but aside from her comment about "bring[ing] the political process forward," Merkel did not remark on upholding the Russian sanctions. Many of her counterparts supported loosening the sanctions against Russia, but Merkel, along with Obama, believed that the sanctions must remain until Putin agreed to abide by the conditions of the Minsk agreement.

On the matter of the free trade agreement between the United States and the EU, Merkel emphasized the importance of signing the Transatlantic Trade and Investment Partnership sooner rather than later. She argued that its passage was vital to help both the German and the European economies grow:

I think we all ought to have an interest in speeding matters up. And
I hope and trust that the American president will continue to support
these negotiations. We should do our bit in order to make this a success.[16]

Merkel's emphasis on the importance of quickly forming a trade agreement demonstrated that she understood that the two nations had business to address, and despite the prior uncertainty of Obama and Merkel's relationship, past personal conflicts could not force them to lose sight of the professional issues that faced them.

Obama's opening remarks at the press conference were exceedingly generous toward Merkel, and he spent a large portion of his time reflecting on his partnership with the German chancellor. He thanked Merkel for her welcome and commented on his gratitude as the first US president, "at Angela's invitation," to visit Hannover and cosponsor the Hannover Messe.[17] Obama's presidency was in its final months, and with the 2016 elections just six months away, his trip to Hannover would be the final "first" the two would share during his tenure. Perhaps that is why he then shifted gears and complimented Merkel directly:

> *It is always a great pleasure to be back with my friend and partner,*
> *Angela. I have valued Chancellor Merkel's thinking and perspective on*
> *a whole range of global issues throughout my presidency. You have been*
> *a trusted partner throughout my entire presidency—longer than any*
> *world leader—and I value your judgment. I thank you for your com-*
> *mitment to our alliance and the values and human rights for which we*
> *stand. And I'm grateful for our personal friendship.*[18]

Unlike their 2009 meeting in Baden-Baden, when Obama had first used the term "friend" to refer to the then-apprehensive Merkel, this statement illustrated that their relationship had evolved from a polite and obligatory one to a true and enduring friendship and alliance.

On the issue of T-TIP, Obama reminded the press that Germany and the United States were "among each other's largest trading partners" and professed that moving forward with the trade agreement would help foster the relationship between the two nations to create prosperity and jobs.[19] He also reminded the press that since their previous meeting, both the United States and Germany had signed the Paris climate agreement, and that both he and Merkel believed it too should be implemented quickly.

Obama then acknowledged that Germany had been a vital member of the coalition to destroy ISIL, and summarized all the ways in which Germany had aided in the fight, from German aircraft supporting the air campaign to German personnel training local Iraqi forces to Germany providing assistance to stabilize and rebuild Iraq in areas liberated from ISIL.[20] The president referred to Germany as "a strong partner in international efforts to provide humanitarian relief to the people of Syria and Iraq" and reiterated that with the increased terror attacks—including in Paris, California, and Brussels—"strong security cooperation" between the two nations was important:[21]

[W]e're committed to using all the tools at our disposal to prevent ter-
rorists from traveling and plotting attacks. And that includes improved
information-sharing between our countries and within Europe. And, as
always, we'll do so while upholding our values and civil liberties, includ-
ing the privacy of citizens here and in the United States.[22]

Obama knew the importance of the relationship between the United States and Germany. With that relationship nearly destroyed by the government's NSA spying, Obama was once again prepared to take the necessary steps to restore it. So, he then did exactly what Merkel had called him to Germany to do—he publicly supported her controversial position on the refugee crisis. Obama offered these opening remarks for the case he would make in his speech before members of the EU the following day:

I want to once again commend Angela for her courageous leadership as
Germany and Europe respond to migrants who are desperately fleeing
the Syrian conflict and conflicts elsewhere in the region. Perhaps because
she once lived behind a wall herself, Angela understands the aspirations
of those who've been denied their freedom and who seek a better life. And
I know the politics around this issue can be difficult in all of our coun-
tries. We did discuss the EU's recent agreement with Turkey, and Angela
and I agree that our nations can respond to this challenge in a way that
is both humane and ensures our security.[23]

These remarks adequately set the tone for the further remarks he would make during this historic visit.

Next, the president admitted that the crisis in Ukraine remained an ongoing problem, but he acknowledged that because of the hard and relentless work of Merkel and French president Hollande, Ukraine had a new government.[24] In regard to the Russian sanctions, Obama again supported Merkel and agreed that "all sides need to uphold commitments made, and . . . sanctions on Russia can and should only be lifted once Russia fully complies with its commitments under the Minsk agreement."[25] As Merkel had implied in her remarks, she remained more united on this point with Obama than with her European counterparts. Because the United States does not share a border with Russia and therefore is not as reliant on the Russians for natural resources and trading goods, economic sanctions did not have as negative an impact on the United States as they did on European countries. The lengths Merkel and Obama went to in order to convince other European nations to abide by the sanctions further showed the humanitarian commonality between them.

Finally, Obama thanked Merkel for her friendship:

> *Tomorrow, Chancellor Merkel will host our meeting with Prime Minister Cameron, President Hollande, Prime Minister [Matteo] Renzi [of Italy], as we discuss the full range of challenges that we face together. And it will be another reminder of how grateful I am for Angela's partnership, and how much the United States values our enduring transatlantic alliance, including with Germany.*[26]

When the two began to answer questions from the media, a reporter asked Obama about the anti-T-TIP protests that had broken out in Germany since the president's arrival. The president pointed to "the benefits [of free trade] to the United States or to Germany," explaining that "typically, jobs that are produced from exports have higher wages and better benefits."[27] He acknowledged that

> *people visibly see a plant moving and jobs lost and the narrative develops that this is weakening, rather than strengthening, the position of ordinary people and ordinary workers, and it's forcing them to compete with low-wage labor. And that, I think, is what drives a lot of suspicion, understandably, of these trade deals. . . . But if you look at the benefits to the United States or to Germany of free trade around the world, it is indisputable that it has made our economies stronger.*[28]

Obama thought the ratification of the T-TIP in 2016 was unlikely but that having an agreement before the German Bundestag and the US Congress seemed feasible by the year's end, by which point "we will have the negotiations completed, and people will be able to see why this would be good for our two countries."[29]

Since Obama's visit to Germany came at the height of the US political primary process, and because Republican presidential candidate Donald Trump had been campaigning fiercely against the T-TIP, Obama had to address the political cycle when he spoke to the press:

> *Now, with respect to the politics of it, recent surveys in the United States [showed that] the majority of people still favor trade. They still recognize, on balance, that it's a good idea. During presidential elections, it's always tough. When we're in the heat of campaigns, people naturally are going to worry more about what's lost than what's gained with respect to trade agreements.*[30]

Since Obama's trip came just months before the 2016 presidential election, everyone assumed it would be his last trip to Germany as president. As such, it seemed to serve as a "reflective" moment for him with regard to his relationship with the chancellor as much as it was a morale booster for Merkel.[31] One article reported that the chancellor's request for Obama's presence pointedly demonstrated "how the often-fraught relationship between Washington and Berlin has evolved into one of the world's most important strategic partnerships," and asserted that in many ways, "Obama's close ties with Merkel reflect one of the most dramatic shifts in US engagement with Europe during the post-World War II era."[32]

The media finally understood the closeness of the bond that had developed between the two and appreciated the full extent of their relationship:

> *From the global financial turmoil and the Eurozone crisis to Russia's intervention in Ukraine and now the flood of Syrian refugees into*

*Europe, Obama has turned more often to Germany than to other Euro-
pean countries, such as the UK.*[33]

In fact, prior to Obama's final European visit to Greece and Germany,
he had snubbed the UK when he named Merkel as his "closest international
partner of the past eight years."[34] Additionally, he had neglected to mention
his upcoming meeting with leaders of the UK and France and only spoke of
his meeting with the German chancellor.

In contrast, the more subdued version of Merkel emerged when a journalist questioned her about her relationship with the US president and asked
her to take stock of her best and worst experiences working with Obama. Her
short, curt reply illustrated her discomfort. "I have the impression that we're
actually quite busy with the conflicts that we need to solve in the world as of
today," she said. "And we have new tasks all the time on our agenda, so I am
not in a position to draw stock now."

Merkel did not want her attention distracted by "frivolous" matters, though
she did speak openly about their working relationship:[35]

> *What you see is a testimony to our close partnership and cooperation and
> friendship based on mutual trust. And I'm very grateful for this because
> it helps us to solve international issues. Germany—as I look at the term
> of office of President Barack Obama—in many instances has become
> a more active partner, I think one can safely say, because we are also
> threatened, our own security is threatened, and we realize that we can-
> not ensure this on our own. We have to do this in alliance.*[36]

Although Merkel willingly elaborated on the strength of the relationship between the United States and Germany, and how that had expanded
during Obama's tenure, her initial "short, remarkably unsentimental answer"
explained to one *Washington Post* reporter

> *why she has become Obama's closest overseas ally and the president's
> political and ideological soul mate on critical issues such as Syria,*

terrorism and containing Russian aggression in Ukraine. More than
most American presidents, Obama disdains what he regards as needy,
showboating allies. Merkel is most definitely neither.[37]

Although there is probably a fair amount of truth to that statement, their chemistry was likely based on more than just that. Merkel, like most Germans, tends to have little use for gestures of superficiality; perhaps Merkel viewed the request to "take stock" as trivial.

When Obama responded to the same reporter's question about the crisis in Syria, however, he tied his answer back to his relationship with Merkel:

The concept of ultimately bringing some safety and security within
[Syria] is entirely consistent with what we're trying to do in our
negotiations. Now, with respect to the US–German relationship
and my relationship with Chancellor Merkel—I've said this before,
I will repeat—this is as important a relationship as I've had during
the course of my presidency. Merkel has been consistent. She has been
steady. She is trustworthy. She has a really good sense of humor that
she doesn't show all the time at press conferences. She's a little more—
she's much more serious in front of all of you—which probably serves
her well. That's why she's been such a long-lasting leader, because she
watches what she says.[38]

As Obama spoke those words, Merkel smiled sheepishly while the combined noise from the laughter of the media and the sounds of clicking cameras became deafening.[39]

Since he thought this would be his final press conference with Merkel, Obama reminisced about many of the challenges the two had handled. He mentioned the economic crisis both leaders faced when he first took office, and how the two of them managed to conquer it—together:

But if you think about the first time I came here, we were in the midst
of a potential collapse of the global economy. And I believe that it was in

*large part because of our joint leadership, because of Europe and the US
and other partners around the world coming together and having a clear
vision, that we were able to stabilize the global financial system. And
our two countries now have been able to grow steadily and reduce unemployment and recovered much better than a number of other countries.*[40]

Obama interestingly pointed out how they addressed the financial crisis
together, but while he did not romanticize their working relationship during
the crisis, he did not mention the tension and disagreements that erupted over
the negotiations either.

Indeed, a certain bittersweetness flavored his words as he reflected on these
various issues he and Merkel had tackled together. He argued that the Paris
Agreement would not have happened without a "strong US–German cooperation, and making sure that we are arresting the pace of climate change is
as important as any issue that we're going to face in the decades to come."[41]
Additionally, Obama maintained that getting a nuclear deal signed with Iran
"occurred because of the partnership of the P5+1 and the leadership that Angela
and others have shown."[42] He also reasoned that the peace process in Ukraine
worked in part "because the United States stands shoulder-to-shoulder with
Angela and President Hollande to draw a very firm line about the basic principles of territorial integrity and sovereignty."[43]

Following Obama's remarks, a *Wall Street Journal* reporter questioned
Merkel:

*You both have spoken about the strong working relationship that the
two of you have. As you look ahead to 2017 and the end of Obama's
term, how do you view the possibility of working with a new US president who has called your refugee policy "insane" and has raised the
specter of dissolving NATO?*[44]

The room erupted in laughter, and Obama flashed his wide smile and
laughed along as Merkel shifted uncomfortably—perhaps to buy some time
to construct a diplomatic answer. If the question amused or annoyed Merkel,

her body language did not indicate so, as she changed from her "poker face" with a nod and nervous smile—a look she often reserves for when she needs to answer a question she would prefer not to have to address. More telling, however, is the fact that promptly after she finished her response, she looked over at the president, who, with a nod and smile, precisely mimicked her body language as if to say to her, "Well done." While Merkel's physical display to the reporter is ambiguous, her body language combined with her curt response could leave one to surmise that she refused to take the dangerous bait the journalist had hoped she would. Instead, she stated:

> Let me make two remarks. First I concentrate on the task ahead for 2016. I'm quite busy with that—thank you very much. And I'm looking with great interest at the American election campaign.[45]

For the second time during their press conference, the clicking sounds of the cameras were deafening.

When asked about his imminent departure from office, Obama yet again praised the German chancellor, whose political role has no term limits like those set by the US Constitution:

> I love this job. . . . But I have come to appreciate, at least in the United States, the wisdom of our founders. I'm glad Angela is sticking around, because I think the world benefits from her steady presence. And she is to be admired for her remarkable endurance. And as a private citizen, I will continue to admire her and appreciate the work she's doing.[46]

If Obama's promise to continue following Merkel's career and achievements did not speak highly enough to the level of his admiration for her, he then ended the press conference by offering his unconditional support to Merkel, particularly when he called out her stance on the Syrian refugee crisis:

> By the way, what's happening with respect to her position on refugees here in Europe—she is on the right side of history on this. And for her to

take on some very tough politics in order to express not just a humanitar-
ian concern but also a practical concern—that in this globalized world,
it is very difficult for us to simply build walls—she is giving a voice, I
think, to the kinds of principles that bring people together rather than
divide them. And I'm very proud of her for that. And I'm proud of the
German people for that.[47]

As stated previously, German author Hans W. Gatzke claimed that while it is considered uncharacteristic for Germans to brag or assume credit for one's achievements, it is not the case for Americans. While Merkel had failed to mention her humanitarian efforts regarding the refugee crisis, Obama made sure to tell the world—and most important, the German people—that they should be proud of the chancellor. As he had said earlier in the press conference:

There's not an issue in which we've worked together where I have not
been hugely appreciative of Angela's steady leadership and trustworthi-
ness. . . . I have a strong partner in Angela Merkel.[48]

Following their meeting and their appearance before the press, Obama and Merkel attended the opening ceremony for the technology trade show at the Hannover Congress Centrum. Merkel opened the festivities with a few words, where she welcomed "*lieber* Barack" and expressed her gratitude for the United States and its agreement to cosponsor the event.[49] In her speech, Merkel underscored the importance of a transatlantic partnership for indus-trial production and said, "We in the EU want to lead the way, together with the USA."[50] At one point during her speech, she looked up from her notes and looked into the audience, directly at Obama, with a mischievous smile as she declared, "We love competition. But we also like to win."[51]

Obama flashed his famous smile back toward her. The brief exchange between the two of them was yet another example of the friendly, informally competitive relationship the two had developed over the years.

Obama spoke after Merkel and thanked his "great partner and friend, Chancellor Merkel" for the invitation and the honor of being the first American president to attend the technology fair:[52]

> I'm pleased that this year the United States is the official partner country for the very first time. And it is an honor to be the first United States president ever to attend the Hannover Messe.[53]

Obama used the ceremony as an opening to mention the economic growth that had occurred in the United States since he took office in 2009—over fourteen million private-sector jobs, including hundreds of thousands of manufacturing jobs—before he discussed some of the displays participants would see at the event.[54] When he talked about the 3D-printed electric car, he joked to laughter and applause about taking a ride with Merkel, saying, "Angela, maybe you and I, we can go driving. I'll have to ask Secret Service."[55]

Then, in the competitive nature that had developed between them, Obama acknowledged that "German investment in the United States now supports more than 600,000 American jobs" and that for the first time in recent memory, the United States was "the top market for exports of German goods." He urged members of the audience to consider American locations "as you look around the globe and try to decide where to invest," before he tossed a lighthearted joke in Merkel's direction:[56]

> I would imagine the chancellor makes a pretty strong case for investing in Germany, and there are a lot of good reasons for that. But as president of the United States, I've got a pretty strong argument as well. So, Angela, with your understanding, I'm going to give everybody here the best pitch I can.[57]

The following morning, the two leaders made brief remarks once more before they visited the various exhibits of the German and American companies. Obama, still in the jovial, competitive mode he had been in the previous night, stated:

> *Last night, I also talked about why companies around the world that are looking for where to set up shop should select America. . . . Of course, Angela may have different ideas when we go to the German pavilion. But this friendly competition is healthy. It is what has made our two countries some of the most competitive in the world, our workers the best in the world, our products the best in the world. So again, I want to thank Angela and everyone at Hannover Messe. I expect as a result of this great event, we'll see more partnerships, more trade, and more good jobs for our people on both sides of the Atlantic.*[58]

While Merkel's remarks were more welcoming than competitive, she was clearly in good spirits as she addressed Obama in her cordial terms:

> *Mr. President, dear Barack, I am delighted that we are able to welcome so many guests from the United States here today. You have more than 400 exhibitors, more than 400 companies that are presenting their goods. . . . I think I can safely speak on behalf of the German business community as well when I welcome you most cordially—you, the representatives of your companies here—as friends. We know you are our friends, you are partners.*[59]

Then in a rare move, she claimed in English, "And now I learn the proof of the pudding is the eating. Let's start."[60] Although Merkel did not quite pull off the idiomatic phrase "the proof is in the pudding," the audience understood her point.

The two leaders experienced several exhibitions while they strolled through the trade fair and interacted with one another on a personal level—a demonstration that was rarely on view for the public. One of the companies that presented at the fair was IFM Electronic. Representatives demonstrated their latest three-dimensional glasses, which used cameras to detect items and then displayed them as 3D images within the glasses. The interaction between Obama and Merkel was quite entertaining, as the president tried the glasses and saw their impact when he shook hands with the demonstrator; he passed the glasses to Merkel for her to try. As she experimented with the full effect of the glasses, Obama stepped in to help, grasped her hand, and shook it in a friendly, joking manner—to chuckles from the onlookers.[61]

Obama and Merkel also stopped at the booth for German software company Siemens, where representatives educated the pair about project and product development software that can improve the design and production process through simulation and automation. The Siemens CEO proudly presented a golf club that had been manufactured in the United States, which they had named "Yes We Can" after Obama's 2008 campaign slogan. As Obama was presented with the golf club, Merkel beamed as Obama joked that he must "teach Angela how to play" golf, to which Merkel shrugged her shoulders as if to say, "We'll see about that."[62]

The two leaders also visited the German company Phoenix Contact, where representatives eagerly explained how the electrical connectors made by their company are used for quickly charging electric vehicles. The company representatives made many references to the 1980s American movie *Back to the Future* and its star character, Marty McFly. When the German chancellor, who obviously had no idea what the reference meant, greeted these comments with a blank stare, Obama stepped in, told her it was a great movie, and promised he would send her the DVD[63]—more evidence of the jovial attitude that had become commonplace between them.

Following their visit to various booths, Obama gave a speech that is now known as an address to "the people of Europe."[64] While the president's remarks at the joint press conference the previous day had demonstrated his support for Merkel and her decision to admit one million refugees into

Germany, those comments proved to be only his opening arguments for the full case he made before the audience in this remarkable April 25 speech.

In his usual fashion, he thanked, on behalf of the American people,

> *Angela for being a champion of our alliance. And on behalf of all of us I want to thank you for your commitment to freedom, equality, and human rights, which is a reflection of your own inspiring life. . . . And over the last seven years, I have relied on your friendship and counsel and your firm moral compass. So we very much appreciate your chancellor, Angela Merkel.*[65]

Obama also professed his personal fondness for the German people, who now held "a special place" in his heart, before he confessed yet again that his

> *only regret is that I have never been to Germany for Oktoberfest. So I will have to come back. And I suspect it's more fun when you're not president. So my timing will be good.*[66]

The president's remarks emphasized the mutual love and respect between him and the German people and spoke to his knowledge of and interest in experiencing an important part of German culture, a gesture that the German people appreciated.

Yet he wanted to discuss not just the European culture of the past but what Europe's future would look like:

> *And now, as Europe confronts questions of immigration and religion and assimilation, I want you to remember that our countries are stronger, they are more secure and more successful, when we welcome and integrate people of all backgrounds and faiths, and make them feel as one. And that includes our fellow citizens who are Muslim.*[67]

With this in mind, and as the end of his eight years in office grew near, the president saw a need to make the following appeal:

> *A strong, united Europe is a necessity for the rest of the world because an integrated Europe remains vital to our international order. Europe helps to uphold the norms and rules that can maintain peace and promote prosperity around the world.*[68]

Obama acknowledged the havoc such a rapid influx of new immigrants could create for the status quo, when he said that "the sudden arrival of so many people from beyond our borders, especially when their cultures are very different—that can be daunting. . . . And I know the politics of immigration and refugees is hard."[69]

Obama continued to passionately plead the case for countries to open their doors to more Syrian refugees within their borders, even though up to the point of this speech the United States had failed to admit even 10,000 such individuals—and he did not state any reason for this failure to offer asylum to a greater number of migrants.[70]

> *And just as a handful of neighborhoods shouldn't bear all the burden of refugee resettlement, neither should any one nation. All of us have to step up; all of us have to share this responsibility. This includes the United States.*[71]

Nevertheless, Obama once again declared his respect and overwhelming support for Merkel's actions:

> *Chancellor Merkel and others have eloquently reminded us that we cannot turn our backs on our fellow human beings who are here now, and need our help now. We have to uphold our values, not just when it's easy, but when it's hard. In Germany, more than anywhere else, we learned that what the world needs is not more walls. We cannot define ourselves by the barriers we build to keep people out or to keep people in. At every crossroads in our history, we've moved forward when we acted on those timeless ideals that [tell] us to be open to one another, and to respect the dignity of every human being.*[72]

The president concluded by enumerating the many nations and cultures of Europe that had struggled to achieve their freedom in the past:

> *That's who you are. United, together. You are Europe—united in diversity, guided by the ideals that have lit the world, and stronger when you stand as one. As you go forward, you can be confident that your greatest ally and friend, the United States of America, stands with you shoulder-to-shoulder, now and forever. Because a united Europe—once the dream of a few—remains the hope of the many and a necessity for us all.*[73]

Merkel's humanitarian immigration policies—an approach she had decided to take regardless of the potential political and personal fallout—brought the refugee issue to the fore going into Germany's next election cycle. According to a 2017 PBS interview, Merkel oversaw the largest European economy, with record low unemployment and a five-year budget surplus.[74] Nevertheless, for the first time in her chancellorship, she faced a serious challenge from the far-right populist party Alternative for Germany (*Alternative für Deutschland*, or AfD), which had emerged in 2013 with a primarily anti-immigrant platform.[75] In fact, one of the party's cofounders, Alexander Gauland, insisted that Germans "should be proud of the achievements of German soldiers in two world wars"—including in the Nazi era.[76]

Although Merkel remained the leading candidate for what would become her fourth term, pundits feared that the AfD candidate would obtain more than the necessary 5 percent vote needed to gain a seat in the Bundestag—becoming the first far-right populist member of parliament since World War II.[77] While many viewed Merkel's position as humane, others, particularly those in the opposition party, viewed it as fiscally and culturally irresponsible. Between the monthly living expense stipends and housing subsidies provided by the German government, more than €30 billion had been attributed to the cost of maintaining the influx of refugees.[78] As a result, for the first time in her tenure in office, the German chancellor faced strong opposition in 2017.

Merkel had requested Obama visit Hannover because she needed his assistance with support of their shared principles, and most believed it would be his last trip to Germany. But with populism rising on both sides of the Atlantic, Obama would make one final trip to Berlin to see his friend and partner—following the surprise victory of presidential candidate Donald Trump in November 2016. They would have one more press conference and two more dinners together, and they would write one joint op-ed piece for a German newspaper. There, the two would argue that it was crucial that the transatlantic relationship remain intact.

13

"DEMOCRACY LIVES OFF CHANGE"

NOVEMBER 2016

The victory of Republican presidential candidate Donald Trump over his Democratic challenger Hillary Clinton on November 8, 2016, was one of the biggest political upsets of modern times. Shortly following the surprise election result, President Obama made his final presidential overseas trip to Greece, Germany, and Peru. The trip had been scheduled long before the results of the election and with far different goals, as Michael Memoli and Christi Parsons argued in the *Los Angeles Times*:

> *Under different electoral circumstances, Obama's trip this week . . . could have been something of a valedictory march: a sweeping speech on democracy in its birthplace, Greece; a final fond farewell and early endorsement in Berlin for his most important partner, German Chancellor Angela Merkel; and an economic summit in Peru of Asian and Pacific leaders.*[1]

Furthermore, Anthony Faiola and Juliet Eilperin for the *Washington Post*, too, claimed that advisors planned the trip as a way to boost Merkel's chances in the national election several months down the road—and a way for Obama to repay a leader described by former deputy national security advisor for strategic communications Ben Rhodes as "the president's closest partner over the course of his entire presidency."[2] However, after Clinton's surprise upset, the focus of Obama's final official trip abroad shifted. Rather than passing the baton of "leader of the free world" to former secretary of state Clinton, who had campaigned on continuing Obama's legacy, the president would have to pass the baton to Merkel instead.

Additionally, and perhaps more importantly, a greater portion of Obama's time overseas would be spent calming the fears of allied nations. "Mr. Obama's visit is about showing that not everything will change overnight," said Almut Möller, head of the Berlin office for the European Council on Foreign Relations (ECFR), according to *The Irish Times*.[3] But that fear of overnight change was widespread; it "dominated" Obama and Merkel's November 18 morning meeting—leaving journalists to write about "group therapy" for the "rattled leaders visiting from France, Britain, Spain, and Italy."[4]

While he would naturally spend some time reminding his fellow world leaders that Trump's election victory did not mean the end of modern Western civilization, Obama would also be "warning about the threats to democracy in an era of 'active disinformation' that left the public struggling to separate fact from fiction."[5]

Despite the shift in agenda for the president's last state visit to Berlin on November 16 through 18, he and Merkel managed to make the most of their bittersweet parting meeting. During his two-day stay, they held one final joint press conference, followed by two intimate dinners where they reminisced about their working relationship. They also co-authored one final joint op-ed piece for the German weekly magazine *Wirtschaftswoche* to emphasize the importance of the transatlantic alliance in an effort to maintain world order.

With the uncertainty created by both the Brexit vote and Trump's election victory, pundits believed Merkel would be the last remaining world leader who could stand up for the democratic principles that had created a bond between the United States and the EU nations since the end of World War II. According to Faiola and Eilperin in the *Washington Post*:

> *Trump's victory is set to usher into the White House a worldview very different from the liberal democratic consensus that was the cornerstone of Obama's partnership with Europe. With Britain disengaging after its vote to leave the European Union and other regional leaders mired in domestic battles, Obama's exit is set to leave Merkel as the world's most influential standard-bearer of those principles.*[6]

As the ECFR's Möller claimed, "Mr. Obama comes to town with expectations that Berlin will do more to hold the threads together, particularly after Brexit."[7] Again, the comments from journalists demonstrated the widespread fear of what would accompany the election of this new American president and the completion of Brexit.

Before Obama boarded Air Force One for his final overseas voyage, he made some telling comments with respect to his relationship with the German chancellor. Much to the dismay of the British, he reiterated that Merkel was "his closest international partner of the last eight years."[8] Furthermore, Obama failed to mention that following his meeting with Merkel, he had meetings scheduled with other EU leaders, including French president François Hollande and UK prime minister Theresa May, which worsened the situation—insinuating that his meetings with other leaders were so unimportant they were not even worth mentioning.[9]

Considering the "rock star" welcome then-candidate Obama had received in 2008, it seemed only fitting for Berlin to be his last European stop as president. Yet Obama had formed a bond not just with the German chancellor but also with the German people. As an article in *Die Welt* pointed out:

> *Berlin residents are not known for being particularly sentimental, but Obama hit the right notes. He understood the "spirit" of the city. That was the start of what would become a long friendship. Obama likes Berlin, and Berlin residents like him. And they had high expectations of the Democrat who entered the White House with a message of peace.*[10]

Despite the controversy and conflicts over the years, the German people—and perhaps Berliners in particular—tended to retain a genuine affection for the outgoing president. When reporters from *Die Welt* interviewed Germans about Obama's imminent departure, one such citizen—an engineer and an "Obama fan"—lamented, "We won't get another one like him again."[11]

Germans are notoriously suspicious of outsiders; thus it often takes them a considerable length of time to develop a rapport with newcomers. Nevertheless, it is no secret that the German people had formed bonds with previous presidents, most notably Kennedy and Reagan, though it took time for that fondness to grow. On the other hand, Obama had managed to win the hearts and confidence of Germans upon their very first meeting. They quickly and overwhelmingly welcomed Obama, which said as much about the chemistry between Obama and the Germans as it did about the ties that linked the two nations.

Obama's aides had hoped to coordinate a symbolic visit for the president in front of the Brandenburg Gate, but unfortunately it could not be organized. Overall, the "celebratory nature of the US president's final world tour was significantly dampened down in light of the US election results."[12] Nonetheless, reporter Derek Scally argued that there was still something special about this last trip. While plenty of world leaders, including Prime Minister May, had talked about supporting Obama, Merkel had actually done it. She was there from the beginning of his presidency, and now she was beside the president at the end to say goodbye.[13]

It is true that in democratic societies leaders come and go, and Obama and Merkel were among the only two who had remained in office throughout the eight years of Obama's presidency. This provided them a longer opportunity to work with each other than other world leaders, and this additional time had allowed a tighter bond to form, especially given the typical German apprehension toward outsiders. Yet despite the sheer length of their relationship, the mutual affinity and respect the two had for each other arguably played a bigger role in their bond.

Memoli and Parsons further added that the primary goal for this visit had been for Obama to reassure European allies that Trump understood the importance of NATO to the global community. Using the information Obama obtained from his one-on-one meeting with Trump in the Oval Office shortly after the election, the outgoing president told his colleagues that he believed Trump would remain committed to the NATO alliance.[14]

However, Scally went further and suggested that Obama would warn allies that Trump would unquestionably discuss the ongoing battle between the EU and the United States over defense spending. More importantly,

> *What we don't need, [Obama] added, was the world described by W. B. Yeats "where the best lack all conviction, and the worst are full of passionate intensity."*[15]

Although Obama may have also been concerned about Trump's campaign rhetoric, he pragmatically encouraged his European colleagues to employ a "wait and see" approach before they judged the newly elected president—a philosophy similar to Merkel's when Obama had been elected, although the outcome would prove to be much different. Merkel, in her practicality, had feared that Obama would be unable to deliver on what she viewed as mere campaign rhetoric. Now, in contrast, Germans feared that the new president would act on his campaign promises—promises that would inherently compromise the democratic principles of Germany and the EU. Ever the diplomat, Obama served as the voice of reason and encouraged the Germans to give Trump a chance. This shared trait of pragmatism, discovered upon their very first meeting, continued to unite Obama and Merkel in the final stages of their working relationship.

When Merkel welcomed Obama to Berlin for his final visit, both she and the president were more subdued than in their recent encounters. Obama and Merkel had spent three hours together on Wednesday evening in the prestigious restaurant Adlon. They had dinner and talked, informally and privately, just as the White House had requested. Ben Rhodes said that he couldn't remember Obama ever sitting down with someone for so long during his entire eight years as president[16]—yet another example of the strength of the bond between the two.

Their November 17 press conference lasted just over an hour—approximately twenty minutes longer than their average in the past. Normally, the cameras focused primarily on the person speaking, either Merkel or Obama, only occasionally shifting their attention to the other person. During the majority of this press conference, however, the camera focused on both leaders, giving the viewer a more complete picture of the interaction between the two.

Over the years of her political career, Merkel had earned the reputation of having a "poker face" for her neutral expressions. Throughout her eight-year working relationship with Obama, that shell had broken from time to time—in sorrow and respect when she and Obama stood shoulder to shoulder together at Buchenwald and, on the other extreme, in joyful affection in the Bavarian Alps in Krün prior to the G7 summit in 2015. As the two stood side by side for their final press conference together, both leaders, but Merkel in particular, were clearly more solemn.

On more than one occasion when the camera zoomed in on the chancellor for her reaction to something the president had said, her eyes almost looked wet with tears. Similarly, several times, she bit her lip and smiled awkwardly as she acknowledged the president's remarks. From their welcoming remarks to their final handshake, viewers could clearly see the bittersweet sentiment behind the event.

Merkel began by reminiscing about the visits Obama had made to Germany during his tenure:

> *In his capacity as president of the United States, let us remind ourselves—visiting us in his capacity as candidate here in Berlin; we then met in Baden-Baden. We then met in Dresden and Buchenwald. We saw each other when he gave a speech at the Brandenburg Gate. In Elmau we met again at the G7. Then Hannover Fair comes to mind. And today he is again in Berlin.*[17]

Then, in an unusual moment, she grew emotional, which left little doubt about the level of profound respect and admiration Merkel had for her American colleague:

> *So eight years are coming to a close. This is the last visit of [President]*
> *Barack Obama to our country. I am very glad that he chose Germany as*
> *one of the stopovers on this trip. . . . Thank you for the reliable friend-*
> *ship and partnership you demonstrated in very difficult hours of our*
> *relationship. So let me again pay tribute to what we've been able to*
> *achieve, to what we discussed, to what we were able to bring about in*
> *difficult hours.*[18]

Immediately following these opening remarks, Merkel alluded to the NSA controversy. Although the privacy issue had not been entirely resolved, shared intelligence provided a benefit for both nations, and thus there had to be coordination between them. With the controversy largely in the past, the relationship between the two countries truly did remain strong:

> *I'm very grateful that Barack Obama, as president, very much put pro-*
> *tection of privacy on the agenda today. Due to the fact of Islamist terror-*
> *ism all over the world and threat of ISIL, we recognize how important*
> *the cooperation with intelligence services, first and foremost, [and] also*
> *with the services of the United States is. We need this cooperation. And*
> *we say this from a German perspective very clearly and unequivocally.*
> *Our bilateral relations are very good; they're very close.*[19]

Merkel then turned to an important issue that she and Obama had worked on: the Transatlantic Trade and Investment Partnership. The incoming US president, Donald Trump, had campaigned against T-TIP, and the chancellor's remarks illustrated her concern that trade talks would not immediately resume under the Trump administration, but they also indicated that the issue was of utmost importance to her, and as such she was unwilling to abandon her hopes just yet. Merkel continued to plead her case:

In the areas of business, of the economy, the United States of America last year [was] our most important trading partner . . . which is why I've always come out strongly in favor of concluding a trade agreement with the United States of America. We have made progress, quite a lot of progress. They cannot be stopped, those negotiations. But we'll keep what we have achieved so far, and I'm absolutely certain that one day we will come back to what we have achieved and build on it.[20]

Changing course, Merkel addressed another hot-button issue on which she and Obama had worked side by side: climate change. She openly acknowledged that without Obama's leadership "this Paris Agreement would never have come about,"[21] and turned to Obama, who stood at the podium to her right and nodded in agreement.

Merkel then shifted to their work together as an alliance—for example, on the issue of Russia's illegal annexation of Crimea, where the interests and cooperation of the two nations were aligned. The number of troops and the military involvement Germany provided in Afghanistan had been a point of contention between the two leaders, and here Merkel confessed that Germany had not pulled its weight—and that it would be necessary to do so going forward. She promised to build upon what they had already achieved and expressed the willingness to work with the new administration:

There are a lot of areas where we cooperate—the fight against ISIL, for example. Germany was able to contribute [and] will continue to do so—in supporting the Peshmerga [Kurdish fighters in Iraq], in air policing. . . . But we also have to acknowledge the United States bears most of the burden. They bear the brunt of this responsibility. So I take your remarks seriously, Barack, that the European Union as a whole, but also Germany, needs to recognize that this is our alliance, our common alliance, our transatlantic alliance—that we have to step up our engagement. Because in the long run, we will not be allowed to accept this imbalance as regards the contributions we give to this alliance.[22]

The chancellor then admitted that the end had come for their close working relationship, but she chose to view the positive side.[23] Merkel could have chosen to explore the entire course of their relationship, but rather than reference her initial apprehension that Obama made promises he could not keep or her early concerns over his policies designed to solve the economic crisis, she focused solely on the strength of their partnership and the positive policies that had developed as a result:

> From a German point of view, German–American and European–American relations are a pillar to our foreign policy—a foreign policy that is obviously guided by interests, but that is very much also committed to shared values. So we have a platform—democracy, freedom, respect of human rights. . . . We have shared those values; we continue to share those values. And obviously we will continue to cooperate with the new administration. But today, I think, a word of gratitude is at hand. Thank you very much for this very close, very intensive cooperation.[24]

This was not only a thank-you to Obama but also a reminder to the next administration of the importance of a continued relationship between the two nations based on their shared principles. While she spoke those words, the cameras shifted toward Obama, who smiled as a very emotional Merkel turned the floor over to the president for the very last time.

In a relatively melancholy tone, the president expressed his pleasure at being

> back with my great friend and ally, Chancellor Merkel. As I reflect back over the past eight years, I could not ask for a steadier or more reliable partner on the world stage, often through some very challenging times. So I want to thank you for your friendship, for your leadership and your commitment to our alliance. And I want to thank the German people.[25]

DEAR BARACK

The cameras captured a somber Merkel, who stood at the podium looking as if she were biting her lips to fight back tears. Obama discussed the fact that the twenty-seventh anniversary of the fall of the Berlin Wall had happened the week prior and emphasized the strength of the commitment between the two nations:

> The United States was proud to stand with Germans as this nation and the continent reunited, and rebuilt, and reached for a better future. And it's a reminder that the commitment of the US to Europe is enduring and is rooted in values we share—values Angela just mentioned: our commitment to democracy . . . rule of law . . . the dignity of all people—in our own countries and around the world.[26]

It had become common for the two leaders to emphasize shared values between their two nations when they spoke publicly alongside one another. With the rise of human rights violations in countries such as Ukraine and Syria, and in light of the concerns that faced EU nations and the United States with regard to the rise of populism and extreme right political parties, both leaders knew they must emphasize the importance of democratic principles.

Obama's successor had campaigned on the notion that NATO had become obsolete, and discussed the possibility of withdrawing the United States from the alliance. Thus, Obama reaffirmed his support for NATO just as the pundits had predicted and said that:

> Our alliance with our NATO partners has been a cornerstone of US foreign policy for nearly seventy years—in good times and in bad, and through presidents of both parties—because the US has a fundamental interest in Europe's stability and security. The commitment that Angela and I share to this guiding principle has formed the basis for our conversations this afternoon.[27]

Perhaps Obama's emphasis on NATO's importance was an effort to counter Trump's attempt to undermine the organization before the public

216

and the media. The president shared that he and Merkel had also discussed T-TIP and ways to create jobs and opportunities on both sides of the Atlantic while keeping both the United States and the EU competitive. He acknowledged, as if trying to convince skeptics, that such trade agreements are challenging, but that markets demonstrated that commerce and trade can create growth in all countries involved, and thus these agreements are a solution where everyone benefits.[28]

The president summarized a list of other topics they addressed and thanked Merkel for her leadership with each policy—from global warming, where he argued, "With the threat of climate change only becoming more urgent, Angela and I focused on the need for American and EU leadership to advance global cooperation," to security, where the president acknowledged their shared commitment to preventing challenges on every front, including ensuring that Iran lived up to the terms of the nuclear deal and countering cyber threats.[29] Obama then complimented Merkel on her leadership with regard to Ukraine, and he confirmed that both leaders supported maintaining sanctions until Russia fully complied with the Minsk agreement.[30] As mentioned previously, Merkel had been under enormous pressure to lift sanctions against the Russians, and Obama once again went out of his way to reinforce to the world his support and endorsement of her actions. He still believed Merkel standing her ground and imposing those sanctions had been the right thing to do, and the president wanted the public to understand that.

Obama then gave his unwavering support for how Merkel handled the Syrian crisis:

> *I want again to commend Angela and, more importantly, the German people for the extraordinary leadership and compassion that you have shown in the face of what I know is a very difficult challenge. You are not alone in trying to deal with this challenge. This is not an issue that any one country should bear, but is in need of an international response. And I not only intend to make sure that we have put in place more robust support from the United States, but I'm hoping that continues beyond my administration.*[31]

The president's final remarks on the Syrian refugee crisis at this press conference were his closing arguments in the case he had made before the European people during his visit to Germany six months earlier for the technology fair. He summarized the importance of Merkel's policy, emphasized the impact of her decisions, and pleaded with his government to continue supporting her even after he left office, since it was unreasonable to expect one person or one country to bear all the burden of the enormous human suffering.

Obama then echoed the comments he made at the Victory Column before 200,000 Germans as a presidential candidate:

> On this final visit, I am reminded of the visit I made here before I became president. It was eight years ago. I had no gray hair. But I believe today what I said then: If you want a model for what is possible, if you want to see how to build a peaceful and prosperous and dynamic society, then look at Berlin and look at Germany.[32]

Then, for the last time, Obama publicly voiced his admiration for Merkel as a shining example of someone from the former East Germany who grew up to become the chancellor of a free and united Germany—and soon the leader of the free world upon Obama's exit:

> Look at Chancellor Merkel. Her personal story helps to tell the story of incredible achievement that the German people have embarked on and, I think, is something you should be very proud of. . . . And on behalf of the American people, I want to thank the German people. I want to thank Chancellor Merkel, for your deep friendship and your steadfast partnership. Vielen Dank.[33]

Just as the normally stoic Merkel had thanked Obama for his friendship, he returned the gratitude.

Obama and Merkel then opened the discussion to the media, whose questions reflected the melancholy air in the room. At the time of Obama's visit, Merkel had yet to announce whether she had planned to seek reelection for a fourth term the following year. One of the first questions posed by a journalist elicited the following response from Obama, about whether he thought the chancellor should seek another term:

> *I try to make it a rule not to meddle in other people's politics. All I can say is that Chancellor Merkel has been an outstanding partner. . . . And although we have not always been in sync on every issue, in terms of our core values, in terms of her integrity, her truthfulness, her thought-fulness, her doing her homework, knowing her facts, her commitment to looking out for the interests of the Germans first, but recognizing that part of good leadership on behalf of the nation requires engag-ing the world as a whole and participating effectively in multilateral institutions, I think she's been outstanding. . . . If I were here and I were German, and I had a vote, I might support her. But I don't know whether that hurts or helps.*[34]

During Obama's comments, Merkel nodded and smiled regretfully—particularly when he mentioned the fact that the two had not always agreed on important issues—which demonstrated that despite current popular opinion, politicians do not have to agree on every issue to form solid work-ing relations or friendships. Due to the strength of their relationship, it is easy to forget that, officially, Merkel and Obama belonged to opposing political parties. However, they put their differences aside and concentrated on what they had in common rather than what divided them to form a formidable bond—and to share an important lesson that seems lacking in much of today's politics.

Asked whether she hoped to make the EU and Germany less dependent on the United States, Merkel responded with her standard answer: that Ger-many could not have been reunited without the support of the United States.

> *The fact that we were able to enjoy German unification is due first and foremost to the help of the United States of America. And ever since Ger-many was able to regain its unity, it is in an even stronger position to*

give its contribution to upholding this order to which we feel committed,
and for which particularly people in the German Democratic Republic
stood out there in the streets to keep this up, to maintain this order, par-
ticularly also in our country. Now, we're trying to do more than it used to
be twenty-six years ago. And there are a number of areas where we have
to also make a stronger contribution.[35]

Merkel's next words, which addressed the disparities of wealth and
human rights in the digital age, sent a stark warning to the Trump administration about his isolationist principles and how that would likely play out
in the complicated modern world. Both Merkel and Obama had repeatedly
argued that because of the increasingly global challenges of the twenty-first
century, it is impractical for a nation to keep to itself—that organizations
like NATO are more important than ever, not less, in securing world peace.
Merkel insisted:

Each and every one of us must be given an opportunity to participate—
which is why Germany's fate, in many ways, depends on the firmness of
its alliance with NATO, with the European Union. We cannot stand
alone with 80 million people. In this world today, you cannot, when you
just stand on your own, achieve much—even though you may be econom-
ically strong. So alliances are part of our destiny as a nation, part of our
future as a nation. And this is what guides me in my policy, what guides
my government as a whole.[36]

When a journalist noted Merkel's somber disposition and asked about the
difficulty of leaving her partner today, Merkel answered with a smile:

Now, taking leave from my partner and friend—well, yes, it is hard. If
you've worked together with somebody very well, leave-taking is very
difficult. But we are politicians. We know that democracy lives off change.
The US constitution has clear stipulations on this. It's a tough rule—eight
years and that's it. Out goes the president and a new one comes in.[37]

As Merkel diplomatically explained the democratic process, Obama smiled, nodded his head, and even winked—appreciating her straightforward ways as always. Merkel continued:

But personal—we have freedom of movement in the whole of Germany, so if we want to see each other, well, I'm game. So we're not completely out of this world, as we would say.[38]

As the chancellor spoke, the president made a gesture with his hand, pantomiming a phone call—as if to confirm that the two would remain in touch after he left office—and the noise from eagerly clicking cameras filled the room. The two shook hands as they ended their final joint press conference.

But their public remarks did not quite end there. Understanding the world's concerns over the wave of populism that stretched across Europe, as well as the isolationist principles upon which Donald Trump had campaigned and ultimately won the presidency, Merkel and Obama co-authored a November 17 op-ed piece where they emphasized the importance of the transatlantic relationship without mentioning Trump by name.

The article describes how the link between their two countries had been joined together through good and bad times, which ultimately resulted in the "deep friendship we enjoy today."[39] In it, Merkel and Obama argued that the alliance between the two countries had been rooted in their joint commitment to individual liberties that only exist in democratic societies, and that Germany and the United States have "a joint responsibility to protect and preserve our way of life."[40] They urged worldwide respect for these universal principles, as such concepts were requirements for stability and prosperity.[41]

Merkel and Obama also emphasized their commitment to the collective defense principles underlying NATO, which they believed was vital to maintaining the security of the EU.[42] The piece suggested that out of "deep respect for human dignity" countries were required to offer humanitarian relief and aid to refugees.[43] Understanding that the integrity of the US involvement in the Paris Agreement was in jeopardy, Merkel and Obama addressed that issue as well and wrote that a "US–German partnership was essential to achieving a global agreement in Paris that offers the world a framework for protecting the planet."[44] Obama and Merkel's piece emphasized the importance of alliances based on shared values, which were necessary not just for maintaining the democratic way of life but also for conquering challenges, such as climate change, that faced everyone.

In the final paragraphs, Obama and Merkel reasoned that the world has become so globalized it is imperative that the two nations work not only with each other but with other nations of the world:

> *Simply put: we are stronger when we work together. At a time when the global economy is evolving more quickly than at any point in human history, and the scope of global challenges has never had higher stakes, such cooperation is now more urgent than ever. . . . Together in the G20 we are working to both strengthen global growth and make it more inclusive, while also addressing pressing, broad global challenges like climate change, migration, and global health security.*[45]

Times were changing, they professed, and never would the world go back to individual countries living in a vacuum. Therefore, working and collaborating with other nations was not only the morally responsible thing to do but the practical one as well.

> *Today we find ourselves at a crossroads—the future is upon us, and we will never return to a pre-globalization economy. Germans and Americans . . . must seize the opportunity to shape globalization based on our values and our ideas. We owe it to our industries and our peoples—indeed, to the global community—to broaden and deepen our cooperation.*[46]

In writing their article, Merkel and Obama, point by point, addressed the platform of nationalist and isolationist principles that had gained momentum on both sides of the Atlantic, and argued that such practices were impractical in the twenty-first century. It was a litany of all the issues they had collaborated on over the past eight years and a way to preserve their shared legacy, particularly given the threat that they seemed to expect from the new occupant of the Oval Office.

Following their joint appearance before the press corps, Merkel and Obama had a final dinner together—this time in the Chancellery, surrounded by guests. As reported by *Der Spiegel*, this final evening together in Berlin, behind closed doors, demonstrated the bond that the world had witnessed firsthand over the course of the two leaders' eight-year working relationship:

> *They reminisced about years [past], but there were no speeches and no cameras. With Americans, who are constantly full of praise and who claim everyone is a good friend even if they aren't always sincere, real emotion isn't measured in words, but in time. As such, Thursday evening was a rare display of affection, almost tenderness, between two heads of government.*[47]

As Klaus Brinkbäumer and Holger Stark pointed out, there was another profound reason for the US president's visit: Obama did not want his legacy diminished, and Merkel appeared to be the most logical way to prevent that from happening—at least on the European front. And no one was better positioned to protect Obama's legacy than Merkel, claimed Faiola and Eilperin of the *Washington Post*: "No other world leader so closely matches Obama's ideology of tireless diplomacy with an emphasis on human rights, tolerance and equality."[48] In addition to their similar beliefs on human rights, their "similar temperaments" helped them form a friendship that assisted with several major agreements, including sanctions against Russia and a deal on Iran's nuclear program.[49] Some saw "the level-headed Merkel emerging as a possible counterpoint on the world stage to the steady global march toward personality-based populism, including in the United States."[50]

Obama encouraged Merkel to run for reelection in 2017. Although he had acknowledged during the press conference that he normally did not get involved in other countries' domestic politics, he did publicly ask the Germans to demonstrate more respect for their chancellor. He understood that Merkel's approval ratings had declined significantly, both within her party and in her role as chancellor. Therefore, in his final trip to Germany, Obama took full advantage of the popularity he had with the German people and encouraged his friend and partner to continue in her role. Since he would no longer be there to battle for the shared values the two nations held so dearly, he wanted Merkel to continue the fight.

"WE CAN'T HIDE BEHIND A WALL"

A s is tradition with many former US presidents, Barack Obama had committed to establishing a presidential library after he left office, and according to the mission statement on the Obama Foundation's own website, "Our mission is to inspire, empower, and connect people to change their world." As evidenced by the various programs the foundation has embarked upon in Africa, Asia, and Europe, as well as the United States, the Obamas' hope to share their vision of leadership and involvement on the international stage is clear. So, when Germany's top Lutheran bishop, Heinrich Bedford-Strohm, invited Obama to speak at a program celebrating the five hundredth anniversary of the Protestant Reformation at the Brandenburg Gate with Chancellor Merkel, the former US president gladly accepted. It provided an opportunity to expand the global component of his presidential library—while also reuniting with his friend and partner.[1]

On the morning of May 25, 2017, Merkel met with Obama for a panel discussion titled "Being Involved in Democracy: Taking on Responsibility Locally and Globally."[2] Although the purpose of Obama's visit was supposed to be educational and celebratory, sadly, the tragedies that face world leaders in the twenty-first century rose yet again. The day before the *Kirchentag* (church congress) event, a terrorist attack struck the British city of Manchester shortly after a concert given by American singer Ariana Grande. An off-duty police officer and an eight-year-old girl were among the twenty-two casualties.[3]

Obama and Merkel took the opportunity to express their condolences in a brief joint statement with Archbishop Justin Welby. In his concise statement, the former president reassured Manchester residents that the world stood behind the victims and the families impacted by the attack. Merkel, too, expressed her sympathies when she stated that all Germans grieved with the citizens of Manchester, and while they mourned the loss, they stood together as well for the sake of freedom.[4] The archbishop summed up the tone when he concluded, "Love conquers hate."[5] Although an unfortunate attack clouded this reunion of these two world leaders, they both clearly still understood the significance of demonstrating unity among allied nations—even though Obama was no longer president.

The Kirchentag is an event that is held every two years in a different German city, and over 100,000 people of different faiths, ages, and backgrounds come together for multiple activities that occur during the festival.[6] Because 2017 marked the five hundredth anniversary of the Reformation, organizers expected the festivities and turnout to be more expansive than usual, with Obama and Merkel's discussion likely to be the most popular event.

After she spent the morning with Obama in Berlin, Merkel would be flying to Brussels for a NATO summit with Trump and other world leaders; it was Trump's first overseas trip as president. Both German and US officials denied the intentionality of the schedule and insisted it was a coincidence. Nonetheless, CNN argued that the appearances "do come as ties between Washington and Europe enter an uncertain phase, spurred by Trump's vague pronouncements of foreign policy and a contentious election season for European leaders."[7] And Polish political analyst Professor Jan Hartman of Jagiellonian University insisted:

> *I think that former president Obama is trying to do his utmost to pre-*
> *vent the splitting of the West, to keep the US and Europe pursuing the*
> *transatlantic line. Obama has probably tried to convince Merkel that*
> *despite the unpredictability of the new US president, the US remains*
> *a stable state and Trump is unable to ruin the long-term political and*
> *cultural alliance between . . . Western Europe and the US.[8]*

Because Merkel faced a possibly contentious election the following September, and given Obama's tremendous popularity among the Germans, many of Merkel's opponents viewed the joint appearance between the two as a publicity stunt intended to garner support for her campaign.

The two leaders, along with some key figures within the faith community, participated in a question-and-answer session with four seminary students—two from the United States and two from Germany. Obama and Merkel also shared the stage with two facilitators: Professor Dr. Heinrich Bedford-Strohm, bishop of the Evangelical Lutheran Church in Bavaria and chair of the Council of the Evangelical Church in Germany, and Kirchentag president Christina Aus der Au.[9] A modest crowd of approximately 70,000 people had gathered—many of them held banners that read WE MISS YOU ... WELCOME BACK, MR. PRESIDENT ... CAN WE KEEP YOU? ... *DU BIST EIN BERLINER.*[10]

From the moment Obama and Merkel took the stage, it was clear that nobody was happier over the reunion than the two of them. Merkel acknowledged in her opening remarks that she had attended previous Kirchentag events, but this one was particularly important to her because not only was it the five hundredth anniversary of the Reformation but Obama was there as well. Moreover, her reference to explorer Christopher Columbus as a contemporary of theologian Martin Luther, who both managed to build bridges between America and Europe, brought a huge smile to the former president's face.[11]

What followed was a question-and-answer session where Obama and Merkel discussed issues such as religion, inclusion, and the future of democracy. On the subject of religion, Obama explained that his public life began as a church worker in Chicago and that it had instilled in him the value of working toward making the world a better place.[12] Then, in a very bold statement for a religious event to celebrate the five hundredth anniversary of the Reformation, Obama acknowledged, "Personally, in my own faith, I believe that it is always good to have a little bit of doubt."[13] After an awkward pause, as though the spectators were unsure how to react, came thunderous applause. Obama had confidently stated a position that might be construed as controversial given his audience, illustrating his apparent ease with his hosts.

When the discussion turned to more pressing political problems, Merkel defended her position on the refugee crisis in Germany. She acknowledged that some of her positions were not always popular, but she pleaded for patience while the situation worked itself out. Obama also spoke about the challenges heads of state face when accepting refugees, and acknowledged the balance needed between doing the humanitarian thing versus doing what the current resources and citizens could handle.

Although Obama did not refer to his successor by name at any point in the ninety-minute presentation, he made a couple of remarks that indicated to whom he was referring. For example:

> *We make investments to try to deal with climate change and the displacement of farmers, and people whose way of life is being changed because the weather patterns are changing. Those things we do are not just for charity. But also, because if there are disruptions in these countries, if there is conflict, if there is bad governance, if there is war, and so on, then in this new world that we live in, we can't isolate ourselves. We can't hide behind a wall.*[14]

Obama's remarks referenced one of the cornerstones of Trump's campaign promises: building a wall along the southern border the United States shared with its southern neighbor, Mexico. Audience members greeted his passionate disagreement with cheers and applause; clearly, others shared his concerns.

During the second part of the program, an interactive discussion between the two leaders and four seminary students, Obama found himself defending positions he had taken as president, including his controversial use of drone strikes, which had been extremely unpopular with German citizens—particularly given the innocent lives lost. "One of the biggest challenges as president of the United States," Obama replied, "is how you protect your country and your citizens from the kinds of things that we just saw in Manchester, England, just a few days ago, or the things that we saw in Berlin or in Paris or in Nice."[15]

And even though Merkel's citizens had vehemently disagreed with Obama's actions, Merkel once again stepped in and defended her friend:

We are dealing with opponents who want to destroy our entire way of life. And what worked during the Cold War—deterrence . . . prevented war, because both sides wanted to stay alive. That doesn't exist with the terrorist groups. They are ready to give up their own lives to destroy the lives of others, as we have just seen in Manchester, of young people, families, ordinary people.[16]

As outlined in this book, the friendship and partnership between Obama and Merkel did not start off under the best circumstances but gradually evolved over the course of their eight-year working relationship. Even after Obama left office, that bond remained.

As Jon Meacham argued in his book *Franklin and Winston: An Intimate Portrait of an Epic Friendship,* American president Franklin D. Roosevelt and British prime minister Winston Churchill had a similarly complex partnership:

> *By the time they met during World War II, neither Churchill nor Roosevelt could really separate their political lives from their private ones. The demands of office and ambition determined the shape of their emotional spheres. Their relationship was like many friendships among the powerful, ones in which public figures conduct statecraft within a framework of professed regard and warmth. There is almost always a practical element in a politician's connection to other people, particularly to other politicians.*[17]

Just as Churchill and Roosevelt discovered, Merkel and Obama learned of not only the practicality but also the necessity of bonds between allies. Yet if necessity first drew Roosevelt and Churchill together, the genuine friendship that developed between them strengthened that initial bond.

Over the years, Merkel and Obama's relationship underwent a similar transformation. As difficult as it is for elected officials to have private lives,

Merkel succeeded in at least one way: her husband, who preferred the quiet private sector, rarely made a public appearance. Yet the bond between Merkel and Obama was so strong that on several occasions, Professor Sauer broke his personal rule to accompany the chancellor when she had an engagement with the president. Although Michelle Obama was more publicly engaged than Professor Sauer, she, too, tended to surface especially when the president was meeting the German chancellor. These appearances indicated that Merkel and Obama's ties went into the private sphere as well as the public sphere. The interconnectedness of the two leaders and their spouses emerged not only publicly throughout their eight-year working relationship but personally as well—both First Lady Michelle Obama and Professor Joachim Sauer joined the president and the chancellor on their farewell call together on January 19, 2017.[18]

As Meacham points out, "C.S. Lewis noted that [Ralph Waldo] Emerson once observed, *Do you love me?* actually means *Do you see the same truth?* 'Or at least,' Lewis wrote, 'Do you *care about* the same truth?'" Although Roosevelt and Churchill had their differences, Meacham concludes, "they cared passionately about the same overarching truth: breaking the Axis."[19] He continues:

> *They also shared the conviction that they were destined to play these roles. A friendship like Roosevelt and Churchill's is rightly understood as a fond relationship in which two people have an interest not just in each other (though they do) but also . . . in a shared external truth or mission. Victory was the common goal, and only Roosevelt and Churchill knew the uncertainties that came with ultimate power.*[20]

Fast-forward seventy years, one could say something similar about Merkel and Obama's relationship.

Together, Merkel and Obama—like their World War II–era counterparts—encountered many obstacles that threatened the democratic principles that united their two nations. They fought against the worst economic recession the world had seen since the Great Depression. They stood firm against

Vladimir Putin and his illegal annexation of Crimea. They shared a united drive to provide humanitarian support for the refugee crisis that erupted due to the Syrian civil war. And they worked closely on passing the Iran nuclear deal and the Paris Agreement.

Whereas Roosevelt and Churchill disagreed over colonization—according to Meacham, "Churchill wanted the British empire to survive and thrive; Roosevelt largely favored self-determination for colonial peoples around the world"[21]—Merkel and Obama clashed over economic policies, particularly regarding the eurozone. Tensions between Germany and the United States reached heights unseen since the Cold War over the NSA scandal, but just as Roosevelt and Churchill remained united in the common goal of defeating the Axis powers during World War II, Obama and Merkel remained united in their conviction to stand up for their democratic principles of tolerance, dignity of man, and rule of law. Because of their commitment to maintaining these principles, they managed to put differences aside—all for the sake of democracy.

Despite the political and ideological differences between the two, the similarities they share overshadowed the conflicts. And regardless of the opposites within their nature, they share personal characteristics as well. Neither has patience for political posturing—both are cut-to-the-chase types of people. Because both remain calm and collected under pressure, the media often used the term "poker face" to describe Merkel's emotionless demeanor, whereas the American media coined the term "no drama Obama."

And so they grew to trust one another. As Klaus Brinkbäumer and Holger Stark argued in their article for *Der Spiegel*:

> *Despite their many differences, this discretion was something that bound him to Merkel and grew over eight years into what was, for Obama, an unusually deep sense of trust.*[22]

Meacham argued that Churchill had been the "warmer human being," whereas Roosevelt had been the better politician. As Hitler's power spread across Europe, Churchill "stood alone" to give Roosevelt enough time to marshal American forces for the war. "Together they preserved the democratic experiment."[23]

Like Churchill, Obama had been the charismatic public speaker, while Merkel had been the deal-maker akin to Roosevelt. As foreign policy expert John Hulsman noted, "Mrs. Merkel is not a great orator, she's not flashy, but she's incredibly effective in meetings," adding that with her grasp of policy detail she can not only hold her own against Obama but also put pressure on the president himself.[24] Nonetheless, during their tenure together, both granted the other an opportunity to excel at something that was not their known forte—such as when Merkel gave her exceptional speech before Congress in 2011, and when Obama demonstrated his deal-making skills at the G20 summit in Strasbourg in 2009. Obama and Merkel complemented each other with their respective skill sets, but they also provided each other an opportunity to grow, learn, and develop skills that had been each other's weak points.

Merkel has a playful side, while Obama, on the other hand, is privately the more reserved, introverted of the two. Indeed, as Kevin Liptak remarked:

> For the famously reserved commander-in-chief, German Chancellor Angela Merkel has become his closest global partner, an alliance-turned-friendship forged by mutual political interests and parallel personalities. . . . [The president's enjoyed certain successes] because the two leaders have formed something rare for Obama: a genuine international friendship that both have leveraged to their own advantage.[25]

It was apparent from their customary greeting of a kiss on each check, ending with a firm handshake, that the two had a remarkable bond. It was these similarities that helped to form the strong partnership that the world became accustomed to witnessing.

So, it was only natural that Merkel would step in to fill the hole left by Obama's departure from politics. That transfer of power had been a long time in the making. When the crisis in Ukraine developed, Merkel "wielded significant global influence as mediator between Russia and the West"[26] and eventually became Obama's surrogate. She stood her ground against her European counterparts about the need to continue sanctions—with Obama standing by her side. According to Brinkbäumer and Stark:

> *To the chagrin of conservatives in Congress, Obama initiated an orderly retreat from the world stage, in part because of his trust in Merkel. In the Ukraine crisis, she grew into her role as mediator and, more recently, as Obama's surrogate. In conversations with Putin, she translated Obama's positions into a language that the Russian leader could understand.*[27]

Ironically, the rapport between Merkel and Obama had granted Germany the pre-eminent role in the US–Europe relationship—a rank previously reserved for the UK or France.[28] As Julianne Smith, a former deputy national security advisor to Joe Biden, explained in 2016:

> *You feel increasingly [that] the center of the trans-Atlantic relationship rests in many ways on the Berlin-Washington axis a little bit more than it has in the past. And I think Obama and Merkel are responsible for that because of that tight relationship.*[29]

Additionally, Brinkbäumer and Stark argue that Merkel had a superficial bond with her European counterparts, such as François Hollande and Matteo Renzi, but that Obama was a "true partner" to the German chancellor, thereby making their relationship different from any other of her career.[30]

With all the uncertainties facing the global community in the twenty-first century, including negotiations for the UK's exit from the EU, the problems created by global warming, the Syrian civil war continuing with no end in sight, increasing aggression from Russia, and interference in democratic elections in the West—what the future holds for democracy is uncertain. And without Obama and Merkel in office to face these challenges together, it is even more so.

Merkel reluctantly agreed to run for a fourth term as chancellor after the burnout and fatigue from twelve grueling years in the role—according to Ben Rhodes, she admitted her uncertainty to Obama but now felt an obligation to do so after the Brexit vote and Trump's surprising election victory.[31] Indeed, Rhodes reveals, when Merkel bade Obama farewell in Berlin, "A single tear appeared in her eye—something that none of us had ever seen before."[32]

Obama, understanding the grimness of the circumstances ahead, shook his head and said, "Angela. She's all alone."[33] He understood the predicament his partner was in and appeared frustrated he could do little to help her.

Concern over the transitional period between the Obama administration and the Trump administration, and the impact on Merkel, caught the attention of America's longest-running satirical television series, *Saturday Night Live*. In one TV news lampoon, host Colin Jost asked Chancellor Merkel (played by actress Kate McKinnon) whether she had heard from Hillary Clinton. The chancellor replied, "No . . . I was so sure we were going to be besties, staying up all night eating junk food. . . . Of course, we would talk about Barack. Oh my Barack!"[34]

In another episode, Donald Trump (portrayed by actor Alec Baldwin) telephoned McKinnon in the role of Chancellor Merkel. Merkel answered the phone, "Is this my sweet Barack? Barack Obama, I miss you." When Trump responded, "No, it's Donald Trump," Merkel replied, "Oh gross."[35]

The fact that Obama and Merkel's relationship had drawn attention outside of the mainstream media outlets further demonstrated the level of friendship between these two leaders and a partnership that captivated many aspects of American culture and society. It also spoke to the challenge that Merkel faced once Obama left office.

History has shown that long-lasting friendships and trusted partnerships among key allied world leaders help make the world a safer place. Churchill and Roosevelt's relationship helped keep the Axis and imperialist Japan at bay during World War II. Some forty years later, Reagan and Thatcher's relationship helped to keep the Soviet Union's aggression to a minimum during the Cold War. And Obama and Merkel's bond, which helped minimize the military threat Putin represented, followed. It appears as if such partnerships between world leaders come around only once a generation.

Who will the next international partners be? Will they be able to replace Obama and Merkel? There are many unknowns, but given the uncertain times facing the world today, until allied nations successfully calm the populist movement sweeping across the Western world, we should take this opportunity to plead with our leaders that, in today's complicated world, the global community cannot wait another forty years for another such relationship to form.

AFTERWORD

"I OFFER
A CLOSE COOPERATION"

2016-2020

Following Barack Obama's historic 2008 presidential victory, the German people saw him as "a healer of transatlantic relations that had been deeply tested during the presidency of George W. Bush," and became "some of Obama's fiercest supporters, with his popularity ratings in Germany almost always higher than they ever were at home."[1] On the other hand, Donald Trump's upset win eight years later "had the opposite effect, provoking a sense of trepidation" that, as many speculated, could influence Merkel's interactions with the president-elect.[2]

The Germans' apprehension toward the president-elect stemmed in part from the fear of his pro-nationalist and isolationist principles, ideas that their country had endured in the period leading up to World War II. German citizens had witnessed firsthand, and had spent decades atoning for, the results of those extreme policies. Many feared it could happen again.

Due to Chancellor Merkel's notorious pragmatism, however, she would inevitably develop some kind of relationship with the new president. After Trump's victory, Merkel publicly congratulated him but also reminded the world that the United States and Germany "are connected through values [of] democracy, freedom, [and] respect for the rights and dignity of men, independent of their origin, skin color, religion, gender, sexual orientation, or political attitude."[3]

To the new president, she pledged, "I offer a close cooperation."[4] Yet she tempered her remarks with a stark warning to the president-elect: her administration would be willing to work cooperatively with the new administration only if he adhered to the democratic principles of tolerance that united the two countries.

Donald Trump had campaigned on a populist "America First" platform that had little in common with the democracy Merkel and Obama had long envisioned. As part of his Republican agenda, he routinely spoke bombastically, berating American allies and policies that Obama had implemented—and because of the interconnectivity of today's world, any decision Trump made on said policies would undoubtedly impact EU nations, including Germany.

For example, Trump opposed free trade and supported strong tariffs; one of the first things he threatened to do, if elected, would be to withdraw the United States from T-TIP—the trade agreement that Obama and Merkel had worked so hard on during the final years of Obama's presidency. Candidate Trump also disparaged global warming as a hoax invented by the Chinese[5] and threatened to withdraw the United States from the Paris Agreement. He argued many times on the campaign trail that the 2015 Iran nuclear deal was one of the most disastrous ever made, and he threatened to pull the United States out of that agreement as well. Trump also promised to move the US embassy in Israel from Tel Aviv to Jerusalem—a change that would make a two-state solution in the Middle East impossible.

One of Trump's biggest concerns as a presidential candidate had been the ineffectiveness of NATO. Time and again he argued that the seventy-year-old treaty that created NATO had become obsolete. The primary focus of NATO had been to prevent Soviet aggression on other European countries during the Cold War—a threat Trump believed no longer existed.[6] Additionally, Trump repeatedly complained that NATO members failed to pay the agreed amount of 2 percent of their GDP for its defense and—in light of this objection— hinted at withdrawing the United States from the alliance if he was elected.[7]

While Foreign Minister Frank-Walter Steinmeier of Germany expressed concern over Trump's rhetoric, Merkel pragmatically promised to refrain from comment until after Trump's inauguration,[8] maintaining the same "wait and see" position with Trump that she had with Obama following his first election victory.

Besides Trump's threats to withdraw from NATO, as a candidate Trump had characterized Merkel's immigration policy as "catastrophic" and viewed her willingness to take in "all of these illegals" as a "mistake."[9] When questioned about the president-elect's remarks, Merkel replied, "We have known what his position is for some time, and my position is also known."[10] Her firm statement affirmed that she and Trump had a clear difference of opinion over the issue, and the two would have to agree to disagree on the topic since she had no intention of changing her position.

Merkel's first visit to Washington on March 17, 2017, to meet with the new president could be characterized as discomfiting.

The strained interactions began in the Oval Office after their first bilateral meeting, when the media asked for a photo of a handshake between the two world leaders and Trump refused to comply, which led to such headlines as the one in the *Huffington Post*: DONALD TRUMP'S AWKWARD MERKEL MEETING IS A FAR CRY FROM HER MOMENTS WITH OBAMA.[11] But during the joint press conference, much to Merkel's relief, Trump expressed his support for NATO.

"I was gratified to know that the president had aligned [sic] how important he thinks NATO is," she said, and continued:

> *NATO is of prime importance for us, and it was not without very good reason . . . that also Germany needs to increase its expenditure. We committed to this 2 percent goal until 2024. Last year we increased our defense spending by 8 percent, and we're going to work together again and again on this.*[12]

While nobody can know for certain what happens behind closed doors, it is clear that Merkel's acknowledgment of Germany's need to increase its funding to NATO certainly helped ease Trump's concerns about the effectiveness of the United States' continued involvement in the organization.

Trump, too, pledged his support to NATO—but with a caveat:

> *I reiterated to Chancellor Merkel my strong support for NATO, as well as the need for our NATO allies to pay their fair share for the cost of defense. Many nations owe vast sums of money from past years, and it is very unfair to the United States. These nations must pay what they owe. . . . I thanked Chancellor Merkel for the German government's commitment to increase defense spending and work toward contributing at least two percent of GDP.*[13]

Trump's remarks calmed the fear of many European leaders, including Merkel, and indicated that he would not immediately withdraw the United States from the alliance, while at the same time he expressed his frustration about other countries not paying for NATO's support.

In the chancellor's very brief remarks during the press conference, she began with a subtle jab at the new president: "In the period leading up to this visit, I've always said it's much, much better to talk to one another and not about one another, and I think our conversation proved this."[14] Notwithstanding any concern with the newly elected president, her remarks indicated that she would give him a chance.

> *[L]et me look back into the past. We, the Germans, owe a lot to the United States of America, particularly as regards the economic rise of Germany. . . . We were also able to regain German unity after decades of the United States standing up for this, together with other allies, and standing by our side during the period of the Cold War. And we are very gratified to know that today we can live in peace and freedom as a unified country due to that.*[15]

When the two fielded questions from the media, a German reporter made a stab at examining Trump's isolationist principles: "'America First'—don't you think that this is going to weaken also the European Union?"[16] To this, Trump replied:

> *Well, first of all, I don't believe in an isolationist policy, but I also believe*
> *a policy of trade should be a fair policy. And the United States has been*
> *treated very, very unfairly by many countries over the years. And that's*
> *going to stop.*[17]

The same reporter asked Merkel, "How dangerous do you think this isolationist policy of the US president is, what with the import of terrorists that he plans—and with the fact that he doesn't . . . deal with the EU in a very respectful way?"[18]

Before Merkel addressed the question, she put forth her notorious "poker face" to diplomatically answer:

> *Migration, immigration, integration has to be worked on, obviously.*
> *Traffickers have to be stopped. But this has to be done while looking*
> *at the refugees as well, giving them opportunities to shape their own*
> *lives where they are, [while helping] countries who right now are not*
> *in [a position] to do so—sometimes because they have civil war. I think*
> *that's the right way of going about it. And this is obviously what we*
> *have exchange of views about, but my position is the one that I have*
> *just set out to you.*[19]

The polite smile Merkel gave to Trump as she turned the floor over to him offered a sliver of hope that perhaps the two could come to some sort of an agreement simply to disagree on the issue. The ever-pragmatic Merkel made it clear that her own position was not open to debate, but at the same time, she would not publicly criticize the American president for his position.

Another awkward exchange occurred at the podium when Trump responded to an inquiry about a tweet he had written where he accused his predecessor of illegally wiretapping his apartment in New York. "As far as wiretapping," he said, "I guess, by this past administration, at least we have something in common perhaps."[20] Trump's comments had been meant as a joke as he referred to his allegations about the Obama administration's wiretapping of both him and Merkel. Nevertheless, the scathing expression on Merkel's face implied she did not view Trump's remarks in the same light.

The initial joint press conference between Merkel and Trump was full of halting, uncomfortable moments, and this event was not to be the last of its sort. In all fairness, though, Obama and Merkel's relationship had also begun on shaky ground; it took a good two years before they truly forged a strong working relationship. Based on first impressions of Trump and Merkel's encounter, it would take time for them to develop an amicable working relationship as well—if they ever would.

As it turned out, from the moment he took office in January 2017, President Trump did his best to undermine both the foreign and domestic policies the Obama administration implemented. Many key European allies, including Germany, stated throughout Trump's presidency that Europe needed to discuss ways to continue without US assistance because leaders did not feel that the United States could be counted on as a reliable ally.

As part of Trump's "America First" campaign rhetoric, he promised to withdraw the United States from the Trans-Pacific Partnership trade agreement, which Merkel had once pinned her hopes on in the belief that it signaled America's willingness to negotiate the T-TIP, or Transatlantic Trade and Investment Partnership, that Merkel and Obama had worked so closely on. True to his word,

With the stroke of a pen on his first full weekday in office, Mr. Trump signaled that he plans to follow through on promises to take a more aggressive stance against foreign competitors as part of his "America First" approach. In doing so, he demonstrated that he would not follow old rules, effectively discarding longstanding Republican orthodoxy that expanding global trade was good for the world and America—and that the United States should help write the rules of international commerce.[21]

Upon hearing of the plans for the US withdrawal from the agreement, Merkel said:

> *I am not happy that the Trans-Pacific agreement now will probably not become reality. I don't know who will benefit from that. I know only one thing: there will be other trade agreements, and they won't have the standards that this agreement and the hoped-for T-TIP agreement have.*[22]

Ultimately, negotiations over the T-TIP went no further.[23] But more conflicts were still to come.

Following his first G7 summit in May 2017 in Hamburg, Germany, Trump formally withdrew the United States from the Paris Agreement. Shortly after his announcement, the leaders of France and Italy—President Emmanuel Macron and Prime Minister Paolo Gentiloni, respectively—joined Germany and released a joint statement that rejected Trump's claim that the climate deal could be renegotiated: "We deem the momentum generated in Paris in December 2015 irreversible, and we firmly believe that the Paris agreement cannot be renegotiated, since it is a vital instrument for our planet, societies and economies."[24] The three leaders called on their other allies to speed up efforts to combat climate change and promised to do more to help developing countries adapt.

Additionally, Merkel spoke before a group of party members at a CDU rally in Munich, where she passionately articulated:

> *The times in which we can completely rely on others are over. . . . We Europeans truly have to take our fate into our own hands.*[25]

Although Merkel did not mention the United States specifically, it was clear she was referring to its withdrawal from the Paris Agreement. That was the first time Merkel expressed such remarks, but it would not be the last.

In May 2018, Trump withdrew the United States from the Iran nuclear deal that Obama and Merkel had helped guide to fruition three years earlier.[26]

World leaders responded to that decision with rage, and Merkel appeared to be especially angered. In a speech she gave in honor of President Macron of France, she stated once again the United States could not be relied upon, but this time, in a bold move, she referred to the country by name:

> *It is no longer such that the United States simply protects us, but Europe must take its destiny in its own hands. That's the task of the future.*[27]

Der Spiegel indicated that Trump's "decision to withdraw from the Iran nuclear deal marks the temporary suspension of the trans-Atlantic alliance," and showed no restraint in its belief that the US president was bringing "chaos where there was once order."[28]

> *The West as we once knew it no longer exists. Our relationship to the United States cannot currently be called a friendship and can hardly be referred to as a partnership. . . . It is impossible to overstate what Trump has dismantled in the last 16 months.*[29]

One of the biggest challenges that faced world leaders in the early years of the Obama administration had been the financial crisis, and at the time the United States had passed the Dodd–Frank Wall Street Reform and Consumer Protection Act as a measure to help restore the American economy and place safeguards to ensure another such crisis never occurred again. Nevertheless, despite the fact that the bill had helped the government avert the brink of financial disaster, on May 24, 2018, Trump signed a bill that had received rare bipartisan support in both houses of Congress and would roll back many of the regulations of Dodd–Frank.[30] The key rollbacks of this new legislation raised the threshold at which banks are considered too big to fail from $50 billion in assets to $250 billion. With these new relaxations in the law, only a dozen of America's largest banks, including Bank of America, Wells Fargo, and JP Morgan Chase, would be subjected to oversight.[31] With the bipartisan support and an overwhelming number of votes in favor of these rules, (67–31 in Senate and 258–159 in the House), evidently, both political parties had forgotten about the consequences unleashed by a lack of financial guidelines and now sided with Trump, who had campaigned on a platform of reversing undue government regulation. As illustrated through the painstaking work Obama and Merkel performed to bring their countries back from the brink of economic failure, described throughout the course of this book, the world has become so globalized it is unlikely that changes in one country will not impact the global economy as well.

Equally as important, and perhaps more consequential, on May 31, 2018, Trump further compromised the transatlantic relationship, as well as the US relationships with Canada and Mexico, when he proposed tariffs on imported steel and aluminum. Implementation of this policy was consistent with his dubious campaign rhetoric that imported products hurt American industry and eliminated American jobs. Needless to say, members of the EU pledged retaliation against the United States and placed a 25 percent tariff on American products, including peanut butter, denim, cigarettes, cranberry juice, and motorcycles.[32] EU trade commissioner Cecilia Malmström promised the tariffs would be "proportionate"; she also insisted that they had done everything possible to prevent the outcome, and called it "a bad day for world trade."[33] Based upon this reaction from the world leaders impacted by Trump's policy, while they still viewed the US as a viable ally and trade partner, they would not sit by and be bullied by the United States either.

In early June, shortly following Trump's controversial decision to impose tariffs on America's closest trading partners, the US president attended the G7 summit in Ottawa, Canada, with other world leaders. Prior to boarding Airforce One before his trip, he addressed reporters on the lawn at the White House and took the opportunity to publicly condemn the past decision world leaders had made to expel Putin from the G7, and to advocate for Russia's reinstatement.[34] These remarks demonstrated yet another deviation from the effective foreign policy strategy of not just Obama but other allied nations and leaders as well.

In the hours following the G7 summit, Merkel's staff shared with the public a photo of Trump sitting down at a table with his arms crossed angrily, with other world leaders standing by—most notably, Merkel standing over him.[35]

According to CBS News correspondent Ian Bremmer, this photo resulted when Merkel and Prime Minister Justin Trudeau of Canada attempted to persuade Trump to commit the United States to adhere to a rules-based international order. According to Bremmer, Trump felt that Trudeau and Merkel were ganging up on him, which ultimately annoyed him, and in his account Trump begrudgingly agreed to sign the communiqué and as he stood up, "he put his hand in his . . . suit jacket pocket and he took two Starburst candies out, threw them on the table and said to Merkel, 'Here, Angela. Don't say I never give you anything.'"[36]

The photo in question immediately hit the mainstream media and went viral on social media, becoming as much a sensation as the photo of Obama's "phone me" photo with Merkel during their final press conference in Berlin. The contrast—between a photo that captured the friendship and partnership of two world leaders who admired and respected one another, and a photo that showed two world leaders who appeared to have only disdain for one another—was unfortunately a sign of a decline after seventy years of amicable and necessary diplomatic relations. Despite the differences and coldness between Merkel and Obama in the beginning, it never sunk to these infantile levels—not even after the Snowden allegations. The two always spoke professionally of each other and worked together, and they demonstrated respect not just for each other but for the partnership between their nations.

In the eighteen months that followed Obama's exit from the political stage, Merkel faced challenges of her own besides just the destabilizing presence of Trump. She managed to win her own reelection campaign in September 2017, but with numbers lower than her party had seen in over seventy years.[37] As a result, it took several months and multiple attempts for her to successfully form a coalition and thus a viable government that would serve throughout her four-year term.

Perhaps more troubling for Merkel was the momentum the far-right, anti-immigrant AfD and the far-left Green parties were gaining across the nation. Just a year later, in the September 2018 state elections of Bavaria and Hesse, the results indicated that Germans had lost faith in the traditional German parties, when these extremist parties achieved far more of the vote than usual—and the anti-immigration AfD received 10.2 percent of the Bavarian vote and thus its first seat in the Bundestag.[38] These results caught the attention of political leaders, but the real tipping point came when Hesse reported similar results two weeks later. In that state election, both Merkel's party (CDU) and the coalition party (SPD) suffered drastic defeats to the benefit of both the Green party (19.5 percent) and the AfD. Much to the dismay of mainstream political party members, the AfD managed to secure 13 percent of the vote—enough to entitle it to representation in the state parliament—for the first time granting it representation in all sixteen German states.[39]

Many of Merkel's own party members believed that Merkel had moved the conservative party too far to the left, and blamed her liberal refugee policy for the rise of the AfD. Following those elections, it became abundantly clear that Germans wanted change, and Merkel was prepared to give it to them. In a press conference in late September 2018, she announced her plans to step down as party leader at the CDU annual meeting later that year and retire from public life.[40]

On December 7, 2018, Merkel's life came full circle. She returned to Hamburg—the city where she was born—to give her final speech as party chair. More than 1,000 party delegates, 1,600 journalists, and hundreds of diplomats from around the world gathered to see Merkel's final farewell.[41] Supporters held signs that read THANK YOU, ANGIE and THANKS, BOSS, FOR 18 YEARS OF LEADERSHIP.[42]

Just as Merkel fought back tears in her and Obama's final press conference together, she fought them back again in this final speech. In her thirty-minute statement, she justified her open-door policy for the 1.6 million migrants from the Middle East who had entered Germany since 2015 when she explained that the country had responded to a "humanitarian catastrophe."[43] In her parting words, followed by a standing ovation that lasted for over ten minutes, she declared:

> *I wasn't born chancellor or party chairman. I always wanted to bear my offices with dignity and to give them up with dignity. It was an honor.*[44]

Although party leader selections historically had been made in backroom deals—where party members had little or no say—for the first time since 1971, party members voted for their new leader.[45] Merkel refused to publicly endorse a replacement, but she clearly had a favorite: her mentee, Annegret Kramp-Karrenbauer, also known as AKK.[46] With eighteen years of front-line political experience, including six years as leader of the state of Sarrland, Kramp-Karrenbauer (often referred to as "mini-Merkel" or "Merkel's crown princess") shared many of the same values and appeared to be the most logical and consistent person to replace Merkel as CDU party leader.[47]

Just as the rise of the AfD led to Merkel's political downfall, however, Kramp-Karrenbauer later faced a similar fate. In a February 2020 state election, the CDU ignored direction from party leaders and formed an alliance with the AfD to help elect Thomas Kemmerich as premier to the state of Thuringia even though, due to the extreme anti-Islam, anti-immigrant platform of the AfD, the CDU explicitly prohibited its members from working with the right-wing party. When they did so anyway, in a surprising move, Kramp-Karrenbauer resigned, stating, "The AfD stands against everything that we in the CDU stand for. . . . Any form of rapprochement with the AfD weakens the CDU."[48] Her decision to step down was so sudden that even Merkel had been caught off guard and called the decision "regrettable."[49] Merkel, on a state visit in South Africa, labeled the alliance "unforgiveable" when she heard of it.[50] Moreover, the chancellor took her rage a step further when she professed "that you don't win majorities with the help of Alternative für Deutschland."[51] Rather than blame the collaboration on the breakdown in communication among coalition and party members, pundits quickly pointed toward Kramp-Karrenbauer's failure of leadership, stating that this defiance illustrated the "shortcomings of her leadership and proved she did not have full control over the party on such a significant issue."[52] Kemmerich, the newly elected premier of Thuringia, ultimately resigned from the position because of the controversy, but only after the damage had been done. As Jen Kirby argued in her article for *Vox*, "AKK will take the fall for Thuringia, but Germany's post-Merkel future is uncertain."[53] While Merkel and the rest of the German politicians struggled to make sense of the chaos and what it would mean for Merkel's legacy, the Covid-19 pandemic hit the world—and addressing this public health crisis became far more important than any instability within the German political structure. Merkel was forced into crisis management mode yet again—and one more time she rose to the occasion.

When news surfaced that Germany too had been hit with the deadly virus, Merkel managed the difficulties of Covid just as she had handled every other crisis in her nearly twenty-year tenure in office—as a problem solver. She relied on her scientific training, and she immediately began to work with experts and public health officials to find an appropriate response. She quickly implemented a plan to combat the illness that included almost a complete lockdown of the country; only essential businesses remained open, and as a result, the Covid-19 death rate in Germany remained relatively low compared with other countries.[54]

Throughout her chancellorship, Merkel had traditionally given a prerecorded New Year's speech to the people of Germany, but nothing live. However, in March 2020, Merkel did something she had never done before—she publicly addressed her country in a live, unscheduled, televised address.[55] Building from her own experience growing up in the former East Germany, she reassured the German people of both the necessity and the temporary nature of the shutdown, and her approval ratings improved dramatically: 80 percent to 90 percent of people believed Merkel could effectively handle the crisis.[56] In her remarks, she appeared poised, calm, serious, and most importantly, honest, all characteristics people look for in a leader during turbulent times.

Later that spring, when much of the world still remained in lockdown, Germany began to slowly, cautiously attempt to return to a state of normalcy, with parks, businesses, museums, and restaurants reopening. "We can afford a bit of courage," Merkel stated.[57] Still, she warned, with her typical, innate caution:

> We have to watch that this thing does not slip out of our hands. The first phase of the pandemic is behind us but we are still at the beginning and it will be with us for a long time.[58]

Much of Merkel's jump in popularity during the first spike of Covid could be attributed to the poor leadership exhibited by the United States. As Professor Andrea Römmele of the Hertie School in Berlin argued:

> She started a massive revival, not just in Germany, but also in the world, because for the first time in 150 years, the world is facing a global crisis and people are not looking towards the US for global leadership. They are looking to Merkel.[59]

While Merkel relied heavily on information from scientists and public health professionals, Trump continued to label the pandemic a hoax. As further indication that he did not take the crisis seriously, he ignored the warnings of his own intelligence community,[60] cut funding for programs to address the public health emergency,[61] and laid off key employees in the department responsible for handling such a crisis.[62] When the epidemic became so widespread that even Trump had to acknowledge the severity, he began to routinely suggest scientifically unproven medication as a viable treatment option for the virus. During a press conference, in a statement heard around the world, Trump suggested that people ingest disinfectants as a method to combat the illness.[63] While the vast number of Americans rolled their eyes or shuddered at the remarks made by a man many did not consider their president, poison control hotlines were flooded with inquiries by those who believed Trump's claims. The president later walked back his remarks, claiming he was "being sarcastic," and once again refused to take responsibility for his words.

Even after four years, Trump had yet to realize that as the leader of the free world, there were consequences to his actions, and one of them was that people listened—regardless of how ludicrous or appalling his remarks were— that people looked up to the president, and with that level of authority, as both Obama and Merkel well knew, comes a certain level of responsibility. Partly as a result of the Trump administration's failures, the United States continued to tally the highest number of both infections and deaths of any country in the world—with over thirty million cases and more than 500,000 deaths as of this writing.[64]

In times of uncertainty and crises, when people are frightened, they want a strong leader to look to for answers, reassurances, and most importantly, honesty—not the tribalism and partisan finger-pointing demonstrated by the Trump administration. During this difficult time, many Americans found themselves without a present leader—so they turned to someone on whom they knew they could rely: former president Obama.

In addition to the death, suffering, and economic hardship felt by so many, the business shutdowns and closures of schools were particularly difficult for young Americans—especially high school seniors, who missed many of the rite-of-passage events such as prom and graduation. In an effort to demonstrate some level of normalcy and reassurance to these young adults, Obama presented a prerecorded national graduation speech for the high school class of 2020, which aired on every major network in the country. In his brief remarks, without mentioning the US president by name, Obama took a jab at the Trump administration's handling of the crisis:

> *Doing what feels good, what's convenient, what's easy—that's how little kids think. Unfortunately, a lot of so-called grown-ups, including some with fancy titles and important jobs, still think that way—which is why things are so screwed up. I hope that instead, you decide to ground yourself in values that last, like honesty, hard work, responsibility, fairness, generosity, and respect for others.*[65]

It is virtually unheard-of for a former US president to speak out about another administration, but the country needed leadership—they needed reassurances that everything would be OK, and since the Trump administration was unable to provide that, Obama stepped in. His remarks seemed to be what the country so desperately needed and had been lacking ever since he left office. The fact that Germans turned to Merkel for leadership in times of crisis, and Americans still turned to former president Obama for similar reassurances, confirmed that the two had powerful connections with their nations, and helps to further explain the connection they had with one another.

Differing leadership styles in addressing the Covid-19 pandemic made a significant impact on foreign diplomatic relations as well as domestic affairs. Much to the irritation of Trump, Merkel declined his invitation to attend the G7 summit in Washington at the end of June 2020. When the media initially reported the story, Merkel cited concerns about the fact that Covid was still circulating, and claimed June was too premature to reopen and hold large gatherings.[66] Trump reportedly was "furious" over the German chancellor's snub and argued that "there would be no 'greater example of reopening' than holding a G-7 summit at the end of June in Washington."[67] Nevertheless, Merkel remained unpersuaded by the president's arguments and stayed firm in her refusal to attend. Although Merkel cited Covid as her justification for declining Trump's invitation, sources in the White House later revealed a contentious phone call between the two leaders earlier in the week in which they had disagreed on important international policies such as a gas pipeline between Germany and Russia, relations with China, and NATO.[68]

Over the course of his presidency, Trump made numerous unilateral decisions about the United States' involvement in key foreign policy issues—decisions that had negative implications for other countries. As a result of these controversial decisions, allied leaders became more skeptical of Trump and of their continued relationship with the United States, perhaps wondering particularly whether they could trust a leader who, in the midst of a unique pandemic, had withdrawn from the World Health Organization.[69] After more than three years of interactions with the Trump administration, Merkel had developed plenty of reasons for wanting to limit ties with the United States, including having no desire to engage in Trump's anti-China rhetoric campaign and not wanting to get dragged into the politics of the 2020 presidential election.[70] Additionally, as one German analyst argued, Merkel had "been hurt" by Trump, and they simply "don't get along and they disagree on many policies."[71]

When asked about the significance of Merkel's refusal to visit Washington, former Obama administration official Julianne Smith, now a senior advisor at the German Marshall Fund in Washington, DC, argued Merkel's stance "says a lot about how fed up multiple leaders are around the world, who have seen how little in return they have gotten on their investments they made into a relationship with Trump."[72] Considering the totality of the circumstances, it is no wonder that Merkel told French president Macron, "I don't want to be in the room with the guy."[73]

It is painful to reflect on the symbolism in this breakdown of diplomatic ties. Less than four years earlier, Merkel cried when she said goodbye to Obama for the final time—and now, in an unprecedented event, a leader of one of the United States' closest allies refused to meet with the president because she could not even bear to be in the same room with him. This breach in protocol spoke volumes not just about the lack of relationship between Trump and Merkel but about the absence of trust between the two nations. In four short years, it seemed a seventy-year-old bond between nations had become severed, possibly beyond repair.

Still in the shadow of the diplomatic disaster the Trump administration embarked upon, American society continues to face myriad domestic challenges, from the highest pandemic death toll since 1918 to record unemployment because of Covid. As problematic as those issues are, it appears that they may pale in comparison to the heightened racial tensions facing the country after four years of Trump—and as a result of the ongoing police brutality toward people of color. Obama's victory and overwhelming popularity once gave the United States a false sense of security that racism had finally become a thing of the past in American society. Unfortunately, the four years of unrest created by Trump and his administration illustrates just how fragile and fragmented American society remains. With President Joe Biden now in the White House, however, civility in domestic policies may at last be a top priority again. While Obama routinely referred to Merkel as his best friend on the international stage, the unique rapport between Obama and his vice president suggests that Biden was Obama's best friend on the domestic front and is perhaps prepared to carry Obama's legacy forward.

Second only to restoring this civility, repairing America's image abroad with key allies should be a top policy agenda item as well. It may still be possible to reverse the trend of nations turning away from the United States, but it will take quite a bit of work by President Biden and others to restore these international ties.

When examining the strength of Merkel's guidance, it is no wonder the world has turned to her and to Germany rather than the United States. Pragmatically speaking, turning to Merkel for reassurance in times of crisis simply has seemed like the logical approach to take. "She will be remembered as a true crisis manager," according to Professor Andrea Römmele of the Hertie School in Berlin. "She is incredible; whenever there is a crisis, she does her best."[74] Whether or not one agrees with Merkel's policies, it is fair to say that she faced more than her fair share of crises and, more often than not, came out on top.

During her four terms as chancellor, Merkel's policy making and leadership skills were tested time and again. During the financial crisis of 2007 and 2008, when Spain, Italy, Portugal, and Greece faced unstable economic times, Germany's austerity policies helped provide stability. Under Merkel's leadership, Germany began to phase out nuclear power following the Fukushima, Japan, catastrophe in 2011. And prior to the Covid pandemic in 2020, Merkel most likely would have been remembered for her willingness to open the German borders to over one million Syrian refugees. Her ability to weather crises was tested again in 2020, when she handled the Covid pandemic and reestablished her credibility as a strong leader in turbulent times. And whether transatlantic alliances and economic recovery can be established now that Trump has left office, Obama will go down in history as not just the first Black president but a successful leader who steered the United States to economic recovery after one of the greatest recessions in history. Yet nontraditional, extremist parties continue to take hold across America and Germany alike, indicating that people want change.

As the dust settles from Covid-19 and people begin a new normal life without social distancing or face masks, it is unclear what will happen to the traditional mainstream political parties in Germany. Merkel will not be there to lead them anyway, as she stepped off the world stage in late 2021, like her friend and partner Obama nearly five years earlier.[75] Whether she will take a political role in Belgium as a member of the EU government, return to academia, or retire from public life remains to be seen as of this writing. What can be said is that Merkel's leadership provided an anchor of stability through some of the most turbulent times in the modern age. Merkel will be missed throughout the world and will leave a gap that will be difficult to fill.

There is a political slogan used in the United States by liberals and conservatives alike and normally said by the members of the victorious party to others who dare to challenge policy proposals of the ruling party—"elections have consequences." It is true. As witnessed in both the 2016 and the 2020 US presidential elections, elections do have consequences. Those who opposed the Trump administration's agenda and viewed many of his positions as threats to democracy often argue that Trump failed to do one positive thing while in office. That statement is not entirely true. Yes, most of his principles and executive orders violated many of the founding ideals upon which the US was built. However, the one positive thing to emerge from those four years is that many everyday citizens became engaged in the democratic process for the first time. From his first weeks in office to his final days, people took to the streets to protest a variety of Trump's controversial policy implementations, including the Muslim ban, the family separation at the southern border, and the budgetary cuts to science and education. Ordinary citizens challenged the administration's agenda. Additionally, people showed up to vote in record numbers; according to the US census, only 61.4 percent of eligible participants cast their votes in the 2016 presidential election,[76] compared to the staggering 81,284,000 votes—or 51.3 percent of the total vote—that Biden alone received in 2020.[77]

While these numbers seem impressive by US standards, they fail to compete with the 76.2 percent of German citizens who participated in the democratic process in the last federal election in 2017, a number fairly consistent with the average voter turnout in the past several decades, which has stayed at around 70 percent.[78] Germany's high participation could stem from the fact that elections are held on Sunday—a day of rest for Germans—so nobody is working, and it is easier for them to participate. Perhaps it is because the Germans remember living through the demise of the dictatorship of the Cold War and have learned not to take democracy for granted. Or it may be that Germans remember that Hitler was defeated in 1923 after the failed Beer Hall Putsch coup attempt only to legally seize power in 1932.[79] Generally speaking, older Germans tend to avoid using what they refer to as the "H-word" unless specifically discussing the time leading up to and following World War II. The one exception to this is when they point out, often to Americans, the failed coup. Their openness to address these issues and educate others demonstrates a willingness for them to let others learn from Germany's mistakes.

Whatever the reason, American voters can learn something from German voters. The 2020 US presidential election illustrated that democracy works when its citizens actively engage in the process. When people benefit from living in a free society, as illustrated through the course of this book, freedom is something that cannot and should not be taken for granted. Unfortunately, there has been a rapid wave of voter suppression laws introduced and enacted in several states over the past few years, and citizens need to take an active stand and fight against these modern forms of voter suppression. In order for citizens to reap the rewards of democracy, they must assume some level of responsibility—most importantly, they must vote. History tends to repeat itself, but if US citizens learn from the Germans now, and remain diligent and not complacent, then, as the 2020 elections illustrated, democracy can indeed prevail.

Trump and Merkel's failure to form the same kind of partnership as Obama and Merkel only highlighted the sore need for partnership in today's unstable times, whether that means world leaders coming together to defend their democratic values or citizens working as one to defend the right to vote. Obama and Merkel did not always agree on key issues, but they developed a solid relationship and worked together to make informed decisions that benefited not just their own nations but other allied nations as well. Their relationship is one that other world leaders should learn from—and hopefully, one day, emulate.

ACKNOWLEDGMENTS

When I decided to undertake a project of this magnitude, little did I realize there were many people whose help and support I had relied on often and whose encouragement and assistance at different points in my life served as the foundation that made this book possible. Therefore, for ease and fairness, people are grouped based upon the roles they played in my life.

First of all, I would like to thank my publisher, Disruption Books, and all the people responsible for overseeing this book and for having faith in both the project and my ability as an author and a historian—most importantly associate publisher Alli Shapiro. I would also like to thank my social media and public relations assistants: Mitzi Valentin, Mike Onorato, and the other members of the Smith Publicity firm.

Over the years, academia and many of my former professors played vital roles in helping me to develop the necessary skills to take on such a task, including: Dr. Lisa Fine, history professor and chair of the history department at Michigan State University, who first introduced me to the field of women's history when I was an undergrad more than twenty-five years ago; and Michael Unsworth, history bibliographer emeritus at Michigan State University, who taught me the necessary skill of plowing through historical and congressional records and always acted as my own personal librarian for the numerous history and public policy papers I wrote during my undergraduate studies. I also owe my sincerest gratitude to both my history thesis advisor at San Jose State University, Dr. Patricia Evridge Hill, and Michael Reisch, former social work professor at the University of Michigan, who served as an incredible mentor and advocate for me in my community organizing and social justice campaigns.

My political and professional colleagues served as both mentors and sources of inspiration, including Judy Pipkin, Santa Clara County Democratic Party administrator; Kevin Mullin, speaker pro tem of the California State Assembly; Sergio Jimenez, San Jose city council member; Andrew Byrnes, former chair of the San Mateo Democratic Party; and Sabrina Kochprapha, political consultant.

I would also like to thank my friends on both sides of the Atlantic: David Mikosz, Harry Joel, Karen Routt, Susan Garmo, Karsten Scheibler, Robert Schumann, Angelika Purtell, Patrick Oberlaender, Emily Froemel, Janet Day Strehlow, Shari Temple, Candice Kerestan, and Matt and Kim Hudson. Most importantly, I would like to thank my oldest and dearest friends—Jennifer Blum, Athena Trentin, and Rebecca Perry. Although our lives have taken us all in different directions, they continued to support and encourage me, and I knew they were always only an email or a phone call away.

It would be irresponsible for me to not include my social media community when I thank my friends. Thanks to social media, activists who otherwise felt isolated or helpless in light of the various injustices over the past few years have outlets. It has been reassuring to see the lengths that like-minded people will go to to stand up and affirm others—often people they do not physically know. This book would not have been possible without the support from my #resister family.

I would like to thank my mother's close circle of friends, who served as surrogate mothers to me as a child, and as I grew up served as some of my own closest friends as well, including Mary Black Juntonnen, Lillian Damer, Kriss Ostrom, Carolin Sage, Nancy Lucas, Janet Bordner, and Cindy Stone.

President Obama and Chancellor Merkel often referred to one another as partners and friends. I would like to thank my partner, friend, and the woman who translated the manuscript into German, Désirée Karge. Désirée and her husband immigrated to San Jose, California, from Hamburg, Germany, over twenty years ago, and we were neighbors until my husband and I moved to Germany in 2017. The fact that an American living in Germany wrote an English version of a book translated by a German living in the United States further illustrates the interconnectedness of the United States and Germany.

It is important for me to acknowledge Sophie Karge. Technically Sophie should be acknowledged with the other members of my social media and publicity campaign as she helped me tremendously in that role. However, Sophie served as much more than that, and I think it is only fair to single her out. Not only has Sophie been like the daughter I never had, she is also an amazing resource, excellent social media assistant, and friend as well.

I would like to thank my mother, Judith Clark, who not only instilled in me from a very early age the importance of social justice but also had the patience and tolerance for my many causes. Whether it was my refusing to buy a particular brand of tuna fish because it was not dolphin safe or her taking me to seventeen different stores without complaining when I tried to find an American-made jacket and not one made in a sweatshop in a developing country, she not only supported me, but encouraged me. When she insisted I visit a concentration camp during my first trip to Germany, she taught me the importance of learning from the negative components of the past as well as embracing the victories, like when she and I went to President Clinton's first inauguration in Washington, DC. I was fifteen when my mother was diagnosed with breast cancer and, at the time, she was not certain she would live to see me graduate from high school. Fortunately, thanks to eleven years of remission, she lived long enough to see me not only graduate from high school but college and graduate school as well. She saw me marry and saw most of my milestones—unfortunately, in 2000, she lost her battle with cancer and did not live to see the US elect the first Black president, nor did she live to see any part of this project. Nevertheless, she is still present in this book.

NOTES

INTRODUCTION

1. "if you want a friend in Washington": Nicholas Wapshott, *Ronald Reagan and Margaret Thatcher: A Political Marriage* (New York: Penguin Group, 2007), ix.

2. "touchy": Gregor Peter Schmitz and Gabor Steingart, "Obama and Merkel: The Trans-Atlantic Frenemies," Spiegel Online, June 3, 2009, http://www.spiegel.de/international/world/obama-and -merkel-the-trans-atlantic-frenemies-a-628301-2.html, accessed June 26, 2017.

3. "difficult": Ibid.

4. single tear: Ben Rhodes, *The World as It Is: A Memoir of the Obama White House* (New York: Random House, 2018), xiv.

5. final call: "Merkel receives Obama's final call to a foreign leader," DW, January 19, 2017, https://www.dw.com/en/merkel-receives-obamas-final-call-to-a-foreign-leader/a-37201219, accessed June 1, 2017.

6. "Obama Lands in Berlin for Farewell Visit to Closest Ally Merkel": *China Daily*, November 17, 2016, http://www.chinadaily.com.cn/world/2016-11/17/content_27402257.htm, accessed April 25, 2017.

7. "16 Heartwarming Photos of Barack Obama and Angela Merkel's Friendship": Charles Clark, Business Insider, November 22, 2016, https://www.aol.com/article/news/2016/11/25/16 -heartwarming-photos-of-barack-obama-and-angela-merkels-frien/21612734/#slide =4287211#fullscreen, accessed June 22, 2017.

8. "Now, taking leave from my partner and friend": Remarks by President Obama and Chancellor Merkel of Germany in a Joint Press Conference, German Chancellery, Berlin, Germany, YouTube video, November 17, 2016, https://www.youtube.com/watch?v=WN3Cp7B2ZnE&t=4s, accessed June 30, 2017.

9. "Dans ses adieux": Thomas Wieder, "Dans ses adieux à l'Europe, Obama loue Merkel, 'partenaire extraordinaire,'" *Le Monde*, November 18, 2016, https://www.lemonde.fr/europe/article /2016/11/17/dans-ses-adieux-a-l-europe-obama-loue-merkel-une-partenaire-extraordinaire _5033071_3214.html, accessed June 1, 2017.

10. "There was no foreign leader": Rhodes, *The World As It Is*, 230–231.

11. find Merkel: Matthew Karnitschnig and Edward Issac Dovere, "How Obama Wooed Back Merkel," *Politico*, June 6, 2015, https://www.politico.com/tory/2015/06/how-obama-wooed-back -merkel-118698, accessed January 20, 2018.

12. "one up each other": Ibid.

13. "awkward, cold and unapproachable": Stefan Kornelius, *Angela Merkel: The Chancellor and Her World* (Richmond, UK: Alma Books, 2016), 128.

14. "which of the two European leaders would prove to be": Barack Obama, *A Promised Land* (New York: Crown, 2020), 335.

15. "a genuine international friendship both have leveraged to their own advantage": Kevin Liptak, "How Obama and Merkel Learned to Love One Another," CNN Politics, April 24, 2016, https://www.cnn.com/2016/04/24/politics/barack-obama-angela-merkel-germany-europe, accessed January 31, 2018.

16. "It would be more correct to say that human factors": Kornelius, *Angela Merkel*, 127.

17. They have similar approaches to solving problems: Liptak, "How Obama and Merkel Learned to Love One Another."

18. Furthermore, both leaders are cerebral: Ibid.

19. "the arc of our lives speaks to this spirit": Remarks by President Obama and Chancellor Merkel in Official Arrival Ceremony, YouTube video, June 7, 2011, https://www.youtube.com /watch?v=qBRzUjqZXUE&t=239s, accessed June 15, 2017.

20. "Germany can no longer simply react": Tom O'Connor, "U.S. 'Will Never Be the Same' After Trump, Germany Says," December 5, 2017, https://www.newsweek.com/us-will-never-be -same-after-trump-germany-says-735881.

CHAPTER 1: "THE ARC OF OUR LIVES"

1. "My father was preaching": Matthew Qvortrup, *Angela Merkel: Europe's Most Influential Leader* (New York: Overlook Duckworth Publications, 2016), 39.

2. "Those who do not understand the difference": John F. Kennedy, "*Ich bin ein Berliner*" speech, June 26, 1963, YouTube video, https://www.youtube.com/watch?v=f57Keqijogg, accessed May 24, 2017.

3. "Mr. Gorbachev, tear down this wall": Ronald Reagan's Address at the Brandenburg Gate, June 12, 1987, YouTube video, https://www.youtube.com/watch?v=5MDFX-dNtsM, accessed May 24, 2017.

4. transatlantic relations lie at the heart of German foreign policy: Kornelius, *Angela Merkel*, 118.

5. urgent need for Protestant clergy in the Soviet-occupied zone: Qvortrup, *Angela Merkel*, 27.

6. those who traveled to the East: Ibid.

7. "I would have travelled anywhere": Ibid., 26.

8. When Angela was only eight weeks old: Ibid., 27.

9. rare luxury of owning two cars: Ibid., 44.

10. hosted heated political debates: Andrew Marr, *The Making of Merkel*, BBC, 2013, YouTube video, https://www.youtube.com/watch?v=s0N9_V7wlUw&t=771s, accessed June 1, 2017.

11. as the time they "despoke": Qvortrup, *Angela Merkel*, 28.

12. active file on the minister's every move: Ibid., 32.

13. found it difficult to get accepted into institutions of higher education: Marr, *The Making of Merkel*.

14. participation in the Free German Youth: George Packer, "The Quiet German," *New Yorker*, November 24, 2014, newyorker.com/magazine/2014/12/01/quiet-german.

15. "learning Russian was not just an opportune way": Qvortrup, *Angela Merkel*, 37.

16. "most gifted" . . . qualified for the Russian Language Olympics: Ibid., 53.

17. "I wanted to study physics": Ibid., 64.

18. "I wanted to be away": Ibid., 63.

19. "Work and leisure became indistinguishable and became as one": Ibid., 35.

20. while the two were students at the University of Hawaii: Barack Obama, *Dreams from My Father: A Story of Race and Inheritance* (New York: Three Rivers Press, 1995), 9.

21. he expressed bewilderment: Ibid., 12.

22. His father was killed: Ibid., 5.

23. Barack's parents did not officially divorce: Ibid.

24. his mother taught English for the US embassy: Ibid., 43.

25. "He didn't talk much": Ibid., 38.

26. "his true life lay elsewhere": Ibid., 47.

27. while he ate breakfast: Ibid., 48.

28. treated as a unique individual regardless of race: Ibid., 50.

29. Martin Luther King Jr. and gospel singer Mahalia Jackson: Ibid., 50.

30. "that my father looked nothing like the people": Ibid., 10.

31. oldest private schools west of the Mississippi River, and the best in Hawaii: David Remnick, *The Bridge: The Life and Rise of Barack Obama* (New York: Vintage Books, 2010), 71.

32. tenants' rights organization: Linda Matchan, "Law Review Breakthrough," *Boston Globe*, February 15, 1990, http://archive.boston.com/news/politics/2008/articles/1990/02/15/a_law_review_breakthrough/, accessed December 17, 2017.

33. "stripped of language, stripped of work and routine": Obama, *Dreams from My Father*, 302.

34. two other couples: Qvortrup, *Angela Merkel*, 72.

35. "Suddenly one day she packed her bags": Ibid., 78–79.

36. "The prospect of another twenty-five years": Marr, *The Making of Merkel*.

37. a sauna followed by a beer with a co-worker: Ibid.

38. "young enough": Ibid.

39. "She wanted to use power": Ibid.

40. "the magical experience of new beginnings": Ibid.

41. Marr argued that the million-dollar question: Ibid.

42. first international promise to reduce greenhouse gas emissions: Karl Vick and Simon Shuster, "2015 Person of the Year," *Time*, December 21, 2015, 70.

43. "I knew that I had to fight": Ibid.

44. "We can only build a future": Angela Merkel, editorial, *Frankfurter Allgemeine Zeitung*, December 22, 1989.

45. it would be prudent not to rush into anything: Qvortrup, *Angela Merkel*, 162.

46. "No, I had not concluded": Ibid.

47. surrendered to societal pressure: Ibid.

48. "She doesn't take on fights she can't win": Vick and Shuster, "2015 Person of the Year," 70.

49. publicly called her "pitiful": Ibid.

50. the first woman chancellor, and—at age fifty-one—the youngest: Qvortrup, *Angela Merkel*, 208.

51. announced his candidacy in January 2003: Rick Pearson and Ray Long, "Obama: I'm Running for President," *Chicago Tribune*, February 10, 2007, http://www.chicagotribune.com/news /nationworld/politics/chi-070210obama-pearson1-story-story.html, accessed December 17, 2017.

52. "There's not a liberal America": Barack Obama, "The Audacity of Hope" speech in E. J. Dionne Jr. and Joy-Ann Reid, *We Are the Change We Seek: The Speeches of Barack Obama* (New York: Bloomsbury, 2017), 11.

53. projected themes of hope and change: Ibid.

54. "threatened to derail Obama's insurgent campaign": Obama, "A More Perfect Union" speech in Dionne Jr. and Reid, *We Are the Change We Seek*, 51.

55. its citizens as less than human: Brian Ross and Rehab El-Buri, "Obama's Pastor: God Damn America, U.S. to Blame for 9/11," ABC News, http://abcnews.go.com/Blotter/DemocraticDebate /story?id=4443788&page=1, accessed February 12, 2018.

56. "A More Perfect Union": Obama speech in Dionne Jr. and Reid, *We Are the Change We Seek*, 51.

57. "I am the son of a Black man from Kenya": Ibid., 53.

58. embrace the challenges of their past: Ibid., 63.

59. advance the interests of the entire country: Ibid., 65.

60. "Wars can end": Remarks by President Obama and Chancellor Merkel in Official Arrival Ceremony.

CHAPTER 2: "I TAKE RESPONSIBILITY"

1. "Satan's representative on earth": Kornelius, *Angela Merkel*, 113.

2. "An institution like Guantanamo": Ibid., 120.

3. She and Bush had a close relationship: Dirk Kurbjuweit, "A Difficult Friendship with Obama: A Wall Separates Merkel and the Land of Her Dreams," Spiegel Online, http://www.spiegel.de /international/germany/a-difficult-friendship-with-obama-a-wall-separates-merkel-and-the-land -of-her-dreams-a-688393-druck.html, accessed June 26, 2017.

4. "85 percent of the German population": Ralf Beste, Dirk Kurbjuweit, Christian Schwägerl, and Alexander Szandar, "What the President-Elect Wants from Germany: Obama Win Sparks Hopes and Fears," Spiegel Online, November 10, 2008, http://www.spiegel.de/international /world/what-the-president-elect-wants-from-germany-obama-win-sparks-hopes-and-fears-a -589493.html, accessed June 26, 2017.

5. "a truly great hour": "'A Great Hour for America': Merkel Hopes Obama Will Launch Era of Global Cooperation," Spiegel Online, January 2, 2009, http://www.spiegel.de/international/world /a-great-hour-for-america-merkel-hopes-obama-will-launch-era-of-global-cooperation-a-602289 .html, accessed June 25, 2017.

6. "I hope our cooperation": Ibid.

7. "We took our decisions": Spiegel staff, "Obama Has 'Reactivated American Magnetism,'" Spiegel Online, https://www.spiegel.de/international/world/the-world-from-berlin-obama-has-reactivated-american-magnetism-a-602607.html, accessed June 25, 2017.

8. "There is not even a trace of enthusiasm for the man": Spiegel staff (translated by Christopher Sultan), "Squabbling over Obama: Berlin Split over How to Deal with New US Administration," Spiegel Online, http://www.spiegel.de/international/germany/squabbling-over-obama-berlin-split-over-how-to-deal-with-new-us-administration-a-604990-2.html, accessed June 25, 2017.

9. Obama took every opportunity: Ibid.

10. "The White House of Barack Obama": Ibid.

11. "an overly hasty expression of admiration": Ibid.

12. "she dislikes the atmospherics": David Smith, "Hillary Clinton Was Told Angela Merkel Is Against 'Obama Phenomenon,'" the *Guardian*, December 31, 2015, https://www.theguardian.com/us-news/2015/dec/31/hillary-clinton-emails-angela-merkel-obama-phenomenon.

13. "rude and impolitic": Schmitz and Steingart, "Obama and Merkel: The Trans-Atlantic Frenemies."

14. "buy its way out": Wikileaks, Hillary Clinton Email Archive, "H: New Memo on New German Foreign Minister and Other German Matters. SID," email from Hillary Clinton to Sidney Blumenthal, September 29, 2009, https://wikileaks.org/clinton-emails/emailid/7438, accessed May 25, 2021.

15. staggering 10.1 percent: "Euro zone unemployment reaches 15 million," CBC News, July 2, 2009, https://www.cbc.ca/news/business/euro-zone-unemployment-reaches-15-million-1.846854, accessed September 15, 2017.

16. reached 18.7 percent: "A retrospective-youths bore brunt of recession," Age Discrimination (blog), February 16, 2012, https://www.agediscrimination.info/blog/2012/2/16/a-retrospective-youths-bore-brunt-of-recession, accessed April 9, 2021

17. The group quickly determined: Carsten Volkery, "EU Spring Summit: Gearing Up for the G-18 Conference," Spiegel Online, March 20, 2009, http://www.spiegel.de/international/europe/eu-spring-summit-gearing-up-for-the-g-20-conference-a-614446.html, accessed June 30, 2017.

18. all nations should spend 2 percent of their gross domestic product: Ibid.

19. "profound belief that the Obama administration": Smith, "Hillary Clinton was told Angela Merkel is against 'Obama phenomenon.'"

20. eye-catching headline: Nicholas Kulish and Judy Dempsey, "Merkel Is Set to Greet, and Then Resist, Obama," *New York Times*, March 30, 2009, https://www.nytimes.com/2009/03/30/world/europe/30merkel.html, accessed June 25, 2017.

21. Obama would keep his word: Ibid.

22. "When it comes to the regulation of the financial markets": Carsten Volkery, "G-20 Discord: Merkel and Sarkozy Sharpen Their Tone in London," Spiegel Online, April 2, 2009, http://www.spiegel.de/international/world/g-20-discord-merkel-and-sarkozy-sharpen-their-tone-in-london-a-616963.html, accessed June 26, 2017.

23. anyone who "doesn't understand": Ibid.

24. "Sarkozy and Merkel went on a warpath": Ibid.

25. "What Merkel is saying makes it sound": Cristina Kirchner, Marc Hujer, Wolfgang Reuter, and Christoph Schwennicke, "'I Take Responsibility': Obama's G-20 Confession," Spiegel Online, April 6, 2009, http://www.spiegel.de/international/world/i-take-responsibility-obama-s-g-20 -confession-a-617639.html, accessed June 1, 2017.

26. "Nicolas, keep in mind": Ibid.

27. published by the OECD: Ibid.

28. The results produced at the London summit were by no means perfect: Ibid.

29. the world leaders at the summit had avoided open conflict: Ibid.

30. Obama had an obligation: Ibid.

31 "It is true": Ibid

32. Merkel immediately telephoned: Ibid.

33. "It is important that we do not sell short the results": Ibid.

34. "very, very good compromise": Ibid.

35. In fact, he had not even: Erik Krischbaum, "Special Report: Don't Call Him Mr. Merkel," Reuters, May 16, 2012, https://www.reuters.com/article/us-germany-sauer/special-report-dont -call-him-mr-merkel-idUSBRE84F07420120516, accessed January 12, 2018.

36. "Phantom of the Opera": Ibid.

37. "we're pleased to have you": "The President's News Conference with Chancellor Angela Merkel of Germany in Baden-Baden, Germany," April 3, 2009, https://www.presidency.ucsb.edu /documents/the-presidents-news-conference-with-chancellor-angela-merkel-germany-baden-baden -germany, accessed March 29, 2018.

38. "the United States has shown that they are willing": Ibid.

39. "pushed our unemployment rate to 8.5 percent": Ibid.

40. "the US will remain the largest consumer market": Ibid.

41. "If NATO becomes everything": Ibid.

42. "You just heard Chancellor Merkel": Ibid.

43. "What does this mean": Ibid.

44. "I think that was an indication": Ibid.

45. "I want to thank Chancellor Merkel": Ibid.

46. "Americans are more willing": Hans W. Gatzke, Germany and the United States: A "Special Relationship"? (Cambridge: Harvard University Press, 1980), 24.

47. "Compliments are not in keeping": Lisa Schwesig, Frage & Antwort, Nr. 517, "Warum vermeiden Deutsche Komplimente?" January 23, 2018, https://www.n-tv.de/wissen/frageantwort /Warum-vermeiden-Deutsche-Komplimente-article20224273.html, accessed March 20, 2018.

48. "The US president, whose initial goal": Matthias Gebauer, "Agreement Reached on Rasmussen: Obama Saves NATO Governments from Summit Shame," Spiegel Online, April 4, 2004, http://www.spiegel.de/international/europe/agreement-reached-on-rasmussen-obama-saves -nato-governments-from-summit-shame-a-617478.html, accessed June 26, 2017.

NOTES

CHAPTER 3: "WILD SPECULATIONS"

1. "one based on mutual interest": Barack Obama, "A New Beginning," in E. J. Dionne Jr. and Joy-Ann Reid, *We Are the Change We Seek: The Speeches of Barack Obama* (New York: Bloomsbury, 2017), 122.

2. "to listen to each other": Ibid.

3. the United States and Israel share: Ibid., 129–130.

4. the only reasonable solution to this decades-old crisis: Ibid., 130.

5. would benefit not only the Israelis and the Palestinians: Ibid.

6. the United States could not force peace: Ibid.

7. a list of steps: Ibid.

8. Palestinians needed to abandon violence: Ibid.

9. "It is time for us to act": Ibid.,132.

10. "no single nation should pick": Ibid., 133.

11. resulted in the deaths: "The Battle of Dresden," History, https://www.history.com/topics /world-war-ii/battle-of-dresden, accessed March 30, 2018.

12. "an important event": Helma Orosz, "The US President in Germany: Obama Plans to Visit Important WWII Symbols," Spiegel Online, June 4, 2009, http://www.spiegel.de/international /germany/the-us-president-in-germany-obama-plans-to-visit-important-wwii-symbols-a-628499 .html, accessed June 26, 2017.

13. Some Germans viewed the decision as a slight: Ibid.

14. "Dresden: Next Stop": John Hinderaker, "Dresden: Next Stop On Apology Tour?," Power Line (blog), June 2, 2009, http://www.powerlineblog.com/?s=Dresden%3A+next+stop&x=0&y=0, accessed March 30, 2018.

15. "It is so important": Obama and Merkel Remarks at Dresden Press Conference, June 5, 2009, EAWorldView, http://enduringamerica.squarespace.com/june-2009/2009/6/5/video-and -transcript-obama-and-merkel-remarks-at-dresden-pre.html, accessed June 25, 2017.

16. "President Obama yesterday gave a very important speech": Ibid.

17. "Germany will try its utmost": Ibid.

18. "You have a very ambitious plan": Ibid.

19. "We know that it's very much an uphill battle": Ibid.

20. "the beautiful city of Dresden": Ibid.

21. "Germany is a close friend": Ibid.

22. "I think on both sides of the Atlantic": Ibid.

23. importance of NATO: Ibid.

24. "It is a great pleasure": Ibid.

25. "wild speculations": Ibid.

26. "So stop it, all of you": Ibid.

27. "Allow me, if I may": Ibid.

28. "Chancellor Merkel has been open to discussions": Ibid.

29. "I am absolutely confident": Ibid.

30. "I very much appreciate Chancellor Merkel's willingness": Ibid.

31. "I believe that with the new American administration": Ibid.

32. both Israel and the Palestinians had to be willing: Ibid.

33. signature foreign policy items: Ibid.

34. he specifically chose Buchenwald: Gregor Peter Schmitz, "Planned Visit to Dresden: Obama to Trace Family History in Germany," Spiegel Online, May 6, 2009, http://www.spiegel .de/international/germany/planned-visit-to-dresden-obama-to-trace-family-history-in-germany -a-623130.html, accessed June 26, 2017.

35. "[T]his is for me deeply moving": Obama and Merkel Remarks at Dresden Press Conference.

36. "It's March weather in June": "Obama's Buchenwald Visit," Spiegel Online, June 5, 2009, http://www.spiegel.de/international/germany/obama-s-buchenwald-visit-these-sights-have-lost -none-of-their-horror-a-628887.html, accessed June 26, 2017.

37. An emotional Merkel: Ibid.

38. "This appeal of the survivors defines the very special responsibility": Remarks by President Obama, German Chancellor Merkel, and Elie Wiesel at Buchenwald Concentration Camp, June 5, 2009, https://www.ushmm.org/wlc/en/article.php?ModuleId=10007827, accessed June 25, 2017.

39. "It gives me an opportunity": Ibid.

40. A visibly emotional President Obama: President Obama Visits Buchenwald Concentration Camp, YouTube video, June 9, 2009, https://www.youtube.com/watch?v=7VxXZby4shw, accessed June 25, 2017.

41. memorials such as Buchenwald remind people: Ibid.

42. Obama emphasized the prisoners' resilience: Ibid.

43. "the strong, enduring bonds between that great nation": Ibid.

44. "it is now up to us, the living": Ibid.

45. "I want to express particular thanks to Chancellor Merkel": Ibid.

CHAPTER 4: "SEA CHANGE"

1. "return to rational polices": "'Two Different Worlds': Merkel Wants More on Climate from Obama," Spiegel Online, June 25, 2009, http://www.spiegel.de/international/world/two-different -worlds-merkel-wants-more-on-climate-from-obama-a-632566.html, accessed June 25, 2017.

2. If members of the press corps: Gregor Peter Schmitz, "A Trans-Atlantic Show of Friendship: Obama Praises His 'Friend Chancellor Merkel'": Spiegel Online, June 27, 2009, http://www.spiegel .de/international/world/a-trans-atlantic-show-of-friendship-obama-praises-his-friend-chancellor -merkel-a-632961.html, accessed June 26, 2017.

3. mentioned her "leadership," "candor," and "wisdom": Ibid.

4. "Chancellor Merkel's visit is the latest chapter in the long partnership between our two countries": Obama and Merkel Remarks at Washington Press Conference, YouTube video, June 26, 2009, https://www.youtube.com/watch?v=F5DS0yXc48A&t=44s, accessed June 26, 2017.

5. "Chancellor Merkel shares my belief": Ibid.

6. "Merkel's commitment to reform": Ibid.

7. Germany and the other EU countries: Spiegel Online, "'Two Different Worlds': Merkel Wants More on Climate from Obama."

8. "The 40 percent below": Ibid.

9. Environmentalists in Germany expected Merkel to use her influence to convince Obama: Ibid.

10. "We have the impression": Ibid.

11. 17 percent from 2005 levels by 2020: Ibid.

12. According to a report by the US Environmental Protection Agency: United States Environmental Protection Agency, "Inventory of US Greenhouse Gas Emissions and Sinks," https://www.epa.gov/ghgemissions/inventory-us-greenhouse-gas-emissions-and-sinks, accessed May 27, 2018.

13. The legislation also called for measures: Suzanne Goldenberg, "Barack Obama Pleads with Congress to Pass Historic Climate Change Bill," the *Guardian*, June 25, 2009, https://www .theguardian.com/environment/2009/jun/25/barack-obama-climate-change-bill, accessed March 29, 2018.

14. "The stakes could not be higher": Ibid.

15. Yet not a single Republican House member: Ibid.

16. "We have been talking about this issue": Ibid.

17. The legislation failed to meet: Environmental Protection Agency, "Inventory of US Greenhouse Gas Emissions and Sinks."

18. "live in two different worlds": Spiegel Online, "'Two Different Worlds': Merkel Wants More on Climate from Obama."

19. "And let me say": Obama and Merkel Remarks at Washington Press Conference, June 26, 2009.

20. "a sea change ": Ibid.

21. The chancellor mentioned that she had gone through similar debates: Ibid.

22. "I think it's so important": Ibid.

23. "The issue at stake": Farhang Jahanpour, "Iran's Stolen Election, and What Comes Next," Open Democracy, June 18, 2009, https://www.opendemocracy.net/en/iran-s-stolen-election-and -what-comes-next, accessed March 29, 2018.

24. Things had grown so out of control: Ibid.

25. "Today we speak with one voice": Obama and Merkel Remarks at Washington Press Conference, June 26, 2009.

26. coordination between China, Russia, Germany, and the other EU nations: Ibid.

27. two-state solution to one of the biggest problems in the Middle East: Ibid.

28. "And during our recent visit to Buchenwald": Ibid.

29. "I would like to underline that the Iranian people": Ibid.

30. "we have to work": Ibid.

31. "We need Russia, for example": Ibid.

32. "We're on a good path here": Ibid.

33. "Meeting these challenges": Ibid.

34. "And we're more than aware": Ibid.

35. At one point: Ibid.

36. "If this is a commitment": Ibid.

37. "We have to talk about that": Ibid.

38. "I will always have, I think, a warm spot in my heart": Ibid.

39. "My sister, she obviously had a great time": Ibid.

40. "Let me perhaps say something": Ibid.

41. Waxman–Markey American Clean Energy and Security Act by a vote of 219–212: John J. Harsh, "House Passes Waxman/Markey Climate Bill in 219–212 Vote," *Agri-Pulse*, June 26, 2009, https://www.agri-pulse.com/ext/resources/pdfs/2/0/0/h/1/20090626H1.pdf, accessed February 1, 2018.

42. "Today, the House of Representatives": Politico Staff, "POTUS Hails 'Historic Action,'" *Politico*, June 26, 2009, http://www.politico.com/politico44/perm/0609/obama_on_climate_change _bill_6b12b7be-33da-45a1-8460-407370756ca4.html, accessed February 1, 2018.

CHAPTER 5: "WE HAVE NO TIME TO LOSE!"

1. "The US is a republic and a relatively new country": Michael Knigge, "Honor, Yes, but Tough Questions Also Await Merkel in Washington," DW, November 1, 2009, http://www.dw .com/en/honor-yes-but-tough-questions-also-await-merkel-in-washington/a-4841338, accessed March 30, 2018.

2. Merkel would address both houses: Ibid.

3. The headline for one article: Ibid.

4. "Beneath all the symbolism": Ibid.

5. despite the good "chemistry" between Merkel and Obama: Ibid.

6. "Now when practical policies are key": Ibid.

7. "She is going to be the first German chancellor": President Obama and German Chancellor Merkel, November 3, 2009, https://www.c-span.org/video/?289769-1/us-germany-relations, accessed June 26, 2017.

8. "We are now moving towards the twentieth anniversary": Ibid.

9. he emphasized his gratitude for: Ibid.

10. "Chancellor Merkel has been an extraordinary leader": Ibid.

11. "And on economic issues": Ibid.

12. "working with her as a partner": Ibid.

13. "I would also like to say": Ibid.

14. "I am also very much looking forward": Ibid.

15. "I think what she said was good": Ibid.

16. "The Wall, barbed wire, and the order to shoot": Angela Merkel, "Angela Merkel's 2009 Speech to the US Congress," The German Way & More website, https://www.german-way.com /notable-people/featured-bios/angela-merkel/angela-merkels-2009-speech-to-the-us-congress/, accessed June 25, 2017.

17. "This speech was bigger than": Gabor Steingart, "Bravo, Chancellor Merkel: A Timely Commitment to America," Spiegel Online, November 4, 2009, http://www.spiegel.de/international /europe/bravo-chancellor-merkel-a-timely-commitment-to-america-a-659184.html, accessed March 30, 2018.

18. "more clearly than any other head of state": Ibid.

19. "Ladies and gentlemen, to sum it up in one sentence": Chancellor Merkel Addresses Congress (2) on World Issues, Meets with President Obama, YouTube video, November 3, 2009, https://www.youtube.com/watch?v=PMP2G97yR_g, accessed June 25, 2017.

20. "we had to do everything we could": "Angela Merkel's 2009 Speech to the US Congress" The German Way & More.

21. promised that allied nations would be successful: Ibid.

22. "Human dignity shall be inviolable": Ibid.

23. "Zero tolerance": Ibid.

24. "Israel's security will never be open to negotiation": Ibid.

25. as important as freedom is: Ibid.

26. "need to resist the pressure of those who almost led the nations": Ibid.

27. "to prevent competing subsidies": Ibid.

28. "to prepare for the United Nations summit": Jennifer Abramsohn, "Merkel Gives Historic Address to US Congress," DW, November 3, 2009, http://www.dw.com/en/merkel-gives-historic -address-to-us-congress/a-4851428?maca=en-rss-en-top-1022-rdf, accessed March 30, 2018.

29. "a wall . . . separating the present from the future": "Angela Merkel's 2009 Speech to the US Congress," The German Way & More.

30. "In the Arctic icebergs are melting": Ibid.

31. "I am pleased that you in your work": Ibid

32. the camera showed the reactions: Chancellor Merkel Addresses Congress (4) on World Issues, Meets with President Obama, YouTube video, November 3, 2009, https://www.youtube .com/watch?v=fIhFhnPPxHk&t=327s, accessed June 25, 2017.

33. "agree on one objective": "Angela Merkel's 2009 Speech to the US Congress," The German Way & More.

34. "A gift from American citizens": Chancellor Merkel Addresses Congress (4) on World Issues, Meets with President Obama, November 3, 2009.

35. "She reportedly lacked charisma": "What public speakers can learn from Angela Merkel," LeadershipCommunications, December 9, 2015, https://www.gingerleadershipcomms.com /article/what-public-speakers-can-learn-from-angela-merkel, accessed April 18, 2021.

36. "With this speech": Steingart, "Bravo, Chancellor Merkel."

37. "The USA's role at the conference": Abramsohn, "Merkel Gives Historic Address to US Congress."

38. joint but differentiated responsibility: "Introduction to Climate Finance," United Nations Climate Change, https://unfccc.int/topics/climate-finance/the-big-picture/introduction-to-climate-finance/introduction-to-climate-finance, accessed April 18, 2021.

39. both countries continued to pollute: Fiona Harvey, "The Kyoto Protocol is not Quite Dead," the *Guardian*, November 26, 2012, https://www.theguardian.com/environment/2012/nov/26/kyoto-protocol-not-dead, accessed June 30, 2017.

40. "remain[ed] an international frontrunner": Umwelt Bundesamt, "Germany Met Its Kyoto Protocol Climate Protection Obligations in 2008," Joint Press Release by the German Federal Ministry for the Environment, Nature Conservation, and Nuclear Safety (BMU), February 1, 2010, https://www.umweltbundesamt.de/en/press/pressinformation/germany-met-its-kyoto-protocol-climate-protection, accessed June 30, 2017.

41. "Obama is taking the United States in a new direction": Gerald Traufetter, "Copenhagen Climate Cables: The US and China Joined Forces Against Europe," Spiegel Online, December 8, 2010, https://www.spiegel.de/international/world/copenhagen-climate-cables-the-us-and-china-joined-forces-against-europe-a-733630.html, accessed March 16, 2021.

42. "consistent with keeping the increase": Ibid.

43. "The time has come": "Obama's Remarks on the Climate Agreement," *New York Times*, December 18, 2009, https://www.nytimes.com/2009/12/19/science/earth/19climate.text.html, accessed June 10, 2018.

44. "collective commitment": "15th Session of the Conference of the Parties to the United Nations Framework Convention on Climate Change," Center for Climate and Energy Solutions, 2009, https://www.c2es.org/content/cop-15-copenhagen/, accessed July 1, 2017.

45. named other factors: "Why Did Copenhagen Fail to Deliver a Climate Deal?" BBC News, December 22, 2009, http://news.bbc.co.uk/2/hi/8426835.stm, accessed July 1, 2017.

46. "the lowest level of ambition": John Vidal, Allegra Stratton, and Suzanne Goldenberg, "Low Targets, Goal Dropped: Copenhagen Ends in Failure," the *Guardian*, December 18, 2009, https://www.theguardian.com/environment/2009/dec/18/copenhagen-deal, accessed June 10, 2018

CHAPTER 6: "DEAR BARACK"

1. Germany had voted against the West: Russell A. Berman, "Angela Merkel Gets Medal of Freedom Despite German-US Rift," Daily Beast, June 5, 2011, updated April 24, 2017, https://www.thedailybeast.com/angela-merkel-gets-medal-of-freedom-despite-german-us-rift, accessed April 8, 2018.

2. "When German Chancellor Angela Merkel meets with President Obama": Ibid.

3. "Sometimes praise is harder to bear": Kristen Allen, "The World from Berlin: Merkel and Obama 'More Similar Than They Like to Admit,'" Spiegel Online, June 9, 2011, http://www.spiegel.de/international/europe/the-world-from-berlin-merkel-and-obama-more-similar-than-they-like-to-admit-a-767673.html, accessed June 25, 2017.

4. "the excessive American hospitality": Ibid.

5. With US unemployment still high at 9.1 percent : "Obama Presses Europe, Pledges Help for Greek Crisis": *Newsmaxfinance*, June 8, 2011, https://www.newsmax.com/Finance/Headline /Obama-Presses-Europe-Greek/2011/06/08/id/399228/, accessed April 8, 2018.

6. friendships arise as a result of open communications: Allen, "The World from Berlin."

7. "her stolid appearance": Barack Obama, *A Promised Land* (New York: Crown, 2020), 335.

8. "The pragmatic Americans": Allen, "The World from Berlin."

9. "the most successful alliance in human history": Germany Official Visit Arrival Ceremony, YouTube video, June 7, 2011, https://www.youtube.com/watch?v=qBRzUjqZXUE&t=193s, accessed June 30, 2017.

10. "one of my closest global partners": Ibid.

11. "As people around the world": Ibid.

12. "Madam Chancellor": Ibid.

13. "Dear Sir Mr. President": Angela Merkel, "Speech by the Chancellor at the Welcome Ceremony at the White House," Die Bundeskanzlerin website, June 7, 2011, https://www .bundeskanzlerin.de/bkin-de/aktuelles/rede-der-bundeskanzlerin-bei-der-begruessungszeremonie -am-weissen-haus-418670, accessed January 1, 2019.

14. "is just as much part": Germany Official Visit Arrival Ceremony, June 7, 2011.

15. "Mr. President, dear Barack, in Berlin in 2008": Ibid.

16. Even though Merkel's English: Matthew Karnitschnig and Edward-Isaac Dovere, "How Obama Wooed Back Merkel," *Politico*, June 6, 2016, https://www.politico.com/story/2015/06 /how-obama-wooed-back-merkel-118698.

17. "We had a wonderful dinner last night": President Obama and Chancellor Merkel Press Conference, YouTube video, June 7, 2011, https://www.youtube.com/watch?v=m3rPHBvrYsU, accessed June 30, 2017.

18. He acknowledged the alliance: Ibid.

19. He emphasized the "essence" of that alliance: "two peoples": Ibid.

20. "Angela, I believe this is our tenth": Ibid.

21. "Germany is one of our largest trading partners": Ibid.

22. "The chancellor and I have been clear": Ibid.

23. Obama acknowledged his profound respect: Ibid.

24. "Mr. President, dear Barack": Ibid.

25. "Barack, thank you very much": Ibid.

26. tax breaks for certain business: Ibid.

27. "we've seen over the last fifteen months": Ibid.

28. After more than fourteen hours: Alan Crawford and Tony Czuczka, *Angela Merkel: A Chancellorship Forged in Crisis* (West Sussex, UK: Bloomberg Press, 2013), 63–64.

29. "We are on the path": President Obama and Chancellor Merkel Press Conference, June 7, 2011.

30. "We are very well aware of our responsibility": Ibid.

31. "We've seen how interdependent we are": Ibid.

32. "Germany is going to be a key leader": Ibid.

33. "On the international stage": Ibid.

34. "As far as the situation in the United States": Ibid.

35. "[W]hat's also important in this context": Ibid.

36. "a tough and complicated piece of business": Ibid.

37. "Greece has to grow": Ibid.

38. "[We] will be there for you": Ibid.

39. "ward off the worst that could have happened": Ibid.

40. G20 had proved: Ibid.

41. "I think that shows great openness": Ibid.

42. she believed Gaddafi needed to step down: Ibid.

43. "What's important": Ibid.

44. he had not visited Berlin: Kornelius, *Angela Merkel*, 130.

45. "Berlin opens its arms to him every day": President Obama and Chancellor Merkel Press Conference, June 7, 2011.

46. "And I can promise that the Brandenburg Gate will be standing": Ibid.

47. "Sooooo, it's Angela and Barack now": Manuel Roig-Franzia, "Germany's Angela Merkel and President Obama on Friendly Terms during State Visit," *Washington Post*, June 7, 2011, https://www.washingtonpost.com/lifestyle/style/germanys-angela-merkel-and-president-obama-on-friendly-terms-during-state-visit/2011/06/07/AGpPaQLH_story.html?utm_term=.15963a665c64, accessed June 25, 2017.

48. "That's quite a leap in coziness": Ibid.

49. "for a true and lasting *Freundschaft*": Hans W. Gatzke, *Germany and the United States: "A Special Relationship"?* (Cambridge: Harvard University Press, 1980), 2.

50. guest list comprised 208 dignitaries: Kornelius, *Angela Merkel*, 135.

51. "Phantom of the Opera": Erik Kirschbaum, "Special Report: Don't Call Him Mr. Merkel," Reuters, May 16, 2012, https://www.reuters.com/article/us-germany-sauer/special-report-dont-call-him-mr-merkel-idUSBRE84F07420120516, accessed January 12, 2018.

52. "He really treasures you, Angela": Karnitschnig and Dovere, "How Obama Wooed Back Merkel."

53. Merkel joined the ranks: State Dinner for German Chancellor Merkel, YouTube video, June 7, 2011, https://www.youtube.com/watch?v=yfDSfKBHgj8&t=6s, accessed June 22, 2017.

54. "We want to pay tribute to an extraordinary leader": Ibid.

55. Obama then described Merkel's first political experience: Ibid.

56. "Determined to finally have her say": Ibid.

57. "spoke not only to the dreams": Ibid.

58. "Mr. President, dear Barack": Ibid.

59. "Seeing the grownups around me": Ibid.

60. "But imagining that I would one day": Ibid.

61. "My thanks go to the American people": Ibid.

62. "Also today, the yearning for freedom": Ibid.

63. "Neither the chains of dictatorship": Ibid.

64. "the finale to such occasions": Kornelius, *Angela Merkel*, 135.

65. Despite all of the ceremonial activities: Ibid, 136.

66. She told the financier: Qvortrup, *Angela Merkel*, 286.

67. "almost jubilant": Ibid.

68. "I am very aware that the world's attention": Ibid.

69. described as a "breakthrough": Ibid, 287.

70. she received a telephone call: Ibid.

71. Speculation was rife that Greece would leave the eurozone: Ibid.

72. referendum was canceled: Ibid.

73. "It's wonderful to be back together": Remarks by President Obama and Chancellor Angela Merkel of Germany Before Bilateral Meeting, Cannes, France, November 3, 2011, https://ua.usembassy.gov/remarks-president-obama-chancellor-angela-merkel-germany-joint -press-conference/.

74. "And without Angela's leadership": Ibid.

75. "political execution": Kornelius, *Angela Merkel*, 128.

76. Reagan had been under constant attack: Richard Aldous, *Ronald Reagan and Margaret Thatcher* (New York: W. W. Norton & Company, 2012), 148.

77. "Pierre, you're being obnoxious": Ibid.

78. "She and Reagan formed": Ibid., 50.

79. The problem remained unresolved: Qvortrup, *Angela Merkel*, 288.

CHAPTER 7: "WE HAVE HISTORY TO MAKE"

1. Merkel used the more familiar pronoun: Watch Angela Merkel and Barack Obama's Remarks from Brandenburg Gate in Berlin, YouTube video, June 19, 2013, https://www.youtube .com/watch?v=qryJNyDV81U&t=868s, accessed July 1, 2017.

2. She, as usual, emphasized the many years of friendship: "Remarks by President Obama and German Chancellor Merkel in Joint Press Conference," June 19, 2013, https://obamawhitehouse .archives.gov/the-press-office/2013/06/19/remarks-president-obama-and-german-chancellor -merkel-joint-press-confere, accessed July 1, 2017.

3. "our American partners": Ibid.

4. "But we also see that the world": Ibid.

5. "We will throw our effort behind": Ibid.

6. "This is a process": Ibid.

7. "the humbling privilege": Ibid.

8. "When he learned about this": Rhodes, *The World as It Is*, 23.

9. "I've always appreciated the warmth": "Remarks by President Obama and German Chancellor Merkel in Join Press Conference," June 19, 2013.

10. Obama reminded the press: Ibid.

11. rumors within the international community: Ibid.

12. responsible for negotiating treaties with other nations: "Role in The International Arena," Der Bundespräsident, https://www.bundespraesident.de/EN/Role-and-Functions /RoleInTheInternationalArena/roleintheinternationalarena-node.html.

13. "Sometimes there's been talk": "Remarks by President Obama and German Chancellor Merkel in Joint Press Conference," June 19, 2013.

14. thirteen million Europeans and Americans: Ibid.

15. that it would benefit everyone: Ibid.

16. "Our men and women have been serving side-by-side": Ibid.

17. "And I appreciate Germany's interest": Ibid.

18. "We are united": Ibid.

19. "I cannot and will not comment on specifics": Ibid.

20. "Germany has very clear": Ibid.

21. "Madam Chancellor, the Nobel Prize winner": Ibid.

22. "One thing with respect to drone policy": Ibid.

23. "Let me complement": Ibid.

24. "dear Barack Obama": Watch Angela Merkel and Barack Obama's Remarks from Brandenburg Gate in Berlin, YouTube video, June 19, 2013, https://www.youtube.com /watch?v=qryJNyDV81U&t=845s, accessed July 1, 2017.

25. "able to greet": Ibid.

26. "Not yet": Ibid.

27. "[A]lso in the twenty-first century": Ibid.

28. "from a child of the East": Ibid.

29. "As I've said": Ibid.

30. Merkel, who laughed joyously: Ibid.

31. "A rebuilt Reichstag": Ibid.

32. "to stand on the Eastern side": Ibid.

33. "to say complacency is not the character": Ibid.

34. Merkel and Wowereit looked at each other: Ibid.

35. "lift our eyes": Ibid.

36. "When Europe and America lead": Ibid.

37. "example we set here at home": Ibid.

38. "The Wall belongs to history": Ibid.

39. "I'm able to say this": Tischreden von Angela Merkel und Barack Obama beim gemeinsamen Abendessen im Schloss Charlottenburg, YouTube video, June 19, 2013, https://www.youtube.com/watch?v=_Mss9_SOMBM, accessed January 3, 2018.

40. "Barack Obama, I think what was possible": Ibid.

41. "We've come a long way": Ibid.

42. thanking "Angela": Ibid.

43. emphasized the gratitude: Ibid.

44. "Now, on a very personal level": Ibid.

45. "Here in Berlin": Ibid.

CHAPTER 8: "FRIENDS SPYING ON EACH OTHER IS NOT ACCEPTABLE"

1. had monitored thirty-eight embassies and the phones of thirty-five world leaders: "Edward Snowden: Leaks That Exposed US Spy Programme," BBC, January 17, 2014, https://www.bbc.com/news/world-us-canada-23123964, accessed January 29, 2018.

2. collecting the telephone records of tens of millions: Ibid.

3. directly tapped into the servers: Ibid.

4. the NSA used a myriad of spying methods: Ibid.

5. "The NSA does NOT target": Laura Poitras, Marcel Rosenbach, Fidelius Schmid, Holger Stark, and Jonathan Stock, "How the NSA Targets Germany and Europe," Spiegel Online, July 1, 2013, http://www.spiegel.de/international/world/secret-documents-nsa-targeted-germany-and-eu-buildings-a-908609.html, accessed August 1, 2017.

6. Germany, along with many other EU nations: Ibid.

7. "The Americans are collecting metadata": Ibid.

8. "We probably put more listening posts in Germany": Ibid.

9. "The NSA's totalitarian ambition": Laura Poitras, Marcel Rosenbach, and Holger Stark, "Friends or Foes?: Berlin Must Protect Germans from US Spying," Spiegel Online, July 1, 2013, http://www.spiegel.de/international/world/why-nsa-spying-program-must-be-independently-investigated-a-908726.html, accessed February 12, 2018.

10. "The monitoring of friends": Ibid.

11. democracies frequently relied on intelligence agencies: "Merkel Speaks: Chancellor Defends Intelligence Monitoring," Spiegel Online, July 10, 2013, http://www.spiegel.de/international/germany/german-chancellor-merkel-defends-work-of-intelligence-agencies-a-910491.html, accessed June 26, 2017.

12. "America is and has been our truest ally": Ibid.

13. waste of time and resources: Karnitschnig and Dovere, "How Obama Wooed Back Merkel."

14. "For me, there is absolutely no comparison": James Kendrick, "The NSA's an America Stasi? Outrageous," New York Daily News, July 17, 2013, https://www.nydailynews.com/opinion/absurd-attempts-call-nsa-american-stasi-article-1.1400317.

15. many European allies, including Germany and France, had mixed feelings: Adrian Croft and Arshad Mohammed, "France Summons U.S. Ambassador over Spying Report," Reuters, October 21, 2013 , https://www.reuters.com/article/us-france-nsa-idUSBRE99K04920131021, accessed April 29, 2021.

16 French president François Hollande cautioned the United States: Michael Mainville, "France warns US spying claims threaten trade talks," AFP Yahoo News, July 1, 2013, https://sg.news.yahoo .com/frances-hollande-tells-us-immediately-stop-spying-005339477.html, accessed April 29, 2021.

17. "We cannot accept this kind of behavior": Ibid.

18. "she did ask US President Barack Obama": Croft and Mohammed, "France Summons U.S. Ambassador."

19. they emphasized the close and valued partnership: "EU–US Spying Row Stokes Concern over Anti-Terror Campaign," EU Business News, https://www.eubusiness.com/news-eu/us -intelligence.r38, accessed April 29, 2021.

20. "must be based on respect and trust": Ibid.

21. "the encroachment on privacy": Kate Connolly, "Barack Obama: NSA Is Not Rifling through Ordinary People's Emails," the Guardian, June 19, 2013, https://www.theguardian.com /world/2013/jun/19/barack-obama-nsa-people-emails, accessed February 20, 2018.

22. "rifling through ordinary emails of German citizens": Ibid.

23. "Free, liberal democracies": President Obama and Chancellor Merkel Hold a Press Conference, YouTube video, June 19, 2013, https://www.youtube.com/watch?v=p1-omSNkDLk, accessed July 20, 2017.

24. Merkel called Obama: "Obama Assures Merkel Her Phone Will Not Be Monitored, Says White House," the Guardian, October 24, 2013, YouTube video, https://www.youtube.com/watch?v =PLIb7E7mq7E, accessed January 30, 2018.

25. he neither confirmed nor denied: Ibid.

26. German foreign minister: "Embassy Espionage: The NSA's Secret Spy Hub in Berlin," Spiegel Online, October 27, 2013, http://www.spiegel.de/international/germany/cover-story-how -nsa-spied-on-merkel-cell-phone-from-berlin-embassy-a-930205.html, accessed March 3, 2018.

27. "In any previous cases of displeasure": James Rosen, "US Ambassador to Germany Summoned over Merkel Phone Monitoring Claims," Fox News Politics, October 24, 2013, http://www.foxnews.com/politics/2013/10/24/germany-says-us-may-have-monitored-merkel -cellphone.html, accessed March 4, 2018.

28. "Friends spying on each other is not acceptable": "Angela Merkel Phone Bugging: 'Spying on Friends Is Not Acceptable,'" the Guardian, YouTube video, October 25, 2013, https://www .youtube.com/watch?v=GC-YPXXNMVU, accessed February 1, 2018.

29. she was more bewildered: Karnitschnig and Dovere, "How Obama Wooed Back Merkel."

30. "Our efforts will only be effective": Transcript of President Obama's Jan. 17 [2014] speech on NSA Reforms, Washington Post, https://www.washingtonpost.com/politics/full-text-of -president-obamas-jan-17-speech-on-nsa-reforms/2014/01/17/fa33590a-7f8c-11e3-9556- 4a4bf7bcbd84_story.html?utm_term=.cfd2ec0ffed9, accessed March 3, 2018.

31. "Just as [we] balance security and privacy at home": Ibid.

32. "uses signals intelligence": Ibid.

33. use bulk collection of signals intelligence: Ibid.

34. "extending certain protections": Ibid.

35. directed his attorney general: Ibid.

36. "This applies to foreign leaders as well": Ibid.

37. "skeptical, guarded, disappointed": Andrew Kaczynski, "Obama on NSA: 'It's Going to Take Some Time to Win Back Trust,'" BuzzFeed, January 19, 2014, https://www.buzzfeednews.com/article/andrewkaczynski/obama-on-nsa-its-going-to-take-some-time-to-win-back-trust.

38. Obama acknowledged that it would take time: Ibid.

39. Obama conceded that: Ibid.

40. two Germans: Ben Brumfield, "Germany Tells Top US Spy Official to Leave the Country," CNN, July 11, 2014, https://edition.cnn.com/2014/07/11/world/europe/germany-us-spying-investigation/index.html, accessed March 7, 2018.

41. "It's a punitive gesture": Ibid.

42. "unconscionable provocations": Karnitschnig and Dovere, "How Obama Wooed Back Merkel."

43. "This last point was important for Merkel": Ibid.

44. the BND (Bundesnachrichtendienst), may have known: Maik Baumgärtner, Martin Knobbe, and Jörg Schindler, "Spying Scandal: German Intelligence Also Snooped on White House," Spiegel Online, June 22, 2017, http://www.spiegel.de/international/germany/german-intelligence-also-snooped-on-white-house-a-1153592.html, accessed March 11, 2018.

45. The BND used thousands of search terms: Ibid.

46. the BND spied on: "Governments and NGOs: Germany Spied on Friends and Vatican," Spiegel Online, November 7, 2015, http://www.spiegel.de/international/germany/german-bnd-intelligence-spied-on-friends-and-vatican-a-1061588.html, accessed March 11, 2018.

47. "People either knew or likely suspected": Baumgärtner, Knobbe, and Schindler, "Spying Scandal: German Intelligence Also Snooped on White House."

48. "From a common sense standpoint": Brumfield, "Germany Tells Top US Spy Official to Leave the Country."

CHAPTER 9: "A FEW DIFFICULTIES YET TO OVERCOME"

1. The trouble in Ukraine began: Qvortrup, Angela Merkel, 293.

2. Yanukovych blamed oppositional leaders: Ibid.

3. Yanukovych fled Kiev: Ibid.

4. Russian-speaking troops: Ibid.

5. Putin argued that Ukraine: Nicolas Miletitch and Dmitry Zaks, "Putin: Ukraine Is 'On the Verge of Civil War,'" Business Insider, April 15, 2014, https://www.businessinsider.com/putin-ukraine-civil-war-2014-4?IR=T, accessed February 12, 2018.

6. The United States and the European Union imposed: Haroon Siddique, Tom McCarthy, and Alan Yuhas, "Ukraine Crisis: Kerry Says Russia 'Hiding Hand Behind Falsehoods,'" the *Guardian*, March 4, 2014, https://www.theguardian.com/world/2014/mar/04/ukraine-crisis-shots-fired-crimea-airbase#block-5315b852e4b0da1677ed2cfe, accessed March 28, 2021.

7. "To be sure, having your phone bugged": Qvortrup, *Angela Merkel*, 295.

8. "little green men": Ibid., 294.

9. the Obama administration swiftly implemented: Anne Gearan, "Obama Warns of 'Consequences' in Ukraine as US Issues Visa Bans," *Washington Post*, February 9, 2014, https://www.washingtonpost.com/world/national-security/obama-warns-of-consequences-if-bloodshed-continues-in-ukraine/2014/02/19/1ad4e4ee-99aa-11e3-80ac-63a8ba7f7942_story.html?utm_term=.cc6ebadc771b, accessed August 13, 2018.

10. Obama banned or revoked: Jamie Boucher, Brian D. Christensen, Frederic Depootere, and William J. Sweet Jr., "An Update on Economic Sanctions Related to Events in Ukraine," Skadden, Arps, Slate, Meagher & Flom, LLP, March 18, 2014, https://www.skadden.com/insights/publications/2014/03/an-update-on-economic-sanctions-related-to-events, accessed August 13, 2018.

11. The White House then canceled: Evan McMorris-Santoro and Chris Geidner, "US Cancels US Delegation to Sochi Paralympic Games," BuzzFeed, March 3, 2014, https://www.buzzfeednews.com/article/evanmcsan/us-cancels-presidential-delegation-to-sochi-paralympic-games, accessed August 13, 2018.

12. From a defense perspective: Roxana Tiron and Derek Wallbank, "House Passes $1 Billion in Loan Guarantees to Aid Ukraine," Bloomberg, March 6, 2014, https://www.bloomberg.com/news/articles/2014-03-06/house-passes-1-billion-in-loan-guarantees-to-aid-ukraine, accessed August 13, 2018.

13. To complicate the situation: Qvortrup, *Angela Merkel*, 294.

14. In a leaked document: Ibid, 295.

15. "completely unacceptable": Ibid.

16. he was a known quantity: Ibid, 298.

17. Putin's vanity was his soft spot: Ibid, 300.

18. The G8, or Group of Eight, was a prestigious, informal group: Ibid.

19. until Russia complied with international law: Ibid.

20. Hague Declaration: The White House, Office of the Press Secretary, "The Hague Declaration," March 24, 2014, https://obamawhitehouse.archives.gov/the-press-office/2014/03/24/hague-declaration, accessed April 12, 2018.

21. Under the guidelines: Ibid.

22. The foreign ministers: Ibid.

23. "We remain ready to intensify actions": Ibid.

24. to Merkel's dismay: Julian Borger, "Russia Shrugs Off Threat of Permanent Expulsion from G8," the *Guardian*, March 24, 2014, https://www.theguardian.com/world/2014/mar/24/russia-shrugs-threat-expulsion-g8, accessed April 12, 2018.

25. would "plead, talk, and criticize": Qvortrup, *Angela Merkel*, 299.

26. During their first encounter: "That time Putin Brought His Dog to a Meeting to Scare Angela Merkel," Business Insider, July 7, 2017, https://www.businessinsider.com/putin-merkel -meeting-dog-2017-7.

27. Although France, the United States, and Ukraine participated: Qvortrup, *Angela Merkel*, 301.

28. pharmaceutical manufacturers would reportedly lose approximately €2.1 billion: Ibid, 300.

29. German companies held up well: Ibid.

30. "Ever since the Ukraine crisis began last November": "Why Germany Gets Four Hours at the White House," *The Christian Science Monitor*, April 30, 2014, https://www.csmonitor.com /Commentary/the-monitors-view/2014/0430/Why-Germany-s-Merkel-gets-four-hours-at-the -White-House, accessed March 18, 2021.

31. "Angela": President Obama Holds a Press Conference with Chancellor Merkel of Germany, YouTube video, May 2, 2014, https://www.youtube.com/watch?v=hXAwx11O6Dc&t=9s, accessed January 3, 2018.

32. "We agreed to continue the close security cooperation": Ibid.

33. "critical to supporting jobs": Ibid.

34. "Angela, I want to thank you": Ibid.

35. "The ruble has fallen": Ibid.

36. Obama emphasized that NATO allies: Ibid.

37. "So Angela, I want to thank you again": Ibid.

38. Merkel thanked "Barack": Ibid.

39. Merkel said the work of the intelligence services was "indispensable": Ibid.

40. "I think particularly": Ibid.

41. "People have doubts": Ibid.

42. The German chancellor concluded by thanking "Barack": Ibid.

43. When the two opened the floor: Ibid.

44. "The goal": Ibid.

45. "But what has been remarkable": Ibid.

46. "And I thank Chancellor Merkel's leadership": Ibid.

47. she reiterated that the United States and Europe :Ibid.

48. "they are not an end in itself": Ibid.

49. "Germany is one of our closest allies": Ibid.

50. Obama listed the steps taken: Ibid.

51. "And in that, we can only be successful": Ibid.

52. "These are complicated issues": Ibid.

53. "What we do have": Ibid.

54. "I think the whole debate": Ibid.

55. "The two sides were closer on the issue of trade": Jeff Mason and Steve Holland, "Obama, Merkel Still Struggle over Spying but Agree on Trade," Reuters, May 2, 2014, https://www.yahoo.com/news/obama-merkel-still-struggle-over-spying-agree-trade-005259220--business.html, accessed June 30, 2017.

56. Although Merkel had spoken in generalities on overcoming "doubts": Ibid.

57. "one of my closest friends on the world stage": Mark Landler, "Merkel Signals That Tension Persists Over US Spying," *New York Times*, May 2, 2014, https://www.nytimes.com/2014/05/03/world/europe/merkel-says-gaps-with-us-over-surveillance-remain.html, accessed June 20, 2017.

58. While Germany still hoped for a blanket no-spy agreement: Ibid.

59. German officials wanted the United States to refrain: Ibid.

60. "It was the best result for the conservatives": David Crossland, "Election Triumph: Merkel Victorious but Faces Tough Talks," Spiegel Online, September 22, 2013, http://www.spiegel.de/international/germany/merkel-wins-third-term-in-general-election-a-923755.html, accessed April 2, 2018.

61. "Who do people trust to rule calmly": Ibid.

CHAPTER 10: "WHEN FREE PEOPLE STAND UNITED"

1. Putin had a sudden change of heart: "Putin Supports Ukraine election on May 25," Euronews, YouTube video, May 7, 2014, youtube.com/watch?v=n8HXjSAn4G8, accessed February 12, 2018.

2. he appeared to reconfirm the need for a free and fair election: "Putin Promises to Respect Ukraine's Election," Associated Press, May 23, 2014, http://www.dailymail.co.uk/wires/ap/article-2637183/Putin-promises-respect-Ukraines-election.html, accessed February 12, 2018.

3. The United States and the European Union vowed: Maxim Shemetov, "EU Puts Third Round Sanctions Against Russia on Pause," Reuters, May 28, 2014, https://www.rt.com/business/161964-eu-third-round-sanctions/, accessed February 12, 2018.

4. On May 25, opposition supporter Petro Poroshenko declared victory: "Poroshenko Declares Victory in Ukraine Presidential Election," *The Wall Street Journal*, May 25, 2014, wsj.com/articles/SB10001424052702304811904579583413180447156, accessed April 3, 2018.

5. on June 27, President Poroshenko signed: "EU Signs Pact with Ukraine, Georgia, and Moldova," BBC News, June 27, 2014, https://www.bbc.com/news/world-europe-28052645, accessed April 3, 2018.

6. Ukraine and pro-Russian separatists agreed: "Ukraine Deal with Pro-Russian Rebels at Minsk Talks," BBC News, September 20, 2014, https://www.bbc.com/news/world-europe-29290246, accessed April 5, 2018.

7. on November 12, a NATO commander: David S. Herszenhorn, "Fears Rise as Russian Military Units Pour Into Ukraine," *New York Times*, November 12, 2014, https://www.nytimes.com/2014/11/13/world/europe/ukraine-russia-military-border-nato.html, accessed April 5, 2018.

8. Donetsk International Airport fell to rebel forces: James Miller and Pierre Vaux, "The Death of Ukraine's Cyborg Army," *Foreign Policy*, January 22, 2015, https://foreignpolicy.com/2015/01/22/the-death-of-ukraines-cyborg-army-ukraine-russia-donetsk-airport-shelling/, accessed April 8, 2018.

9. allegations of "crimes against humanity": Susannah Cullinane, "Ukraine to ask Hague to investigate 'crimes against humanity," CNN, January 26, 2015, https://www.cnn.com/2015/01/26 /europe/ukraine-crisis/index.html, accessed April 8, 2018.

10. considering providing lethal aid: Michael R. Gordon and Eric Schmitt, "U.S. Considers Supplying Arms to Ukraine Forces, Officials Say," *New York Times*, February 1, 2015, https://www .nytimes.com/2015/02/02/world/us-taking-a-fresh-look-at-arming-kiev-forces.html, accessed April 12, 2018.

11. higher than the 5,000 already killed: "Restrained Optimism Follows Minsk Summit, New Russia Sanctions Off the Table?" RT Question More, February 12, 2015, https://www.rt.com /news/231643-minsk-summit-ceasefire-reactions/, accessed April 12, 2018.

12. Senator McCain expressed support for providing weapons: Soraya Sarhaddi Nelson, "Merkel's US Visit Could Turn Testy," NPR, February 8, 2015, https://www.npr.org/2015/02/08/384695813 /merkels-u-s-visit-could-turn-testy, accessed January 12, 2018.

13. "Look, I'm absolutely convinced" : Nelson, "Merkel's US Visit Could Turn Testy."

14. That agreement stipulated that no new sanctions: Justin Sink, "Obama Threatens to Veto New Iran Sanctions from Congress," *The Hill*, January 16, 2015, http://thehill.com/policy /international/229782-obama-threatens-to-veto-new-iran-sanctions-from-congress, accessed July 3, 2017.

15. Obama had threatened to veto: Ibid.

16. the escalating crisis in Ukraine: Oren Dorell, "5 Things about German Leader's Visit to Washington," *USA Today*, February 8, 2015, https://www.usatoday.com/story/news/world/2015 /02/08/5-things-germany-merkel-visits-washington/23050835/, accessed July 1, 2017.

17. "When Merkel visited President Obama in Washington": Nelson, "Merkel's US Visit Could Turn Testy."

18. "It is long past time": Dan Roberts and Ian Traynor, "Merkel to Meet Obama amid US Skepticism over Ukraine Peace Talks," the *Guardian*, February 9, 2015, https://www.theguardian .com/world/2015/feb/09/merkel-to-meet-obama-to-resolve-ukrainian-differences, accessed July 1, 2017.

19. "if there is no deal in sight": Ibid.

20. "Putin cannot be beaten militarily": Ibid.

21. "my close friend and partner": President Obama Hosts Chancellor Merkel at the White House, YouTube video, February 9, 2015, https://www.youtube.com/watch?v=r23-k6NFa_k&t =68s, accessed July 1, 2017.

22. "Well into her third term": Ibid.

23. The president revealed that the morning's focus: Ibid.

24. "Instead of withdrawing": Ibid.

25. He surmised that Russia's combativeness: Ibid.

26. He reiterated that the United States: Ibid.

27. "to destroy this barbaric organization": Ibid.

28. the important role of Germany: Ibid.

29. "we can help these communities": Ibid.

30. "speaking out forcefully": Ibid.

31. "Obama admired her pragmatism": Rhodes, *The World as It Is*, xiii.

32. "So in a time when conflicts": President Obama Hosts Chancellor Merkel at the White House, February 9, 2015.

33. Merkel began her address when she emphasized her pleasure to be in Washington: Ibid.

34. "After we thought in the nineties": Ibid.

35. "We stand up for the same principles": Ibid.

36. "Thank you for your hospitality": Ibid.

37. "a good cop–bad cop act": Ibid.

38. "Angela" believed the likelihood of "a military solution": Ibid.

39. He even admitted that he asked his advisors: Ibid.

40. "We have the Minsk agreement": Ibid.

41. "But you may rest assured": Ibid.

42. The next journalist: Ibid.

43. Obama appeared slightly flustered: Ibid.

44. "nobody wishes more for a success": Ibid.

45. "And I, as German chancellor": Ibid.

46. Obama then responded, as he had done: Ibid.

47. but he emphasized that his 2014 executive order: Ibid.

48. "[T]he United States has always been": Ibid.

49. "And if we have that fundamental": Ibid.

50. "I'm very glad that with the American President": Ibid.

51. "The point Angela made, I think, is right": Ibid.

52. then someone else would have solved them: Lila MacLellan, "Barack Obama shares his approach to handling tough decisions," Quartz, March 7, 2019, https://qz.com/work/1567301 /barack-obamas-advice-for-handling-tough-decisions/, accessed May 18, 2021.

53. one reporter asked: President Obama Hosts Chancellor Merkel at the White House, February 9, 2015.

54. "I don't see a further extension": Ibid.

55. "there [have] been no cracks": Ibid.

56. "As much as I love Angela": Ibid.

57. "What I do know is": Ibid.

58. Minsk II agreement: "The Economist Explains: 'What Are the Minsk Agreements?'" *The Economist*, September 14, 2016, https://www.economist.com/blogs/economist-explains/2016/09 /economist-explains-7, accessed April 11, 2018.

59. "The Ukrainian crisis was not caused by the Russian Federation": Dan Roberts and Ian Traynor, "Obama Sidesteps Ukraine Military Option but Backs German Diplomatic Effort," the *Guardian*, February 9, 2015, https://www.theguardian.com/us-news/2015/feb/09/obama-support -german-effort-russia-ukraine-military, accessed April 11, 2018.

CHAPTER 11: "THERE'S NEVER A BAD DAY FOR A BEER"

1. "almost two years of frosty public relations": Carrie Budoff Brown and Matthew Karnitschnig, "Obama and Merkel make nice," *Politico*, June 7, 2015, https://www.politico.eu /article/obama-merkel-g7-alliance/, accessed July 10, 2017.

2. The encounter between the two: G7-Gipfel in Elmau: Trachtenempfang von Barack Obama und Angela Merkel am 07.06.2015, YouTube video, June 7, 2015, https://www.youtube.com /watch?v=KYTHe-bdGQw&t=990s, accessed August 1, 2017.

3. played traditional Bavarian music: Ibid.

4. They signed the visitor guestbook: Ibid.

5. "dear Barack": Ibid.

6. "*Barack, du hast das Wort*": Ibid.

7. When Obama addressed the crowd: Ibid.

8. For approximately an hour among the townspeople: Ibid.

9. He expressed regret at forgetting his *Lederhosen*: Ibid.

10. expressed his disappointment: Ibid.

11. "But then again": Ibid.

12. did not allow the relaxed atmosphere: Ibid.

13. "one of the strongest alliances the world has ever known": Ibid.

14. nonalcoholic beer: "Elmau, Germany—Mayor: Obama and Merkel's Pre-G-7 Summit Beer Was Alcohol-Free," *Voz Iz Neias?*, June 8, 2015, https://www.vosizneias.com/205549/2015/06/08 /elmau-germany-mayor-obama-and-merkels-pre-summit-beer-was-alcohol-free/, accessed October 7, 2017.

15. neither raised the issue of the NSA surveillance controversy: Nedra Pickler and Julie Pace, "Obama, with Beer and Wurst, Works to Mend US–German Ties," Associated Press, June 7, 2015, https://federalnewsradio.com/all-news/2015/06/obama-aims-to-mend-us-german-relations-on -bavarian-trip/, accessed July 10, 2017.

16. According to the *New York Times* and White House press secretary: Julie Hirschfeld Davis, "Over Beer, Obama and Merkel Mend Ties and Double Down on Russia," *New York Times*, June 7, 2015, https://www.nytimes.com/2015/06/08/world/europe/on-sidelines-of-g-7-meeting -obama-and-merkel-strengthen-ties.html, accessed July 10, 2017.

17. "There is little doubt": Ibid.

18. the president "continues to reach out": Ibid.

19. "Merkel seemed eager to move on": Pickler and Pace, "Obama, with Beer and Wurst."

20. "Let me begin by once again thanking Chancellor Merkel": The White House, Office of the Press Secretary, "Remarks by President Obama in Press Conference After G7 Summit," June 8, 2015, https://obamawhitehouse.archives.gov/the-press-office/2015/06/08/remarks -president-obama-press-conference-after-g7-summit, accessed June 3, 2018.

21. "agree that the best way to sustain": Ibid.

22. America remained "a major source of strength": Ibid.

23. "We recognize that the global economy": Ibid.

24. Obama stated that the other G7 leaders: Ibid.

25. "As we've done in the US": Ibid.

26. Obama commended Merkel: Ibid.

27. "This is now the second year": Ibid.

28. He promised the people of Ukraine: Ibid.

29. "The ruble": Ibid.

30. Obama also emphasized that although the G7 leaders: Ibid.

31. "stand ready": Ibid.

32. "Iran has a historic opportunity": Ibid.

33. Obama thanked "Angela and the people": Ibid.

34. Iran had a nuclear program of one kind or another: Michael Wilner, "Six World Powers Adopt Nuclear Deal with Iran," *Jerusalem Post*, July 14, 2015, http://www.jpost.com/Middle-East /Iran-nuclear-deal-reached-408871, accessed April 12, 2018.

35. In 2003, diplomacy talks: Ibid.

36. Washington had already imposed sanctions: Ibid.

37. Additional negotiations seemed futile: Ibid.

38. Obama then opened communication lines: Ibid.

39. "amounts to the most significant": Ibid.

40. The JCPOA permitted Iran: Ibid.

41. In exchange for these concessions: Ibid.

42. Obama, who vehemently supported the deal: The White House, Office of the Press Secretary, "Statement by the President On Iran," July 14, 2015, https://obamawhitehouse.archives.gov /the-press-office/2015/07/14/statement-president-iran, accessed July 8, 2018.

43. "If Iran violates the deal": Wilner, "Six World Powers Adopt Nuclear Deal with Iran."

44. "Today, after two years of negotiations": The White House, Office of the Press Secretary, "Statement by the President On Iran."

45. Under the provisions of this climate agreement: Coral Davenport, "Nations Approve Landmark Climate Accord in Paris," *New York Times*, December 12, 2015, https://www.nytimes.com /2015/12/13/world/europe/climate-change-accord-paris.html, accessed July 12, 2018.

46. "So the individual countries' plans": Ibid.

47. Adoption of the historic agreement: Ibid.

48. "the stars for this assembly were aligned": Ibid.

49. scientific studies confirmed: Ibid.

50. Flooding, droughts, and water shortages: Ibid.

51. "That breakthrough announcement": Ibid.

52. "This agreement sends a powerful signal": Ibid.

CHAPTER 12: "ON THE RIGHT SIDE OF HISTORY"

1. "Leaders are tested": Nancy Gibbs, "The Choice: Person of the Year Angela Merkel," *Time*, November 21, 2015, 49.

2. "Every saga has its galvanizing moment": Karl Vick and Simon Shuster, "Person of the Year: Chancellor of the Free World," *Time*, November 21, 2015, 86.

3. Merkel knew it well: Ibid., 88.

4. "Let us be free": Ibid.

5. a decline in Merkel's poll numbers: Gibbs, "The Choice: Person of the Year Angela Merkel," 50.

6. "an audacious act": Ibid.

7. "*Wir schaffen das*": Ibid.

8. Although Obama had been initially ambivalent: Carol E. Lee and Anton Troianovski, "Obama's Trip to Germany Reflects New Closeness," *MarketWatch*, April 23, 2016, https://www .marketwatch.com/story/obamas-trip-to-germany-reflects-new-closeness-2016-04-23, accessed July 12, 2017.

9. Merkel welcomed Obama to Germany: President Obama Holds a Press Conference with Chancellor Angela Merkel, YouTube video, April 24, 2016, https://www.youtube.com/watch?v =l7YjZcw4cjM&t=123s, accessed July 30, 2017.

10. times were "turbulent": Ibid.

11. "But let me tell you, Barack": Ibid.

12. "And this in many ways": Ibid.

13. "But this also means": Ibid.

14. "We are ready and willing to be militarily engaged": Ibid.

15. "We stand by the Minsk agreement": Ibid.

16. "I think we all ought": Ibid.

17. "at Angela's invitation": Ibid.

18. "It is always a great pleasure": Ibid.

19. On the issue of T-TIP: Ibid.

20. summarized all the ways: Ibid.

21. "a strong partner in international efforts": Ibid.

22. "[W]e're committed to using all the tools": Ibid.

23. "I want to once again commend Angela": Ibid.

24. the crisis in Ukraine remained an ongoing problem: Ibid.

25. "all sides need to uphold commitments": Ibid.

26. "Tomorrow, Chancellor Merkel will host our meeting": Ibid.

27. The president pointed to: Ibid.

28. "people visibly see a plant moving": Ibid.

29. "we will have the negotiations completed": Ibid.

30. "Now, with respect to the politics of it": Ibid.

31. a "reflective" moment: Lee and Troianovski, "Obama's Trip to Germany Reflects New Closeness."

32. "how the often-fraught relationship": Ibid.

33. "From the global financial turmoil": Ibid.

34. "closest international partner of the past eight years": Nick Allen, "Barack Obama delivers parting snub to special relationship with Britain by naming Angela Merkel his 'closest partner,'" *The Telegraph*, November 14, 2016, https://www.telegraph.co.uk/news/2016/11/14/barack-obama -delivers-parting-snub-to-special-relationship-with/, accessed July 17, 2018.

35. Her short, curt reply: President Obama Holds a Press Conference with Chancellor Angela Merkel, April 24, 2016.

36. "What you see is a testimony": Ibid.

37. "short, remarkably unsentimental answer": Greg Jaffe, "International Odd Couple: How Obama and Merkel Forged a Special Bond," *Washington Post*, April 24, 2016, https://www .washingtonpost.com/politics/the-international-odd-couple-how-obama-and-merkel-forged-a -special-bond/2016/04/24/9ce8beac-0a4a-11e6-a6b6-2e6de3695b0e_story.html?utm_term= .efaf8c80e30f, accessed April 18, 2018.

38. "The concept of ultimately bringing some safety": President Obama Holds a Press Conference with Chancellor Angela Merkel, April 24, 2016.

39. As Obama spoke those words: Ibid.

40. "But if you think about the first time I came here": Ibid.

41. "strong US–German cooperation": Ibid.

42. "occurred because of the partnership": Ibid.

43. "because the United States stands shoulder-to-shoulder": Ibid.

44. "You both have spoken about the strong working relationship": Ibid.

45. "Let me make two remarks": Ibid.

46. "I love this job": Ibid.

47. "By the way, what's happening ": Ibid.

48. "There's not an issue": Ibid.

49. "*lieber* Barack": Merkel Opens Hannover Fair, YouTube video, April 24, 2016, https://www .youtube.com/watch?v=V6ah4eDm2oY, accessed August 1, 2017.

50. "We in the EU want to lead the way": Ibid.

51. "We love competition. But we also like to win": Ibid.

52. "great partner and friend, Chancellor Merkel": President Obama Speaks at the Hannover Messe Trade Fair, YouTube video, April 24, 2016, https://www.youtube.com /watch?v=F7gBg0RsCow&t=39s, accessed August 1, 2017.

53. "I'm pleased that this year the United States": Ibid.

54. mention the economic growth: Ibid.

55. "Angela, maybe you and I, we can go driving": Ibid.

56. "German investment in the United States": Ibid.

57. "I would imagine the chancellor": Ibid.

58. "Last night, I also talked about why companies": President Obama Delivers Remarks at the Hannover Messe Trade Fair with Chancellor Merkel, YouTube video, April 25, 2016, https://www.youtube.com/watch?v=zY0fanoZcvg, accessed August 1, 2017.

59. "Mr. President, dear Barack": Ibid.

60. "And now I learn the proof of the pudding is the eating": Ibid.

61. The interaction between Obama and Merkel: Germany: Obama and Merkel Geek Out at Hannover Messe, YouTube video, April 25, 2016, https://www.youtube.com/watch?v=BOJYjq58BTM, accessed August 1, 2017.

62. "teach Angela how to play": Obama and Merkel Visit Siemens at Hannover Messe, YouTube video, April 25, 2016, https://www.youtube.com/watch?v=Jj3xpUvgRXs&t=112s, accessed August 1, 2017.

63. promised he would send her the DVD: Carsten Dierig and Ulrich Exner, "Harmonie in Hannover," *Welt*, April 26, 2016, https://www.welt.de/print/welt_kompakt/article154744270/Harmonie-in-Hannover.html, accessed May 17, 2021.

64. "the people of Europe": The White House, Office of the Press Secretary, "Remarks by President Obama in Address to the People of Europe," April 25, 2016, https://obamawhitehouse.archives.gov/the-press-office/2016/04/25/remarks-president-obama-address-people-europe, accessed March 23, 2021.

65. "Angela for being a champion of our alliance": Obama Delivers Remarks at Hannover Messe Building 35, YouTube video, April 25, 2016, https://www.youtube.com/watch?v=jux08I6o8Vw&t=1215s, accessed August 1, 2017.

66. "a special place": Ibid.

67. "And now, as Europe confronts questions": Ibid.

68. "A strong, united Europe": Ibid.

69. "the sudden arrival of so many people": Ibid.

70. had failed to admit even 10,000 such individuals: editorial board, "America has accepted 10,000 Syrian refugees. That's still too few," *New York Times*, September 2, 2016, https://www.washingtonpost.com/opinions/global-opinions/america-has-accepted-10000-syrian-refugees-thats-still-too-few/2016/09/02/470446e2-6fc0-11e6-8533-6b0b0ded0253_story.html, accessed May 16, 2021.

71. "And just as a handful of neighborhoods": Obama Delivers Remarks at Hannover Messe Building 35.

72. "Chancellor Merkel and others have eloquently": Ibid.

73. "That's who you are": Ibid.

74. Merkel oversaw the largest European economy: Christopher Livesay, "Merkel Beating Backlash to Refugee Policy in Reelection Bid," *PBS News Hour*, September 23, 2017, https://www.pbs.org/newshour/show/far-right-party-gains-footing-german-election, accessed July 17, 2018.

75. for the first time in her chancellorship: Ibid.

76. "should be proud": Ibid.

77. Although Merkel remained the leading candidate: Ibid.

78. the monthly living expense stipends: Ibid.

CHAPTER 13: "DEMOCRACY LIVES OFF CHANGE"

1. "Under different electoral circumstances": Michael A. Memoli and Christi Parsons, "Obama's Final Foreign Trip Was His Last Chance to Warn the World about Trump, and to Warn Trump about the World," *Los Angeles Times*, November 20, 2016, http://www.latimes.com/politics/la-fg -obama-trip-20161121-story.html, accessed July 16, 2017.

2. advisors planned the trip as a way to boost: Anthony Faiola and Juliet Eilperin, "Obama to Bid Bittersweet Farewell to Closest Partner on World Stage," *Washington Post*, November 15, 2016, https://www.washingtonpost.com/world/obama-to-bid-bittersweet-farewell-to-closest-partner -on-world-stage/2016/11/14/68df7b4c-a91d-11e6-ba59-a7d93165c6d4_story.html?utm_term= .a01128646dbb, accessed April 20, 2018.

3. "Mr. Obama's visit is about showing": Derek Scally, "Barack Obama to Bid Berlin and Angela Merkel Farewell," *The Irish Times*, November 15, 2016, https://www.irishtimes.com/news/world/us /barack-obama-to-bid-berlin-and-angela-merkel-farewell-1.2869138, accessed April 20, 2018.

4. "dominated" . . . "group therapy" . . . "rattled leaders": Memoli and Parsons, "Obama's Final Foreign Trip Was His Last Chance."

5. "warning about the threats to democracy": Ibid.

6. "Trump's victory is set to usher into the White House": Faiola and Eilperin, "Obama to Bid Bittersweet Farewell to Closest Partner on World Stage."

7. "Mr. Obama comes to town with expectations": Scally, "Barack Obama to Bid Berlin and Angela Merkel Farewell."

8. "his closest international partner of the last eight years": Allen, "Barack Obama Delivers Parting Snub to Special Relationship with Britain."

9. Obama failed to mention: Natasha Clark, "Not So Special Relationship," *The Sun*, November 15, 2016, https://www.thesun.co.uk/news/2189116/barack-obamas-final-snub-to -britain-by-describing-angela-merkel-as-his-closest-political-friend-as-president-embarks-on -farewell-tour-of-europe/, accessed July 17, 2017.

10. "Berlin residents are not known for being particularly sentimental": "Berliners React to Obama's Last Presidential Visit," DW, November 17, 2016, http://www.dw.com/en/berliners -react-to-obamas-last-presidential-visit/a-36431625, accessed July 17, 2017.

11. "We won't get another one like him again": Ibid.

12. Obama's aides had hoped to coordinate: "Trump, Putin Loom Large Over President Obama's Last Germany Visit," CBS News, November 17, 2016, https://www.cbsnews.com/news /obama-merkel-germany-donald-trump-russia-vladimir-putin-europe/, accessed July 17, 2017.

13. still something special: Scally, "Barack Obama to Bid Berlin and Angela Merkel Farewell."

14. the primary goal for this visit: Memoli and Parsons, "Obama's Final Foreign Trip Was His Last Chance."

15. "What we don't need": Scally, "Barack Obama to Bid Berlin and Angela Merkel Farewell."

16. Ben Rhodes said: Klaus Brinkbäumer and Holger Stark, "The End of Power: What Will Remain of Obama's Legacy?" Spiegel Online, November 18, 2016, http://www.spiegel.de /international/world/the-deep-bond-of-trust-between-obama-and-merkel-a-1122000-2.html, accessed August 1, 2017.

17. "In his capacity as president": President Obama and German Chancellor Angela Merkel hold joint press conference, YouTube video, CBS News, November 17, 2016, https://www .youtube.com/watch?v=WN3Cp7B2ZnE&t=1461s, accessed August 1, 2017.

18. "So eight years are coming to a close": Ibid.

19. "I'm very grateful that Barack Obama": Ibid.

20. "In the areas of business, of the economy": Ibid.

21. "this Paris Agreement would never": Ibid.

22. "There are a lot of areas where we cooperate": Ibid.

23. the end had come: Ibid.

24. "From a German point of view": Ibid.

25. "back with my great friend and ally, Chancellor Merkel": Ibid.

26. "The United States was proud to stand with": Ibid.

27. "Our alliance with our NATO partners has been a cornerstone": Ibid.

28. commerce and trade can create growth: Ibid.

29. "With the threat of climate change only becoming more urgent": Ibid.

30. Obama then complimented Merkel on her leadership: Ibid.

31. "I want again to commend Angela": Ibid.

32. "On this final visit": Ibid.

33. "Look at Chancellor Merkel": Ibid.

34. "I try to make it a rule": Ibid.

35. "The fact that we were able to enjoy German unification": Ibid.

36. "Each and every one of us must be given an opportunity": Ibid.

37. "Now, taking leave from my partner and friend": Ibid.

38. "But personal—we have freedom of movement": Ibid.

39. "deep friendship we enjoy today": The White House, Office of the Press Secretary, "Op-Ed by President Obama and Chancellor Merkel: The Future of Transatlantic Relations," November 17, 2016, https://obamawhitehouse.archives.gov/the-press-office/2016/11/17/op-ed-president -obama-and-chancellor-merkel-future-transatlantic, accessed April 20, 2018 (originally published in Wirtschaftswoche, https://www.wiwo.de/politik/ausland/usa-and-germany-the-future-of -transatlantic-relations/14853710.html).

40. "joint responsibility to protect and preserve our way of life": Ibid.

41. respect for these universal principles: Ibid.

42. they believed was vital: Ibid.

43. "deep respect for human dignity": Ibid.

44. "US–German partnership was essential": Ibid.

45. "Simply put: we are stronger": Ibid.

46. "Today we find ourselves at a crossroads": Ibid.

47. "They reminisced about years [past]": Brinkbäumer and Stark, "The End of Power."

48. "No other world leader so closely matches Obama's ideology": Faiola and Eilperin, "Obama to Bid Bittersweet Farewell to Closest Partner on World Stage."

49. their "similar temperaments" helped them: Ibid.

50. "the level-headed Merkel emerging as a possible counterpoint": Ibid.

CONCLUSION: "WE CAN'T HIDE BEHIND A WALL"

1. Germany's top Lutheran bishop, Heinrich Bedford-Strohm: Kelsey Sutton, "Obama Heading to Germany in May to Talk Democracy with Merkel," *Politico*, April 11, 2017, https://www.politico.com/story/2017/04/obama-germany-visit-angela-merkel-237100, accessed September 3, 2017.

2. "Being Involved in Democracy": Ibid.

3. An off-duty police officer and an eight-year-old girl: "Last Manchester bombing victim identified," CBS News, May 26, 2017, https://www.cbsnews.com/news/manchester-victims-ariana-grande-concert-deaths-united-kingdom/, accessed September 3, 2017.

4. the former president reassured Manchester residents: Archbishop Welby, President Obama and Chancellor Merkel Send Message to Manchester, YouTube video, May 25, 2017, https://www.youtube.com/watch?v=5pmyh78jm8o, accessed September 5, 2017.

5. "Love conquers hate": Ibid.

6. The Kirchentag is held: "Angela Merkel and Barack Obama at the Kirchentag: Our Faith Demands That We Act," The Federal Government, May 25, 2017, https://www.bundesregierung.de/breg-en/chancellor/our-faith-demands-that-we-act-422200, accessed July 14, 2017.

7. "do come as ties": Kevin Liptak, "Obama to Visit Merkel during Trump's First European Trip," CNN, April 12, 2017, https://edition.cnn.com/2017/04/12/politics/obama-germany-angela-merkel-trump/index.html, accessed August 7, 2018.

8. "I think that former president Obama": Professor Jan Hartman, "No Coincidence: Why Obama Visited Merkel Hours before Trump Joining NATO Summit," Sputnik News, May 27, 2017, https://sputniknews.com/politics/201705271054040834-merkel-obama-nato-trump/, accessed April 19, 2018.

9. Obama and Merkel also shared the stage: Sutton, "Obama Heading to Germany in May to Talk Democracy with Merkel."

10. many of them held banners: Barack Obama joins Angela Merkel in Berlin, YouTube video, May 25, 2017, https://www.youtube.com/watch?v=3KHI0VtYsWw&t=1152s, accessed September 5, 2017.

11. her reference to explorer Christopher Columbus: The Federal Government, "Angela Merkel and Barack Obama at the Kirchentag."

12. Obama explained that his public life: Ibid.

13. "Personally, in my own faith": Ibid.

14. "We make investments": "Obama: We Can't Hide Behind a Wall," *Washington Post* (video), May 25, 2017, https://washingtonpost.com/video/national/Obama-we-can't-hide-behind-a-wall /2017/05/25/6cb099a0-4156-11e7-b29f-f40ffced2ddb_video.html, accessed May 18, 2021.

15. "One of the biggest challenges": Barack Obama joins Angela Merkel in Berlin.

16. "We are dealing with opponents": Ibid.

17. "By the time they met during World War II": Jon Meacham, *Franklin and Winston: An Intimate Portrait of an Epic Friendship* (New York: Random House, 2003), xvii.

18. First Lady Michelle Obama and Professor Joachim Sauer joined: "Readout of the President and First Lady's Call with Chancellor Angela Merkel of Germany," White House Office of the Press Secretary, January 19, 2017, https://obamawhitehouse.archives.gov/the-press-office /2017/01/19/readout-president-and-first-ladys-call-chancellor-angela-merkel-germany, accessed May 18, 2021.

19. "they cared passionately": Meacham, *Franklin and Winston: An Intimate Portrait of an Epic Friendship*, xix.

20. "They also shared the conviction": Ibid.

21. "Churchill wanted the British empire to survive": Ibid.

22. "Despite their many differences": Klaus Brinkbäumer and Holger Stark, "What Will Remain of Obama's Legacy?" Spiegel Online, November 18, 2016, https://www.spiegel.de /international/world/the-deep-bond-of-trust-between-obama-and-merkel-a-1122000.html, accessed April 20, 2018.

23. "warmer human being": Meacham, *Franklin and Winston: An Intimate Portrait of an Epic Friendship*.

24. "Mrs. Merkel is not a great orator": Knigge, "Honor, Yes, but Tough Questions Also Await Merkel in Washington."

25. "For the famously reserved commander-in-chief": Liptak, "How Obama and Merkel Learned to Love One Another."

26. "wielded significant global influence": Jenny Hill, "Why Germany Is Sorry to See Obama Go," BBC News, November 17, 2016, http://www.bbc.com/news/world-europe-38019605, accessed April 20, 2018.

27. "To the chagrin of conservatives": Brinkbäumer and Stark. "The End of Power."

28. the rapport between Merkel and Obama: Liptak, "How Obama and Merkel Learned to Love One Another."

29. "You feel increasingly": Ibid.

30. "true partner": Brinkbäumer and Stark, "The End of Power."

31. she admitted her uncertainty: Rhodes, *The World as It Is*, xiv.

32. "A single tear": Ibid.

33. "Angela. She's all alone": Ibid.

34. "No . . . I was so sure we were going to be besties": *Saturday Night Live*, "Weekend Update: Angela Merkel on Donald Trump," YouTube video, December 11, 2016, https://www.youtube .com/watch?v=ahZAW0EY4eg, accessed June 3, 2020.

35. "Is this my sweet Barack?": *Saturday Night Live*, "Oval Office Cold Open," YouTube video, February 5, 2017, https://www.youtube.com/watch?v=pZOF9q5fzfs, accessed June 3, 2020.

AFTERWORD: "I OFFER A CLOSE COOPERATION"

1. "a healer of transatlantic relations": Faiola and Eilperin, "Obama to Bid Bittersweet Farewell to Closest Partner on World Stage."

2. "had the opposite effect": Ibid.

3. "are connected through values": German Chancellor Angela Merkel Reacts to Donald Trump as Elected President, YouTube video, November 9, 2016, https://www.youtube.com /watch?v=XpXWTQ64l8k&t=86s, accessed May 7, 2018.

4. "I offer a close cooperation": Ibid.

5. disparaged global warming as a hoax: Edward Wong, "Trump Has Called Climate Change a Chinese Hoax: Beijing Says It Is Anything But," *New York Times*, November 18, 2016, https: //www.nytimes.com/2016/11/19/world/asia/china-trump-climate-change.html, accessed July 2, 2018.

6. a threat Trump believed no longer existed: "Trump Worries NATO with Obsolete Comment," BBC News, January 16, 2017, https://www.bbc.com/news/world-us-canada-38635181, accessed May 18, 2021.

7. Trump repeatedly complained: Krishnadev Calamur, "NATO Shmato? Donald Trump's Apparent Rejection of the Cornerstone of Global Security after World War II Has Stunned US Partners in the Alliance," *The Atlantic*, July 21, 2016, https://www.theatlantic.com/news/archive /2016/07/trump-nato/492341/, accessed January 3, 2018.

8. Merkel pragmatically promised: "Germany's Steinmeier 'Scared' at Prospect of Trump Presidency," DW, October 8, 2016, https://www.dw.com/en/germanys-steinmeier-scared-at -prospect-of-trump-presidency/a-19463287, accessed August 6, 2018.

9. Trump had characterized Merkel's immigration policy as "catastrophic": Jessica Satin, "Trump Calls Merkel's Refugee Policy a 'Catastrophic Mistake,'" *i24 News International*, January 16, 2017, https://www.i24news.tv/en/news/international/135231-170116-trump-calls-merkel-s-refugee -policy-a-catastrophic-mistake, accessed September 1, 2017.

10. "We have known what his position": Ibid.

11. "Donald Trump's Awkward Merkel Meeting": Daniel Marans, "Donald Trump's Awkward Merkel Meeting Is a Far Cry from Her Moments with Obama," HuffPost, March 17, 2017, https://www.huffingtonpost.com/entry/donald-trumps-awkward-merkel-meeting-is-a-far-cry -from-her-moments-with-obama_us_58cc5a86e4b0be71dcf4f138, accessed September 3, 2017.

12. "I was gratified to know": Donald Trump and Angela Merkel's Full Press Conference, March 17, 2017, https://www.govinfo.gov/content/pkg/DCPD-201700178/html/DCPD -201700178.htm, accessed May 18, 2021.

13. "I reiterated to Chancellor Merkel": Ibid.

14. "In the period leading up to this visit": Ibid.

15. "[L]et me look back into the past": Ibid.

16. "'America First'": Ibid.

17. "Well, first of all": Ibid.

18. "How dangerous do you think": Ibid.

19. "Migration, immigration, integration": Ibid.

20. "As far as wiretapping": Ibid.

21. "With the stroke of a pen": Peter Baker, "Trump Abandons Trans Pacific Partnership, Obama's Signature Trade Deal," *New York Times*, January 23, 2017, https://www.nytimes.com/2017/01/23/us/politics/tpp-trump-trade-nafta.html, accessed July 1, 2018.

22. "I am not happy": Samuel Osborne, "TPP: Angela Merkel 'Not Happy' about Possible Demise of Trans-Pacific Trade Deal," Independent, November 23, 2016, https://www.independent.co.uk/news/world/politics/tpp-trade-deal-angela-merkel-donald-trump-not-happy-comments-trans-pacific-partnership-a7433251.html, accessed March 24, 2021.

23. negotiations over the T-TIP: "The Transatlantic Trade and Investment Partnership (TTIP)," European Commission, https://ec.europa.eu/trade/policy/in-focus/ttip, accessed May 18, 2021.

24. "We deem the momentum generated in Paris": "France, Italy, Germany Defend Paris Accord, Say Cannot Be Renegotiated," Reuters, June 1, 2017, https://www.reuters.com/article/us-usa-climatechange-eu/france-italy-germany-defend-paris-accord-say-cannot-be-renegotiated-idUSKBN18S6GN, accessed July 1, 2018.

25. "the times in which we can completely": "Angela Merkel: EU Cannot Completely Rely on the US and Britain anymore," the *Guardian*, May 28, 2017, https://www.theguardian.com/world/2017/may/28/merkel-says-eu-cannot-completely-rely-on-us-and-britain-any-more-g7-talks, accessed September 3, 2017.

26. Trump withdrew: Mark Landler, "Trump Abandons Iran Nuclear Deal He Long Scorned," *New York Times*, May 8, 2018, https://nyt.com/2018/05/08/world/middleeast/trump-iran-nuclear-deal.html, accessed May 18, 2021.

27. "It is no longer such": Kelsey Caulder, "Merkel and Macron Declare Europe Can No Longer Rely on US for Protection and Security," Euronews, May 10, 2018, https://thehill.com/homenews/administration/387067-merkel-europe-cant-count-on-us-to-protect-us-anymore, accessed May 18, 2021.

28. "decision to withdraw from the Iran nuclear deal": Klaus Brinkbäumer, "Trump and Iran: Time for Europe to Join the Resistance," Spiegel Online, May 11, 2018, http://www.spiegel.de/international/world/editorial-trump-deals-painful-blow-to-trans-atlantic-ties-a-1207260.html, accessed August 6, 2018.

29. "The West as we once knew it": Ibid.

30. Trump signed a bill: Jacob Pramuk, "Trump Signs the Biggest Rollback of Bank Rules Since the Financial Crisis," CNBC, May 24, 2018, https://www.cnbc.com/2018/05/24/trump-signs-bank-bill-rolling-back-some-dodd-frank-regulations.html, accessed October 1, 2018.

31. The key rollbacks: Donna Borak and Ted Barrett, "Senate votes to roll back parts of Dodd-Frank banking law," CNN Politics, March 14, 2018, https://edition.cnn.com/2018/03/14/politics/banking-bill-vote-mike-crapo/index.html, accessed October 1, 2018.

32. members of the EU pledged retaliation: Nathan Bomey, "European Union Tariffs Take Effect in Trump Fight: How They Will Hit American Products," *USA Today*, June 22, 2018, https://eu.usatoday.com/story/money/2018/06/22/european-tariffs-donald-trump/725672002/, accessed August 7, 2018.

33. "a bad day for world trade": Doug Palmer, "'Today Is a Bad Day for World Trade': Trump Slaps US Allies with Tariffs," *Politico*, May 31, 2018, https://www.politico.com/story/2018/05/31/trump-hits-us-allies-with-steel-aluminum-tariffs-615327, accessed August 7, 2018.

34. Prior to boarding Airforce One: Julian Borger and Anne Perkins, "Donald Trump Calls for G7 to Readmit Russsia Ahead of Summit," the *Guardian*, June 9, 2018, https://theguardian.com/world/2018/jun/08/donald-trump-shows-no-sign-compromise-flies-in-g7-summit, accessed May 18, 2021.

35. photo of Trump: Jesco Denzel/German Federal Government via AP Images, featured in Liz Zhou, "A Viral G7 Photo Captures the State of Trump's Relationships with World Leaders," Vox, June 11, 2018, https://vox.com/2018/6/11/17448614/trump-merkel-g7-photo, accessed May 18, 2021.

36. "'Here, Angela. Don't say I never give you anything'": Cristina Maza, "Donald Trump Threw Starburst Candies at Angela Merkel, Said 'Don't Say I Never Give You Anything,'" *Newsweek*, June 20, 2018, https://www.newsweek.com/donald-trump-threw-starburst-candies-angela-merkel-dont-say-i-never-give-you-987178, accessed August 7, 2018.

37. She managed to win: Matt Clinch, "Merkel's Conservatives Suffer Worst Election Result Since 1949 as German Far Right Sees Surge in Support," CNBC, September 25, 2017, https://cnbc.com/2017/09/24/german-exit-poll-shows-angela-merkel-is-on-track-for-fourth-term-as-chancellor.html, accessed May 18, 2021.

38. 10.2 percent of the Bavarian vote: Atika Shubert, Nadine Schmidt, and Angela Dewan, "Angela Merkel's Bavarian Allies Lose Majority in Crushing Vote," CNN World, October 15, 2018, https://edition.cnn.com/2018/10/14/europe/bavaria-election-germany-results-grm-intl/index.html, accessed December 27, 2018.

39. These results caught the attention of political leaders: Josie Le Blond, "Merkel Suffers Another Election Setback in Key German State of Hesse," the *Guardian*, October 29, 2018, https://www.theguardian.com/world/2018/oct/28/merkel-suffers-another-election-setback-key-german-state-of-hesse, accessed December 27, 2018.

40. announced her plans to step down: "Angela Merkel to Step Down as German Chancellor in 2021," BBC News, October 29, 2018, https://bbc.com/news/world-europe-46020745, accessed May 18, 2021.

41. More than 1,000 party delegates: Kate Connolly, "Merkel Bows Out to Applause as CDU Votes on Successor," the *Guardian*, December 7, 2018, https://www.theguardian.com/world/2018/dec/07/germanys-cdu-party-to-vote-on-angela-merkels-successor-annegret-kramp-karrenbauer-friedrich-merz-jens-spahn, accessed December 27, 2018.

42. Supporters held signs: Ibid.

43. "humanitarian catastrophe": Rede von Angela Merkel, YouTube video, December 7, 2018, https://www.youtube.com/watch?v=4Inu8b50m0c, accessed January 1, 2019.

44. "I wasn't born chancellor": "Merkel Tells Germany's Ruling CDU to Prepare for 'Time after Me' in Measured Farewell Address," European Views, December 7, 2018, https://www.european -views.com/2018/12/merkel-tells-germanys-ruling-cdu-to-prepare-for-time-after-me-in-measured -farewell-address/, accessed December 27, 2018.

45. for the first time since 1971: Connolly, "Merkel Bows Out to Applause as CDU Votes on Successor."

46. Merkel refused to publicly endorse: Ibid.

47. With eighteen years of frontline: Ibid.

48. In a February 2020 state election: Jen Kirby, "Why Angela Merkel's Successor Resigned: A Controversial Election Shakes Up German Politics," Vox, February 10, 2020, https://www.vox .com/2020/2/10/21131546/angela-merkel-successor-resigned-germany-chancellor, accessed June 2, 2020.

49. "regrettable": Kate Connolly, "AKK's resignation sparks battle for soul of German conservatism," the Guardian, February 11, 2020, https://www.theguardian.com/world/2020/feb/11 /annegret-kramp-karrenbauer-resignation-sparks-battle-for-soul-of-german-conservatism accessed, June 2, 2020.

50. "unforgiveable": Ibid.

51. "that you don't win": Ibid.

52. "shortcomings of her leadership": Kirby, "Why Angela Merkel's Successor Resigned: A Controversial Election Shakes Up German Politics."

53. "Germany's post-Merkel future is uncertain": Ibid.

54. She relied on her scientific training: Ivana Kottasová, "How Angela Merkel Went from Lame Duck to Global Leader on Coronavirus," CNN World, May 7, 2020, https://edition.cnn.com /2020/05/07/europe/angela-merkel-coronavirus-legacy-grm-intl/index.html, accessed June 3, 2020.

55. Merkel did something she had never done: Ibid.

56. her approval ratings improved dramatically: Ibid.

57. "We can afford a bit of courage": Ibid.

58. "We have to watch": Ibid.

59. "She started a massive revival": Ibid.

60. he ignored the warnings: David A. Graham, "Why Trump Was Deaf to All the Warnings He Received," The Atlantic, April 29, 2020, https://theatlantic.com/ideas/archive/2020/04/how -many-warnings-did-trump-ignore/610846, accessed May 18, 2021.

61. cut funding: Emily Cochrane, "Trump Pushes to Cut Funding for Covid-19 Testing and CDC in Latest Senate Relief Package," Baltimore Sun, July 19, 2020, https://www .baltimoresun.com/coronavirus/ct-nw-nyt-trump-funding-covid-19-testing-cdc-20200719 -35n6qxrlkvcexo7e4rg6pvbi2u-story.html, accessed May 18, 2021.

62. laid off key employees: Lauren Weber, Laura Ungar, and Michelle R. Smith (Associated Press) and Hannah Recht and Anna Maria Barry-Jester, "Hollowed-Out Public Health System Faces More Cuts Amid Virus," KHN, July 1, 2020, https://khn.org/news/us-public-health-system-underfunded-under-threat-faces-more-cuts-amid-covid-pandemic, accessed May 18, 2021.

63. he began to routinely suggest: "Coronavirus: Outcry after Trump Suggests Injecting Disinfectant as Treatment," BBC News, April 24, 2020, https://bbc.com/news/world-us-canada-52407177, accessed May 18, 2021.

64. over thirty million cases: Worldometer, https://www.worldometers.info/coronavirus/country/us/, accessed March 24, 2021.

65. "Doing what feels good": President Barack Obama, "Graduate Together Commencement Speech," *New York Times*, May 17, 2020, https://www.nytimes.com/2020/05/16/us/obama-graduation-speech-transcript.html, accessed June 3, 2020.

66. cited concerns: Sarah Al-Arshani, "Trump Reportedly 'Furious' That Germany's Angela Merkel Turned Down His G7 Summit Invitation over Coronavirus Concerns," Business Insider, May 30, 2020, https://www.msn.com/en-au/news/world/trump-reportedly-furious-that-germanys-angela-merkel-turned-down-his-g7-summit-invitation-over-coronavirus-concerns/ar-BB14MP0y, accessed June 3, 2020.

67. Trump reportedly was "furious": Ibid.

68. contentious phone call: J. Edward Moreno, "Trump insulted UK's May, called Germany's Merkel 'stupid' in calls: report," *The Hill*, June 30, 2020, https://thehill.com/homenews/administration/505182-trump-insulted-uks-may-called-germanys-merkel-stupid-in-calls-report, accessed May 17, 2021.

69. allied leaders became more skeptical: David Badash, "'I Don't Want to Be in the Room With the Guy': European Allies, from Merkel to Macron, 'Turning Their Backs' on Trump," New Civil Rights Movement, June 3, 2020, https://www.thenewcivilrightsmovement.com/2020/06/i-dont-want-to-be-in-the-room-with-the-guy-european-allies-from-merkel-to-macron-turning-their-backs-on-trump/, accessed June 4, 2020.

70. Merkel had developed plenty of reasons: Ibid.

71. Merkel had "been hurt" by Trump: Ibid.

72. "says a lot about how fed up": Ibid.

73. "I don't want to be in the room with the guy": Ibid.

74. "She will be remembered": Kottasová, "How Angela Merkel Went from Lame Duck to Global Leader on Coronavirus."

75. as she stepped off the world stage: "Merkel Says She's 'Absolutely Not' Standing for Reelection," *The Local DE*, June 4, 2020, https://www.thelocal.de/20200604/merkel-says-absolutely-not-planning-to-stand-for-reelection?fbclid=IwAR0Tpcp8qSDCe0NGNBz6Gs1mMuDyZy10cJnGE62u2d0TUn5G1Z5tt6r4XAY, accessed June 6, 2020.

76. 61.4 percent of eligible participants: Thom File, "Voting in America: A Look at the 2016 Presidential Election," United States Census Bureau, May 10, 2017, https://www.census.gov/newsroom/blogs/random-samplings/2017/05/voting_in_america.html#:~:text=In%202016%2C%2061.4%20percent%20of,who%20reported%20voting%20in%202012, accessed May 18, 2021.

77. compared to the staggering 81,284,000 votes: Sophie Lewis, "Joe Biden Breaks Obama's Record for Most Votes Ever Cast for a U.S. Presidential Candidate," CBS News, December 7, 2020, https://www.cbsnews.com/news/joe-biden-popular-vote-record-barack-obama-us-presidential-election-donald-trump, accessed May 18, 2021.

78. 76.2 percent of German citizens who participated: Evgenia Koptyug, "German elections: voter turnout 1949-2017," Statista, https://www.statista.com/statistics/753732/german-elections-voter-turnout/, accessed May 10, 2017.

79. Hitler was defeated in 1923: "The Munich Putsch," schoolshistory.org.uk/topics/european-history/weimar-nazi-germany/munich-putsch, accessed May 14, 2021.

INDEX

NOTE: Page numbers in *italics* indicate photographs.

INDEX

INDEX

ABOUT THE AUTHOR

CLAUDIA CLARK is an author, speaker, and activist focused on social justice and democracy. She has served as a field organizer and campaign manager for various progressive groups, including the South San Francisco Unified Schools Campaign, ACORN, the South Bay Labor Organization, and the South Dakota Campaign for Healthy Families. In 2017, Clark and her husband moved from San Jose, California, to Germany, where she served as the national Get Out the Vote (GOTV) coordinator for Democrats Abroad Germany from January 2019 to May 2020. Clark studied history and public policy at Michigan State University and has several advanced degrees with a focus on progressive topics, including an MA in US history with an emphasis on women's history from San Jose State University. She currently lives in Berlin, where she is conducting research for her next book about the rise of the alt-right in Europe.